Félix Ravaisson: *French Philosophy in the Nineteenth Century*

BSHP NEW TEXTS IN THE HISTORY OF PHILOSOPHY

The aim of this series is to encourage and facilitate the study of all aspects of the history of philosophy, including the rediscovery of neglected elements and the exploration of new approaches to the subject. Texts are selected on the basis of their philosophical and historical significance and with a view to promoting the understanding of currently under-represented authors, philosophical traditions, and historical periods. They include new editions and translations of important yet less well-known works which are not widely available to an anglophone readership. The series is sponsored by the British Society for the History of Philosophy (BSHP) and is managed by an editorial team elected by the Society. It reflects the Society's main mission and its strong commitment to broadening the canon.

General editors
Maria Rosa Antognazza
Michael Beaney
Mogens Lærke (managing editor)

ALSO PUBLISHED IN THE SERIES

Leibniz: General Inquiries on the Analysis of Notions and Truths
Edited with an English translation by Massimo Mugnai

Félix Ravaisson

French Philosophy in the Nineteenth Century

Translated with introduction and notes by
MARK SINCLAIR

OXFORD
UNIVERSITY PRESS

Great Clarendon Street, Oxford, OX2 6DP,
United Kingdom

Oxford University Press is a department of the University of Oxford.
It furthers the University's objective of excellence in research, scholarship,
and education by publishing worldwide. Oxford is a registered trade mark of
Oxford University Press in the UK and in certain other countries

© Mark Sinclair 2023

The moral rights of the author have been asserted

First Edition published in 2023
Impression: 1

All rights reserved. No part of this publication may be reproduced, stored in
a retrieval system, or transmitted, in any form or by any means, without the
prior permission in writing of Oxford University Press, or as expressly permitted
by law, by licence or under terms agreed with the appropriate reprographics
rights organization. Enquiries concerning reproduction outside the scope of the
above should be sent to the Rights Department, Oxford University Press, at the
address above

You must not circulate this work in any other form
and you must impose this same condition on any acquirer

Published in the United States of America by Oxford University Press
198 Madison Avenue, New York, NY 10016, United States of America

British Library Cataloguing in Publication Data
Data available

Library of Congress Control Number: 2022942889

ISBN 978–0–19–289884–5

Printed and bound by
CPI Group (UK) Ltd, Croydon, CR0 4YY

Links to third party websites are provided by Oxford in good faith and
for information only. Oxford disclaims any responsibility for the materials
contained in any third party website referenced in this work.

Contents

	Editor's Introduction	1
	French Philosophy in the Nineteenth Century	17
I.	The History of Philosophy prior to the Nineteenth Century	19
II.	Cousin and the Eclectic School	30
III.	Lamennais's Metaphysics and Theology	41
IV.	Socialism: Saint-Simon, Fourier, Proudhon	47
V.	Socialist Philosophy: Leroux and Reynaud	50
VI.	Iatromechanism and Phrenology: Broussais and Gall	54
VII.	Comte's Positivism	55
VIII.	Positivism in Britain	62
IX.	Auguste Comte's Later Philosophy	66
X.	Littré and Philosophy	80
XI.	The Philosophy of Taine	83
XII.	Renan and Philosophy	89
XIII.	Renouvier's Neo-Criticism	92
XIV.	The Philosophy of Vacherot	97
XV.	Claude Bernard's Physiological Doctrine	103
XVI.	Philosophical Theology: Gratry	109
XVII.	Philosophical Theology: Saisset, Simon, and Caro	117
XVIII.	Philosophical Theology: Ontologism	119
XIX.	De Strada's Metaphysics	122
XX.	Magy on Physics and Metaphysics	130
XXI.	Physics and Philosophy: De Rémusat and Martin	133
XXII.	Psychology: Habit, Memory, and the Association of Ideas	134
XXIII.	Animism, Vitalism, and Organicism	139
XXIV.	Old and New Materialisms: On Paul Janet	145

XXV.	Organicism and Animism	148
XXVI.	Neurology after Phrenology	150
XXVII.	Instinct	156
XXVIII.	Sleep	159
XXIX.	Madness	162
XXX.	Genius	164
XXXI.	Language and Physiognomy	166
XXXII.	Science and Probability: Cournot	169
XXXIII.	Epistemology: Analysis and Synthesis	175
XXXIV.	Moral Philosophy	180
XXXV.	Aesthetics	184
XXXVI.	Summary and Manifesto for a New Spiritualist Philosophy	188

Index   209

Editor's Introduction

Félix Ravaisson's *French Philosophy in the Nineteenth Century* is one of the most influential and pivotal texts of modern French thought. Commissioned by the Minister of Public Instruction, Victor Duruy, as one of a series of reports to record the progress of the French sciences and humanities for Paris's second world fair, the 1867 Exposition universelle d'arts et d'industrie, it was published with the others the following year. In the hands of another writer the report could have had all the charm and interest of a catalogue or set of obituaries, but Ravaisson used it as an opportunity to show, with verve and generosity, that the myriad voices in nineteenth-century French thinking were beginning to form a chorus, one that was advancing towards a new, more concrete form of spiritualist philosophy able to resist materialist, mechanist, and sensualist doctrines while incorporating recent developments in the life sciences. 'It is possible', as Ravaisson proclaims in reclaiming the idea of a positive philosophy from Auguste Comte, 'to foresee a philosophical epoch whose general character will consist in the predominance of what may be called a spiritualist realism or positivism, having as its generative principle the consciousness that mind has in itself of an existence, on which all existence depends, which is nothing but its own activity' (Section XXXVI). The final section of the report offers a manifesto for this new spiritualism and ends with a 'hymn to the French genius'.[1] It was these passages in particular that, as Henri Bergson would note, 'twenty generations of students learnt by heart'[2] in the following years in order to pass the philosophy *agrégation*, the competitive examination for positions in the national education system, for Ravaisson was president of the committee selecting the examination questions as well as the successful candidates. Bergson was among the latter, and his 1907 *Creative Evolution*, which made him the world's most celebrated living philosopher at the end of the long nineteenth century, is, with its psychological interpretation of biological evolution, a direct expression of the new philosophical orientation that Ravaisson had divined forty years before.

---

[1] Louis Léger, 'Notice sur la vie et les travaux de Monsieur Ravaisson-Mollien', *Comptes rendus des séances de l'Académie des Inscriptions et Belles-Lettres* 45 (1901), pp. 327–72, p. 360. This is the eulogy delivered by Léger after being elected to replace Ravaisson at the Académie des Inscriptions et Belles-Lettres, the wing of the Institut de France concerned with history and classical studies.

[2] Henri Bergson, 'The Life and Work of Ravaisson' in *The Creative Mind*, trans. M. Andison (New York: Philosophical Library, 1946), p. 246. This is the eulogy delivered by Bergson in 1904 after being elected in 1900 to replace him at the Academie des sciences morales et politiques, the wing of the Institut de France that accommodates philosophers.

Ravaisson's 1868 report was thus enormously influential, and, even though nineteenth-century French philosophy has until recently been neglected, later and more famous developments in twentieth- and twenty-first-century French thinking can be understood adequately only against its background. The report arrived, in fact, at a moment of transition, and even of rebirth, for philosophy in France. Under Napoleon III's Second Empire, as Ravaisson explains in the final section of the report, philosophy had been reduced to logic in the *lycées* and the *agrégation* discontinued. This was a suppression not simply of philosophy in general, but of Victor Cousin's eclecticism in particular, which had dominated the national education system as the *de facto* state philosophy of the July Monarchy, the liberal constitutional order that spanned the revolutions of 1830 and 1848; Cousin's eclectic attempt to find a middle way between British empiricist scepticism and German idealist absolutism, by means of a liberal *bon sens* much influenced by Scottish 'common sense' philosophy, accorded with the 'citizen king' Louis-Philippe's concern to represent a *juste milieu*, a middle way, between reaction and socialist republicanism. Ravaisson does not—and could not—describe the situation so starkly, but Napoleon III's 1851 *coup d'état* brought dark days for philosophy, with those remaining in the national education system having to swear allegiance to the emperor. However, the 1863 appointment of the historian Duruy (whom Napoleon III had previously employed as an assistant in his biography of Julius Caesar) as Minister of Public Instruction represented a thawing of the regime. With recognizably reformist and liberal tendencies, Duruy promptly reinstated the *agrégation* in philosophy, and nominated Ravaisson, an old school friend from the Collège Rollin in the late 1820s, to organize and lead it.

Ravaisson thus also came to enjoy something of a philosophical renaissance. Three decades earlier, he had experienced illustrious beginnings as a philosopher: in 1834, aged twenty-one, he was the remarkably young laureate of a competition organized by the Academy of Moral and Political Sciences on Aristotle's *Metaphysics* and its historical reception with a dissertation that he would later publish in two revised volumes as *Essai sur la Métaphysique d'Aristote* (1837 and 1846); in 1836 he was received by Cousin in first place in the *agrégation* in philosophy; and then in 1838 he gained his doctorate with an undeniably brilliant primary thesis, *Of Habit*.[3] At this time, however, Ravaisson declined to submit to Cousin's discipline, and he pursued a career as a senior civil servant rather than as a university professor; in 1838 he was appointed as principal private secretary to Narcisse-Achille de Salvandy, then Minister of Public Instruction. In 1839 Ravaisson (through de Salvandy rather than Cousin) was appointed to a teaching position at the new Rennes Faculty of Humanities, but in the end the minister's preference, together with, it seems, Ravaisson's urbane horror of living far from

---

[3] Ravaisson, *Of Habit*, ed. C. Carlisle and M. Sinclair (London: Continuum, 2008).

Paris, meant that he remained in the capital.[4] When de Salvandy resigned later in the year, Ravaisson became General Inspector of Libraries, a newly created position which involved cataloguing the exceptional holdings of libraries and archives throughout France, and later, under the Second Empire, General Inspector of Higher Education. Ravaisson had not entirely ceased to write philosophy—he published a long essay on Stoicism in 1856[5]—but his professional activities had facilitated a growing interest in the history of religion and art (Ravaisson was also a practising artist who exhibited under the name of Laché).[6] This led to his nomination in 1870, just a few weeks before the fall of the Second Empire and the Prussian siege of Paris, as Curator of Classical Antiquities at the Louvre. In any case, his lack of teaching experience must have appeared as a strength rather than a weakness to Duruy in 1863, for it meant that he had never been a member of what Cousin liked to call his regiment of philosophy teachers—Ravaisson considered himself a 'stranger to the eclectic school' (Section II)—and thus looked sufficiently like a new broom.

*

In 1840 Ravaisson had, in fact, published a stinging critique of Cousin's eclectic philosophy in the *Revue des deux mondes*, the major venue for philosophical essays before the creation of the *Revue philosophique de la France et de l'étranger* in 1876 and the *Revue de métaphysique et de morale*, for which Ravaisson wrote the inaugural essay 'Metaphysics and Morals', in 1893.[7] Ravaisson returns to this critique in Section II, and again in the conclusion, of the 1868 report. The eclectic school produced a raft of important work in the history of philosophy, which Ravaisson details, but he argues that Cousin's eclectic project of drawing the best from the philosophical systems of the past was never genuinely realized: his relation to the tradition of metaphysics is essentially negative, and even when he appeals positively to Plato and Descartes, he reads them through the lens of Scottish common sense philosophy. With the Scottish philosophers, Cousin accepted the principle that we have knowledge only of phenomena, and that philosophical method, in extending an inductive method from physics to psychology, consists in induction on the basis of the observation of psychological

---

[4] Léger claims that Ravaisson taught for some time in Rennes before returning to Paris ('Notice', p. 354), but Bergson convincingly denies that Ravaisson ever took up the post ('The Life and Work of Ravaisson', p. 279).

[5] 'Essay on Stoicism' in Ravaisson, *Selected Essays*, ed. M. Sinclair (London: Bloomsbury, 2016), pp. 85–144.

[6] According to Léger ('Notice', p. 348), Ravaisson was the name of a small parcel of land on the banks of the Sonnette, in south-western France, a name which Ravaisson's father, Jean-Gaspard Laché, a Crown Prosecutor, added to his own. He died soon after his younger son's birth, but much later Ravaisson added to his patronym his mother's maiden name, Mollien, at the request of his maternal uncle, to become: Jean-Gaspard Félix Laché Ravaisson-Mollien.

[7] See 'Contemporary Philosophy' and 'Metaphysics and Morals' in Ravaisson, *Selected Essays*, pp. 59–84 and 279–95.

phenomena. In this way, in Ravaisson's eyes, Cousin's spiritualist eclecticism was no more genuinely spiritualist than it was really eclectic, for it denied the basic tenet of any 'spiritualist' philosophy since Descartes, namely that the mind has an immediate knowledge of itself as a unity underlying the variety of psychological phenomena. At the beginning of the nineteenth century, Pierre Maine de Biran had developed this position (without, it should be noted, identifying his own position as 'spiritualist'[8]) with the claim that in voluntary agency the mind has an immediate awareness—an 'apperception' that accompanies and conditions sense perception—of itself as activity, as the activity of will meeting resistance in the body. On Ravaisson's account, Cousin fails to grasp this 'primitive fact' of consciousness on his way to an essentially Platonic philosophy separating phenomena from mere conceptions, mere thoughts, whose truth could be revealed only by a sort of 'mysterious, inexplicable revelation, the work of what he called reason'. Certainly, in 1834 Cousin published Biran's manuscripts, and this may have produced a change in his philosophical orientation, but this change, Ravaisson argues, was expressed most clearly in the work of Cousin's most eminent pupil, Théodore Jouffroy, who died before his time in 1842, as well as in the work of Emile Saisset and Adolphe Garnier. Moreover, Ravaisson discerned in the work of the next generation of Cousin's pupils, such as Emile Caro and Paul Janet, who in 1864 replaced Saisset and Garnier at the Sorbonne, the Paris Faculty of Humanities, 'tendencies' that 'increasingly distance them...from the starting point of the eclectic school'. The same applies to Etienne Vacherot, whom Section XIV examines at some length. Cousin, it should be noted, was never able to read this second critique of his work by Ravaisson, but Bergson relates poignantly that in January 1867, 'old and seriously ill, just before leaving for Cannes where he was to die, Cousin made known his desire for a reconciliation; at the station, as the train was ready to leave, he held out his hand to Ravaisson; they exchanged a few words fraught with emotion'.[9]

The philosophical position from which Ravaisson criticized Cousin is partially laid out in Section I of the report, which presents a brief history of philosophy prior to French eclecticism, a history that comprises two chapters. In the first, that runs from antiquity to the seventeenth century, Ravaisson argues that the summit of Greek thinking was attained with Aristotle's apprehension of being as *energeia*, as actuality or activity; as he had first argued in his 1834 Aristotle

---

[8] On this point, see Anne Devarieux, 'Maine de Biran and the Legacy of Ideology' in *The Oxford Handbook of Modern French Philosophy*, ed. M. Sinclair and D. Whistler (forthcoming).

[9] Bergson, 'The Life and Work of Ravaisson', p. 278. In the light of this troubled relationship, and given the specificity of Ravaisson's 'spiritualist positivism' together with his claim that Cousin's eclecticism established only a 'half-spiritualism' (Section XVII), the limitations of the view that as president of the *agrégation* jury he guaranteed the 'influence of Cousin's commitment to spiritualism on French philosophy' for most of the remainder of the century should be clear; see Alan D. Schrift, 'Effects of the *Agrégation de Philosophie* on Twentieth Century French Philosophy', *Journal of the History of Philosophy* 46/3 (2008), pp. 449–74.

dissertation, 'substance' (the Greek term fatefully translated by the Latin *substantia* is *ousia*, which derives from the Greek verb *einai*, 'to be') is not some*thing*, the hidden core or the passive matter of a being, but actuality in contrast to potentiality. As Ravaisson will put it in a later text, Aristotle teaches that 'substance and energy are the same'.[10] This sort of activist interpretation of Aristotle's ontology would later be promoted by thinkers such as Martin Heidegger and Aryeh Kosman.[11] More idiosyncratic, however, is Ravaisson's view that Aristotle's statement that pure *energeia* is divine thought licenses the panpsychic claim—which shaped his reflection on habit in 1838—that actuality, everywhere, is thought, but not always of a self-conscious variety. In any case, in modernity Descartes adds concretion to this activist conception of thought and mind in at least glimpsing the truth that the essence of mental activity is will, and that the will is infinite; infinity can thus be taken in a positive sense, as plenitude, rather than, as it was in Greek thinking, as a lack. Ravaisson briefly suggests—drawing on his 1856 essay—that ancient Stoicism's notion of the 'tension' constitutive of all things points to the recognition of the will as the principle of 'tension and effort', but he also suggests that soon after Descartes, Pascal showed modern thought that the will is not a self-sufficient principle, and that beneath the will lies love and the heart. Although this idea will be crucial in Ravaisson's own philosophical development, he does not dwell on it here, and instead, in the second part of his brief history, traces how Descartes's affirmation of the infinite or absolute had to be 'put to the test and purified more than once' within a brief history of modern philosophy that situates the empiricist tradition from Locke through Berkeley and Hume to Condillac, Scottish 'common sense' philosophy, as well as Kant's critical philosophy, and that ends with Maine de Biran's philosophy of the will, which replaces the Cartesian *cogito ergo sum* by *volo ergo sum*.

Post-Kantian German thought does not appear in Ravaisson's history of modern philosophy, but in conclusion the report briefly addresses the 'great movement of renovation which Kant began', with reference to the work of Schelling, Hegel, Schopenhauer, and Hermann Lotze. Ravaisson was no stranger to German thought since he had gone to Munich to study with Schelling in 1839, but in the report his task, of course, was to elucidate the progress of French philosophy and its principal movements. After eclecticism, the report addresses French socialism; Section IV examines the ideas of Henri de Saint-Simon, Charles Fourier, and Pierre-Joseph Proudhon, while Section V examines what Ravaisson takes to be the more philosophically substantial views of Pierre Leroux and Jean Reynaud. Ravaisson treats the French socialists with sympathy as well as scepticism.

[10] Ravaisson, 'Pascal's Philosophy' in *Selected Essays*, pp. 253–78.
[11] See, in particular, Aryeh Kosman, *The Activity of Being: An Essay on Aristotle's Ontology* (Cambridge, MA: Harvard University Press, 2013). For more on Ravaisson's reading of Aristotle and on Heidegger's interest in the French philosopher's work, see my *Being Inclined: Félix Ravaisson's Philosophy of Habit* (Oxford: Oxford University Press, 2019), particularly the final section of chapter 4.

He was hardly a socialist, and his struggle against utilitarian doctrines relating to the teaching of art, doctrines that promoted forms of technical drawing,[12] highlights his distance from the more technocratic and industrial elements of French socialism. That said, the struggle also expressed a genuine concern for equality of educational opportunity for all, and his own patrician, chivalric ethics of generosity and sacrifice (see Section XXXVI) were not far from some of the Christian impulses of the early socialist thinkers. Moreover, even though Ravaisson pays no attention to socialist feminists such as Flora Tristan, Jeanne Deroin, and Pauline Roland, the promotion at several points in the report (Sections IX, XVII, and XXXII) of the work of the brilliant early nineteenth-century French mathematician, physicist, and philosopher Marie-Sophie Germain—who, as a woman, had been prevented from developing an academic career—seems to express the same concern for equality at a time when Duruy was introducing secondary education for girls in the national education system, and when the Parisian *facultés* (initially the medical faculty) were beginning to accept female students.[13] It should also not pass unnoticed that the report almost completely ignores the Traditionalist, counter-Enlightenment thinkers Joseph de Maistre and Louis de Bonald, who stood opposed to the socialists after the Revolution and Napoleon's First French Empire. Instead, in Section III Ravaisson precedes his treatment of the French socialists with a critical examination of the metaphysical doctrines of Hugues-Félicité Robert de Lamennais, who moved from Traditionalist ideas towards a liberal, reforming, and social Catholicism.

The centrepiece of Ravaisson's project in the report is the confrontation with Auguste Comte and the positivist tradition. This occupies at least six sections of the report. Section VII first shows how Comte departed from the ideas of Saint-Simon and how, in the judgement of the latter with which he concurs, the founder of positivism, with his historical account of the three stages of history—the religious, the metaphysical, and the positive or scientific—articulated a soulless phenomenalism that abjured enquiry into causes beyond visible sequences of phenomena and that assumed that the basic elements of the inorganic realm studied by physics and chemistry could explain existence as a whole. On Ravaisson's account, this phenomenalism, in its thirst for the empirically verifiable data of sense perception, fails to recognize that the most primary and positive fact of experience is the mind's awareness of itself. It is this failure concerning inner experience that contributes to the early Comte's impoverished conception of living beings, since these can be conceived, Ravaisson argues, only by analogy with mind.

---

[12] See 'On the Teaching of Drawing' in Ravaisson, *Selected Essays*, pp. 159–88.
[13] See Sandra Horvath, 'Victor Duruy and the Controversy over Secondary Education for Girls', *French Historical Studies* 9/1 (1975), pp. 83–104. On Tristan, Deroin, and Roland, see Felicia Gordon and Maire Cross (eds), *Early French Feminisms* (Cheltenham: Edward Elgar, 1996).

Comte's ideas, as he acknowledged, owe much to the tradition of British empiricism, and Section VIII charts their influence in Britain, which was more extensive than in France. Comte's doctrine was brought to England by George Lewes and adopted, not without reservations particularly concerning its practical prescriptions, by J. S. Mill, but Ravaisson additionally discusses thinkers such as Alexander Bain, Samuel Bailey, and Herbert Spencer, rather than doctrinaire, card-carrying positivists.[14] On Ravaisson's account, scepticism was the result of Comte's early positivism in Britain, just as a crude materialism was its main result in France. Crucially, however, the later Comte—whom Ravaisson, in opposition to Mill, considers to be the 'good' rather than the 'bad' Comte—had undergone a 'metamorphosis'. On the way to considering human nature in society, he progressively came to recognize that biological life was not merely a modification of inorganic existence: the second, 1838 volume of his *Course on Positive Philosophy* denied this for animal life, whereas the sixth, 1842 volume denied it for life as a whole. In a living being, the whole, and thus a principle of organization, makes possible the parts and their arrangement. Biology thus cannot be reduced to physics and chemistry, and, according to Ravaisson's favourite Comtean formula, the superior cannot be explained by the inferior. On the contrary, the later Comte—whom Georges Canguilhem would describe as the 'most illustrious representative of Montpellier vitalism'[15] in nineteenth-century philosophy of biology—suggests that it is the superior that explains the inferior, that animal life can be grasped only from the perspectives opened by sociology, and that echoes or vestiges of life can be grasped in the inorganic realm. On this basis, although Comte always rejected any appeal to direct knowledge of the mind as offering access to this superior principle, Ravaisson claims that in his later work, concerned as he was with a religion of humanity, with music and the arts, the founder of an originally superficial 'physical positivism' moved towards a 'spiritual or metaphysical positivism', and that he might even have arrived at it had he lived longer.[16]

Post-Comtean French thinkers such as Emile Littré, Hyppolyte Taine, and Ernest Renan were advancing in the same direction, as Ravaisson argues in Sections X–XII. Littré, celebrated more now for his dictionary than for his contributions to philosophy, rejected Comte's 'religion of humanity' and the second phase of his philosophy, like Mill, but in the face of biological facts he was no less forced to admit the reality of a form of purposiveness and thus final causation.

---

[14] See T. R. Wright, *The Religion of Humanity: The Impact of Comtean Positivism on Victorian Britain* (Cambridge: Cambridge University Press, 1986).

[15] This is the concluding affirmation of Canguilhem's 1958 'L'école de Montpellier jugée par Auguste Comte' in *Oeuvres complètes*, vol. 3: *Ecrits d'histoire des sciences et d'épistémologie* (Paris: Vrin, 2019). Montpellier vitalism is discussed in more detail below.

[16] For more on Ravaisson's reading of Comte, and the latter's relation to the spiritualist tradition, see Laurent Clauzade, 'Auguste Comte and Spiritualism', *British Journal for the History of Philosophy* 28/5 (2020), pp. 944–65.

The same can be said of Taine in his concern to replace Comtean agnosticism concerning causes with the view that they can be accounted for in factual, phenomenal terms. Taine's positivist commitments had meant that he did not pass the philosophy *agrégation* in 1851—the last one presided over by Cousin before it was discontinued the following year—and had to earn a living by his pen before being named professor of the history of art and aesthetics at the Paris School of Fine Arts in 1865, but in his 1857 *French Philosophers of the Nineteenth Century*,[17] Taine tried to correct positivism on this score while delivering a broadside against what he construes as the spiritualist tradition. Ravaisson is clearly sympathetic to Taine's critique of Cousinian orthodoxy, but underlines his failure to appreciate the originality of Maine de Biran's work: if Taine had understood Biran, claims Ravaisson, he might have perceived the possibility of a more spiritualist positivism, a genuine and positive spiritualism, that postulates not ghostly entities behind the scenes, but activity, the voluntary activity of mind, as the fundamental fact of experience.

Section XV finds the same movement, most importantly, in the work of France's most prominent French life scientist of the time, Claude Bernard, who wrote the 1867 Exposition universelle report on the progress of physiology. Bernard was influenced by Comte's early positivism,[18] and in the 1865 *Introduction to the Study of Experimental Medicine*[19] he seemed to many to put an end once and for all to traditional vitalist theories by extending the reach of mechanical determinism to all the particular phenomena of living beings. That said, in order to account for the concert and unity formed by these phenomena, Bernard still speaks of an 'organic idea' that is 'creative' of the organism as a whole, and which constitutes, in both morphogenesis and phylogenesis, in Ravaisson's Comtean terms, 'both order and progress, and progress above all'. Even though Bernard does not commit himself to any philosophical elucidation of this principle, Ravaisson argues, following Paul Janet in an 1865 article, and before Bergson,[20] that the great biologist leaves room for a psychological, and in some way purposive, interpretation of life in its 'creative evolution'.

Controversy concerning the nature of life had never abated in the nineteenth century, as Section XXIII shows in examining animist, vitalist, and organicist philosophies. Animism, which supposed that the principle of biological life is one with the mind, was a late seventeenth-century reaction to iatromechanism and had found its most prominent representative in G. E. Stahl in Jena, then Halle;

[17] Hyppolyte Taine, *Les philosophes français du XIXe siècle* (Paris: Hachette, 1857). This pamphlet, much less stately than Ravaisson's report, became *Les philosophes classiques du XIXe siècle en France* in later editions.

[18] In this connection, see Annie Petit, 'D'Auguste Comte à Claude Bernard, un positivisme déplacé', *Romantisme* 21-2 (1978), pp. 45–62.

[19] Claude Bernard, *An Introduction to the Study of Experimental Medicine* (New York: Henry Schuman, 1927).

[20] See Bergson, 'The Philosophy of Claude Bernard' in *The Creative Mind*, pp. 238–47.

vitalism, according to which the principle of life is independent of mind as well as superior to the principles of matter, was a critical reaction to animism and had been promoted most notably in Montpellier since the time of Paul Joseph Barthez; organicism, sometimes discussed as 'plurivitalism', which rejected the vitalist conception of an overarching principle in the organism and explained life by particular properties of the organs, had been promoted in Paris since the time of Xavier Bichat. In 1838, Ravaisson had contributed to the debate by arguing that the vitalists had criticized only a caricature of Stahl's animism in failing to appreciate its distinction of *logismos* and *logos*, of clear and distinct thought, the domain of reason and the imagination, and a kind of pre-reflective intuition, thought without image or distinction, responsible for apparently involuntary vital functions. Ravaisson took this position on the basis of the claim that the gradual acquisition of a motor habit, where by means of its repetition an action becomes more and more—but never totally—independent of will and consciousness, shows that Stahl's distinction between *logos* and *logismos* is really a matter of degree and that there exists a continuity throughout human nature, and even throughout nature as a whole. In 1868 Ravaisson reaffirms his position in the contemporary context: there exists 'between the instinctive and the voluntary a mixture, an intimate fusion, an indivisible continuity' (Section XXVI). Hence Ravaisson can argue that when Francisque Bouillier states that he accepts everything in Stahl's animism except the claim that the vital functions are the work of thought, rather than of soul in a broader sense, he has misjudged Stahl's intentions only slightly less than his recent vitalist critics Albert Lemoine and Charles Lévêque, and failed to see that the purposiveness in vital functions such as instinct means that they have an essential connection to thought. The issue of instinct lies, in fact, 'at the heart of all the philosophical and scientific controversies of the century',[21] as Henri Joly wrote in 1877, and it is crucial to Ravaisson's animist project within his report. Section XXVII addresses recent accounts of it from the perspective of an indivisible continuity between vital functions and reflective thought, while Sections XXVIII–XXX address the related issues of sleep, madness, genius, physiognomy, and language.

Before those discussions, Section XXVI draws the same claim concerning continuity from recent work in neuroscience, which had given the lie to theories of the cerebral localization of mental functions in highlighting what we now call 'neuroplasticity'. In cases of brain damage, research had shown, as Ravaisson relates, that conscious operations usually requiring the cerebrum can be undertaken with lower regions of the cerebrospinal nervous system, normally employed solely for instinctive functions, such as the medulla oblongata. Ravaisson therefore can affirm that 'it is not the organ which causes the function, as materialism

---

[21] Henri Joly, *Psychologie comparée: l'homme et l'animal* (Paris: Hachette, 1877), p. 6.

maintains, but it is the functions, the action, which under certain physical conditions subjugates and appropriates the organ'. This insight will be important for Bergson's conception of the relation between mind and body in *Matter and Memory*, and for his critique of brain-trace theories of episodic memory in particular. The conclusion of the third chapter of that 1896 text cites a memorable line from Ravaisson's own survey of recent work on memory in Section XXII, but extending the citation beyond the semicolon illuminates the full extent of Bergson's inheritance: 'It is materiality, on which our senses are partly dependent, which begets oblivion; pure mind, on the contrary, is all action, and thus all unity, all duration, all memory.' That said, Ravaisson's approach does not sanction the dualist basis of Bergson's reflections in *Matter and Memory* or his concomitant concessions to mechanistic neuro-philosophy concerning habit.[22]

Section XXVI extends this critique of mechanistic neuro-philosophy to the idea of reflex action. Ravaisson has evidently not forgotten that the concept of reflex action (response to stimuli occurring locally within the nervous system and without the intervention of the brain) was the fruit of animist and vitalist, rather than mechanist medical philosophies. He has not been misled by the nineteenth-century legend—promoted by Du Bois Reymond in Germany in 1858, deconstructed by Canguilhem almost a century later—that the origin of modern ideas of the reflex arc is to be found in Descartes.[23] After physiologists such as Robert Whytt, Georg Prochaska, and then Eduard Pflüger in the nineteenth century (who, for all that he seemed to endorse a mechanistic perspective, had written of a 'spinal soul' to account for reflexes), Ravaisson discerns in reflex action, not a blind, mechanical response to stimuli but 'some power to feel, to perceive, and then to aim at a goal, to tend towards an end, and in these depths of the most obscure vitality... something of a glimmer emanating from something that knows and wants'. This licenses the conclusion, 'that at bottom everything comes back to the same principle, but one that is engaged in conditions of existence which, grasped from the point at which it possesses and governs itself, make it more and more external and foreign to itself'. Does Ravaisson thus simply restate, as Canguilhem claims, precisely what 'the notion of reflex had to overcome as its most intimate obstacle', namely the theory that involuntary movement is 'voluntary movement that has become automatic, i.e. unconscious, by habit'?[24] The idea of the vital power 'emanating' from the will invites Canguilhem's reading, but, in truth, Ravaisson does not affirm here that all reflex actions were once voluntary actions. He states only that conscious will and the vital power in reflexes are different functions or levels of one and the same principle, and he held the same

---

[22] On the problematic dualism in *Matter and Memory*, see chapter 3 of my *Bergson* (Abingdon: Routledge, 2020).
[23] Georges Canguilhem, *La formation du concept de réflexe aux XVIIe et XVIIIe siècles* (Paris: Presses universitaires de France, 1955).
[24] Canguilhem, *La formation du concept de réflexe*, p. 149.

EDITOR'S INTRODUCTION 11

view in his 1838 *Of Habit*. Pace Canguilhem, the 'essential idea of *De l'habitude*' was *not* that 'all automatic movement is at bottom only reflection mechanized by forgetting'.[25] Although the text stated hyperbolically that habit leads voluntary action to become instinctive, Ravaisson only emphasized thus that habit and instinct are continuous with each other (that it is impossible to say where habit ends and instinct begins) while remaining different in origin: habits, but not instincts, are acquired in a single life. Ravaisson was not committed in 1838 to the thesis that *all* 'automatic' movement, including all instinctive movements, originated in reflective, voluntary consciousness, whether in the course of a single life or in the evolution of a species (according to a Larmarckian theory of the inheritance of acquired characteristics), and he did not suppose that the lower levels of what he sees as a continuous scale of existence are necessarily or entirely a product of the higher levels.[26] Canguilhem is right to affirm that Ravaisson's doctrine remained unchanged, but he perceives less clearly the details of the doctrine that did not change.

*

The focal point of Ravaisson's *French Philosophy of the Nineteenth Century*, as we have seen, is the development of the positivist tradition in the light of the life sciences, but the report also attempts to incorporate philosophers working independently of that tradition into its grand narrative concerning the progression of French thought. Section XIII addresses Charles Renouvier's neo-Kantian, 'critical' philosophy. Renouvier had initially worked with the socialists Leroux and Reynaud, but had then delineated his own philosophical doctrine in the four volumes of his 1854–64 *Essays in General Critique*.[27] After graduating from the Ecole Polytechnique, he had no university affiliation and was still relatively unknown, but Ravaisson's survey of his work in the report was the first of its kind and changed Renouvier's philosophical fortunes: the report 'marks the moment' when his work 'began to count significantly for university professors. The generation of young philosophers who at this time were preparing for the *agrégation* were to varying degrees influenced by it.'[28] At the same time, in 1868, Renouvier published his own study 'On Nineteenth-Century Philosophy in France' as the inaugural essay of the philosophical yearbook *L'Année philosophique*,[29] a study which criticizes Cousinian eclecticism and then evaluates French socialism and

---

[25] Canguilhem, *La formation du concept de réflexe*, p. 149.
[26] On the subtleties of Ravaisson's position in this connection, see my *Being Inclined*, pp. 99–104. Perhaps Canguilhem's reading would have been more nuanced and favourable if he had referred to Ravaisson's treatment of reflex action in the 1868 report rather than just the remark in the 1899–1900 'Philosophical Testament'.
[27] Charles Renouvier, *Essais de critique générale* (Paris: Armand Colin, 1912).
[28] Gaston Milhaud, *La philosophie de Charles Renouvier* (Paris: Vrin, 1927), p. 15.
[29] Charles Renouvier, 'De la philosophie du dix-neuvième siècle en France' in *L'Année philosophique*, ed. F. Pillon (Paris: Germer Baillière, 1868).

positivism from a Kantian rather than spiritualist perspective. Although from the beginning Renouvier's critical, Kantian perspective restricts knowledge to phenomena, physical and psychological, and denies any direct self-knowledge in rejecting, with the positivists, the possibility of knowledge of anything not merely relative but absolute, Ravaisson senses the possibility of a return to metaphysics in his affirmations concerning a moral absolute and in his concern to reduce the Kantian gulf separating freedom and the empirical world by rooting knowledge itself in freedom and the will.

In addition, Section XXXII turns to Antoine Augustin Cournot, remembered more now as a mathematician and economist rather than philosopher, whose epistemological work stands somewhere between the positivists and Kant. For Cournot, we can have no deductive assurance that what we consider to be laws of nature actually order the phenomenal facts of experience. As a development of his ideas about chance, probability, and indeterminacy in nature, in his 1851 *Essay on the Foundations of Knowledge and on the Characteristics of Philosophical Critique* he argued that there is a non-calculable, non-numerical philosophical probability that what we posit as laws, which are established by induction and analogy on the basis of facts, do conform to the intrinsically unknowable order of the world.[30] There is a philosophical probability, but no certainty, that our rational nature, guided as it is by ideas of order, law, unity, and harmony, corresponds to the order of the universe. Ravaisson, however, sees in this appeal to innate ideas of order, unity, harmony a recognition of moral and aesthetic principles as forming the foundation of knowledge and existence, and a philosophy close to that of the later Comte; do we not see, he asks, in the 'different systems of our time, that there is more agreement than it seems and more than we think?'

When Ravaisson suggests that this turn to moral and aesthetic principles requires a new unifying metaphysics, he writes in a prophetic mode: 'some new Kepler, new Newton' will discover 'the sun of the intellectual and moral world', and reveal why the 'systems initially produced by the most pronounced aversion to metaphysics, ultimately gravitate towards the very idea from which they were supposed to have departed without return' (Section XXXII). For this reason, we should not be surprised that when he attempts to review recent work on morality and aesthetics directly, in Sections XXXIV and XXXV respectively, Ravaisson's own claims leave something to be desired. His arguments that any ethics of duty presupposes an idea of the good will doubtless not convince the deontologist, but Ravaisson replaces what he takes to be an abstract, formal concern for duty with an ethics of sacrifice (see also the conclusion of Section XVI): just as existence as a whole can be thought of as the emptying or relaxation, from top to bottom, of a principle that was once fully in possession of itself, so too human action,

---

[30] Antoine Augustin Cournot, *Essai sur les fondements de nos connaissances et sur les caractères de la critique philosophique* (Paris: Hachette, 1851).

grounded in love, should be based on self-sacrifice and immolation. Ravaisson's claims in Section XXXV about the inner connection of beauty, grace, love, and the good, as well as his attempt to identify the beautiful and the sublime, also require development, but some of these themes he addressed in more detail in his other work on art and aesthetics.[31]

We should also not be surprised that in the report's peroration, Ravaisson falls back on a traditional philosophical doctrine of moral necessity when he outlines the idea of freedom involved in the metaphysical position that grounds his approach to aesthetics and ethics. Following Leibniz, Ravaisson attempts to reconcile an idea of freedom with an idea of necessity: a form of necessity, he argues, conditions what we call 'free will', but this is a moral necessity rather than a mechanical necessity, a necessity that belongs to final causation rather than efficient causation such that the mind has no power to do other than what it apprehends as the best. For Ravaisson, this 'relative necessity', which implies 'contingency and will', is no hinderance to human freedom; the person who perceives the good and has to act accordingly is freer than the one 'enslaved by the passions', torn between 'good and evil'. One might, at the very least, expect more discussion of this classically controversial issue, and it is particularly in this regard true to say that there are 'conventional and rhetorical aspect of certain developments and certain positions...in the *Report*'.[32] Moreover, one might have expected Ravaisson to address the incompatibility of this position with his own metaphysics in *Of Habit*. Although it discussed the force of habit according to an idea of a 'necessity of attraction and desire', this necessity was conceived as being acquired by degree, and as belonging to the force of habit rather than consciousness in general; the argument was that the aim or final cause is *gradually* incorporated into a now habitual action such that reflective thought is no longer required to guide or even to initiate it. Given that necessity cannot admit degrees (something is either necessary or not), the idea of a 'necessity of attraction and desire' could only be an approximation of Ravaisson's real position in 1838. Be that as it may, thirty years later he seems to affirm that it is only conscious awareness and not the attraction and desire that decrease and increase by degrees.

Still, the report retains *Of Habit*'s earlier panpsychic project, for these degrees of consciousness, Ravaisson proclaims, are present throughout nature as a whole: from our own experience of the gradual decline of conscious awareness in the acquisition of a habit, and in recognizing that there is a certain non-mechanical elasticity in bare material things, as Leibniz showed, it is possible to discover by analogy a graduated unitary principle constituting nature as a whole. Ravaisson's

---

[31] See Ravaisson, *Selected Essays*.
[32] Dominique Janicaud, *Ravaisson et la métaphysique: une généalogie du spiritualisme français* (Paris: Vrin, 1997), p. 116. For more on Ravaisson's invocation of moral necessity in the report, see chapter 4 of my *Being Inclined*.

concomitant conception of matter as an emanation and relaxation of mind draws on Stoic and neo-Platonist ideas more than those of Leibniz: 'The Stoics, in their very physical language, defined the first cause, or the Divinity, as a burning ether, at the maximum of tension; matter as the same ether relaxed. Could it not be said, in a similar way, that what the first cause concentrates in its immutable eternity, it unfolds, so to speak, relaxed and diffused in those elementary conditions of materiality which are time and space; that it thus lays down, as it were, the basis of natural existence, a basis on which, by that continuous progress that is the order of nature, from degree to degree, from realm to realm, everything returns from material dispersion to the unity of spirit?' Diffusion and relaxation characterize not only the relation of the human mind to matter, but of the divine mind to the world as a whole. This means, for Ravaisson, that the relation of the divine principle to creation is to be conceived as 'kenotic', as an emptying and diffusion, and that this kenotic descent allows in turn, and in time, for the return of material dispersion to the height and unity of the divine source. It is from this dual perspective, which Section II seems to find in Lammenais's theology, that Ravaisson approaches not just later nineteenth-century theological doctrines, particularly in Sections XVI to XIX of the report, but also evolutionary biology.[33]

This conception of space as relaxation, and thus of extension as ex-tension, will motivate the third chapter of Bergson's *Creative Evolution*, but the vision expressed in the final section of the report found its most immediate prolongation in the work of Jules Lachelier, who is manifestly Ravaisson's protégé in 1868 (see the remarks in Sections X, XIV, and XXXIII). Lachelier's 1871 thesis *On the Ground of Induction* begins with an effusive dedication to Ravaisson and ends in a reassertion of his philosophical vision: the 'true philosophy of nature is a spiritualist realism, in the eyes of which every being is a force and every force a thought that tends towards an increasingly complete awareness of itself'.[34] Lachelier may appear to depart from Ravaisson's ideas when he writes that 'it is not...universal necessity but rather universal contingency that is the veritable definition of existence, the spirit of nature and the last word of thought', but he immediately adds in a Ravaissonian vein that 'what we call contingency in opposition to a brute and blind mechanism is, on the contrary, a necessity of attraction [*convenance*] and choice, the only one that accounts for everything'.[35] The concluding pages of the thesis, in fact, expand on the doctrine of moral necessity in terms borrowed from Ravaisson's report. Lachelier's work, however, clearly expresses the influence of Kant, and his philosophy of nature is more accepting of mechanism and thus more dualist than the one promoted by his teacher. *On the Ground of Induction* argues that our inductions are based on a conception of nature as a nexus of

---

[33] On this point, see 'Philosophical Testament' in *Selected Essays*.
[34] Jules Lachelier, *Du fondement de l'induction* (Paris: Alcan, 1907), p. 102.
[35] Lachelier, *Du fondement de l'induction*, p. 86.

mechanical, efficient causation, but then argues that this conception of nature requires a supplement of final causation in order to explain the harmony in biological life and nature as a whole.

The idea of contingency subsequently takes centre stage in Boutroux's doctoral thesis of 1874, *On the Contingency of the Laws of Nature*, which was also dedicated to Ravaisson. Within the framework of a Ravaissonian philosophy of nature, Boutroux attempts to prise apart final causation and moral necessitation: 'the higher one climbs the scale of beings, the more one sees develop a principle that, in a sense, resembles necessity: the attraction for certain objects. But it is not pushed by something already realized; it is attracted by a thing that is not already there, and that, perhaps, will never be'. Hence 'the idea of necessity...would be, at bottom, the translation, in the most abstract language possible, of the action exerted by the ideal on things'.[36] Moral as well as mechanical ideas of necessitation are merely abstractions and approximations, and although this indeterminist doctrine—which echoes and develops that of Cournot—contrasts with the letter of the 1868 report, it no less discovers its true spirit and does so in returning to the subject of Ravaisson's doctoral thesis, namely habit. It is thus true to say, perhaps despite appearances, that Boutroux was Ravaisson's most 'faithful disciple'.[37] Boutroux was certainly faithful to the report when he extended it in 1908 with his own 'Philosophy in France since 1867',[38] which described a renewal of philosophical activity that in many ways Ravaisson's report had initiated. Within the course of this post-1867 renewal, Ravaisson had tried to draw together a metaphysics, ethics, and aesthetics according to a guiding idea of love within the 'Philosophical Testament' that was found on his desk when he died in 1900, but in many ways it was in the work of his disciples, including Bergson, that the ideas sketched in the report gained their fullest expression.[39]

*

As originally published, *French Philosophy in the Nineteenth Century* contains no titles for its thirty-six numbered sections, but I have provided headings in this edition. Ravaisson would doubtless have found them gauche and compromising, but they are formulated to make it easier for an interested anglophone reader—a reader probably not additionally motivated, unlike Ravaisson's *agrégation* candidates, by fear of failing an examination and having to seek an alternative occupation—to find her way through the text over a century and a half after its

---

[36] Emile Boutroux, *On the Contingency of the Laws of Nature*, trans. Fred Rothwell (Chicago: Open Court, 1916), p. 177.
[37] Denise Leduc-Fayette, 'Loi de grâce et de liberté', *Les Etudes philosophiques* (Jan.–Mar. 1993), pp. 25–34, p. 25.
[38] Boutroux, 'La philosophie en France depuis 1867', *Revue de métaphysique et de morale* 16/6 (1908), pp. 683–716.
[39] See Ravaisson, *Selected Essays*, pp. 295–336.

publication. In the same spirit, when it is not obvious what texts Ravaisson is citing, sometimes loosely, I have provided references to them and to their English translations when possible. The few original footnotes are indicated with an asterisk and labelled [Ravaisson's footnote]. My own interventions, which also contain biographical remarks on the less well-known philosophers mentioned, are numbered footnotes.

I have removed all of the instances of the abbreviated honorifics 'M.' and 'Messrs.' in the translation. This decision to conform to less formal modern usage was supported by the fact that Ravaisson did not always use them consistently. For the sake of readability, titles of books and articles are translated in the body of the text, even when the item does not exist in English translation, with the original French name (and I have often had to correct the titles when Ravaisson names them loosely) appearing, on its first appearance, in a footnote. The same applies to institutions when they are easily identifiable in English; the Académie des sciences morales et politiques is thus rendered as the Academy of Moral and Political Sciences, but the Ecole Normale Supérieure remains as it is, given that Superior Normal School sounds rather odd—and more of a contradiction in terms—in English. In order to avoid confusion, I have not translated either the names of journals or the names of French learned societies. *L'âme* in French suggests something more substantial, to use traditional philosophical language, than *l'esprit*, as does the English 'soul' in relation to 'spirit', but it is not possible to translate these terms consistently, particularly given that English also possesses, and often demands, 'mind' as an alternative translation of both.

For suggesting improvements on earlier versions of this introduction, my thanks are due to Alison Stone, Pietro Terzi, Tatsuya Murayama, Adi-Efal Lautenschläger, Mogens Laerke, and to an anonymous reader employed by Oxford University Press. I am also grateful to Mogens Laerke and to Laurent Clauzade for advice concerning Ravaisson's citation of Leibniz and Comte respectively.

FRENCH PHILOSOPHY IN THE NINETEENTH CENTURY

Félix Ravaisson

I
The History of Philosophy prior to the Nineteenth Century

In order to understand the state of contemporary philosophy, its movement and its progress, it is worthwhile to recall briefly its origins.

Philosophy dates from the quite remote time when it was clearly recognized that there exists in things, besides the various properties studied by the various sciences, something that constitutes their being and their unity, which in all things is considered by a single science. High philosophy dates from the time, still very remote but more recent, when it was recognized that in order to explain being and unity more is required than matter conceived as what things are composed of, and that something else must give to matter a form or a way of existing. This something was at first supposed by the Greek genius—which was all order, all measure, all harmony—to reside in number. This was, instead of getting to the bottom of things, to the principle of their reality and life, to remain satisfied somehow with their traits, their outline, through which our intellect grasps them. Such was the character of Pythagorean and Platonic philosophy; such was also the character of the art—as sublime as the philosophy, but with forms more epic than dramatic, more harmonious though still animated—of the contemporaries of Plato, Sophocles and Phidias.

A little later, at the time when Menander, Praxiteles, Apelles began to express in their moving creations powers of life and soul that had previously been more or less ignored, Aristotle, an attentive observer of realities, in both the physical and moral orders, realized that everything that exists has its being and its unity from movement and by something like a principle of life which binds all the parts together by penetrating them in all their depth. He saw that qualities, quantities, relations—those modes under which objects present themselves to our understanding and which his predecessors believed to be sufficient to explain them—are things which exist only in other things, which, on the contrary, subsist in themselves, separately, independently, and are beings properly so called, substances. This is the great division, established by the author of *Categories*, between that which exists by itself and that which, on the contrary, just as a surface exists only in a solid, exists only in that which exists by itself. Secondly, he saw that, in the category of what exists by itself, of being properly speaking, of substance, it was necessary to distinguish, on the one hand, virtual or potential existence, which is, as it were, only a beginning of existence, and which is all that matter possesses in relation to what it will receive through a particular form; on the other hand, real, actual existence, to which there is nothing more to add, which is the end and perfection, the existence constituted by actuality [*acte*], the source and ground of movement, and the cause, through movement, of being and unity. Consequently, he saw that the name 'substance' is fitting, rigorously speaking, for this actuality only. He then saw, and Plato was not entirely ignorant of this, that complete and perfect activity, whence derives all other activity, to which all movement goes back, is the activity of thought, on which the whole of nature consequently depended, and which, independent of everything, was sufficient for everything and for itself. He thus posited, at a height that neither physics nor logic alone can reach, above material realities and the abstractions by which our understanding measures them, the object of what he was the first to call, with an expressive name, 'metaphysics', and that is to say the science of the supernatural, a science that is as universal as its object, and to which all sciences should be tied as to their common centre.[1]

With Aristotle, however, metaphysics had only just begun.

The art of Praxiteles and Apelles, though it came close to reality, to life, did not yet quite touch it. Similarly, the doctrine of the author of *Metaphysics* quite often did not advance beyond formulae that, though closer to reality than Pythagoras's numbers or Plato's idea-numbers, nevertheless remained far from it, or perhaps touched it without embracing it. How to understand this 'perfection (*entelechia*)' or this 'actuality' that were supposed to account for everything? What does it mean exactly to define light as the 'actuality of the transparent'; sound as the 'common actuality of the air in movement and hearing'; the soul as 'the actuality of an organized body'? It is tempting to say with Leibniz: 'He appeals to his "actuality" too much, which actually says very little.'[2]

Stoicism, instead of this rather obscure 'actuality', and in direct opposition to the 'inertia' of Epicurean materialism, saw everywhere 'tension'. Here the movement and the actuality that generate it are mixed, and it is consequently a more obscure notion than that of actuality, but which, from another perspective, from that of the effort that it involves, led thought to what explains, in the clarity of inner experience, both tension and effort, namely will.

After Stoicism, when Greek science and art was aging and becoming increasingly sterile, Christianity appeared, revealing, above physical and even intellectual life, at a depth that had hardly been suspected, a moral and spiritual life that would shed more and more light on them, and infused them with its force.

---

[1] Now, of course, the orthodox view is that the title *Metaphysics* was invented by the editors of the diverse manuscripts that they gathered together under that title.

[2] Gottfried Wilhelm Leibniz, *New Essays on Human Understanding*, III, iv, §10, p. 298. Here and below I have generally relied above all on P. Remnant and J. Bennett's translation (Cambridge: Cambridge University Press, 1996) of Leibniz's text, but the page number refers to the 1962 Akademie-Verlag of Berlin edition of the *Nouveaux essais sur l'entendement humain* by A. Robinet and H. Schepers.

Such were the elements that antiquity bequeathed to the Middle Ages.

The Middle Ages, a period of renewal—thus, in many respects, of infancy and weakness—possessing only debris from the past, could hardly go further in science than antiquity, could hardly grasp reality more closely and further penetrate it. Also often content, like antiquity, to explain facts by extraordinary actions without determinate conditions, it saw everywhere powers quite similar to those that we find in ourselves, and by which it easily, without incurring the costs of observation and experiment, accounted for all natural phenomena. 'They were helpful goblins which came forwards like gods on the stage, or like the fairies in *Amadis*, to do on demand anything that a philosopher wants of them without ways or means.'[3]

It was not possible, however, given the regularity with which certain physical effects are bound, after all, to particular circumstances, to imagine ascribing reason and freedom to their immediate causes. Only a vague and indeterminate idea of them was gained—as vague, one has to admit, as the ideas that we have, still often now, of what are named forces, which are neither matter, nor mind, but somehow belong to both. With these mysterious powers, *occult qualities* acting without intelligible means, *substantial forms* that are effective and creative all by themselves, scholasticism thought it could explain everything, but it explained nothing. In what it named causes, as soon as it had to withdraw what it had found in them that was analogous to intentional action, it was left with only general expressions of the phenomena themselves, pure logical signs, simple categories, and, instead of solutions to problems, statements in more abstract terms. Often taking thus 'the straw of terms for the grain of things' (Leibniz),[4] it arrived finally at the Art of Ramon Llull, who, taking the terms by which realities can be designated as equivalents of these realities themselves, 'taught', according to Descartes, 'how to speak about everything without knowing anything'.[5] The inventor of this art called it the 'great art'; a great art of transmutation, which was the aim of the ambitious but impotent science of the age, a universal alchemy by which anything could be made from anything. Such were the empty promises of a logic that thought it possible to grasp things by words. This made Leonard da Vinci, the great initiator of modern thought, lover of nature and reality, declare that the intellectual sciences were deceitful (*le bugiarde scienze mentali*).

Among this luxuriance of terms and formulae, it was still possible to discern realities. Beneath all this scholastic dross, there was hidden some gold. Beneath

---

[3] Leibniz, *New Essays on Human Understanding*, IV, iii, §7, p. 382.

[4] Leibniz, *Theodicy* (Illinois: Open Court, 1985), §320.

[5] Ravaisson writes 'Raymond Lulle', but he is referring to the medieval philosopher Ramon Llull (1232–1316), author of *Ars Magna*, a logical system to discover the truth that was intended to aid interfaith dialogue. Descartes's critical comment on Llull is to be found in the second part of the *Discourse on Method*; see *The Philosophical Writings of Descartes*, vol. 1, ed. J. Cottingham, R. Stoothoft, and D. Murdoch (Cambridge: Cambridge University Press, 1985).

so many vain sentences, beneath what one of our contemporaries has called 'a world of foolishness', some wisdom lay dormant. The time had not yet come for it to burst forth.

Descartes appeared, in whom the teaching of the Schools was joined to experience of the world and to a mind that long voyages in many countries, the experience of many different sorts of people as well as of different ways of living and thinking, had liberated from all prejudices. Purged of the many phantoms that haunted the shadowy imagination of the doctors of the Schools, and with which it populated everything, he saw reality as if stripped bare. Beneath the confusion of equivocal, semi-logical, and semi-personal forms, he recognized where to draw the line and the necessity of a grand distinction: on the one hand, thought, this simple and single principle that we know clearly in ourselves; on the other, what we see clearly outside of us, this multiple and diffuse existence that forms body, or extension. Philosophy, which had floated for so long in the air among fictions, thus gained a foothold, became positive. It no longer had to do merely with reasoning, but with fact and experiment.

It had been thought, at least generally, that experience reached only the facts of the physical order, particular and limited facts. Now one sees that mind sees itself, and that in seeing itself it discovers, without a complicated syllogistic apparatus, but as if in bright and brilliant light, the principle of both itself and everything else: on the outside, body, so real, and that can be touched; on the inside, the mind that touches itself, and, in the mind, without separation, God, still more real, and that can somehow be touched more closely. This double realism, so opposed to what can be called the rationalism of the Middle Ages, and even to the greater part of antiquity, constituted the ground of the Cartesian system.

That is not all: in thought, of which reflection gives us immediate knowledge, Descartes distinguishes intellect, wholly passive, and will, essentially active; and while the intellect is always determined, finite, the will, he remarks, is absolutely without hindrance or limitation, free, indeed, with an infinite freedom. Taking up a path that Christianity had prepared, he thereby introduced, as an attribute of the superior principle that is manifest in thought, what antiquity, preoccupied above all by what was determinate and determining in thought and how it is the source of order, had attributed only to the material and inferior principle, as a cause of multiplicity and, consequently, of disorder and imperfection, namely: infinity. Infinity, for the first time, becomes the character of the soul, and still more of God; infinity, as found in perfect and absolute will. We should not, says Descartes, imagine the Divinity making his resolutions conform to what is given to the intellect. This would be to retrieve the Jupiter, subject to Destiny, of the ancients; we should instead admit that any divine operation can be reduced, as if to its sole principle, to an infinitely free will.

Pascal, with his profound vision, saw the infinite in all things; the infinite proper to the divine manifesting itself both in immensity, which imitates it, and in smallness, which, from division to smaller division, tends ceaselessly towards nothingness; these are two infinites between which we are suspended. Moreover, the author of *Pensées* revealed, with Christianity, something that is the source of will itself, something that surpasses both bodies and intellect: 'Charity (love)', he said, 'is of another order, and supernatural.'[6]

In this new principle of the infinite—revealed, in a certain way, by Descartes and generalized by Pascal—Leibniz discovered the ground of all science. There is a more general order in things than Descartes ever saw, more regular than Pascal saw, but to which their principles lead. Everything is proportionate, analogous, harmonious. Everything is bound together and is continuous within a concatenation that nothing interrupts: this is the law of universal continuity, according to which the manifold general rules of movement proposed by Descartes, which would bring disaccord into nature, should be reformed and completed. This law of continuity leads, on the one hand, in mathematics, to the advance of the infinitesimal calculus, wherein the same subsisting relations, whatever the values might be, can be followed beyond any finite quantity; on the other hand, in nature, it leads to the progress by which it stretches out in all directions, not quite to an infinite greatness and an infinite smallness, which are physically as well as numerically unconceivable, but to a greatness and to a smallness that go beyond any determinate value.

Now, if everything is repeated as analogous in the quantitative indefiniteness of time, of space, of all the universe, this is because there is always the same ground for the repetition of identical relations. This ground, in the final analysis, is that in all finite things there is the same ground of being, which is found with particular limitations, but which in itself is exempt from them, and is consequently infinite, and infinite because it is perfect and absolute.

Leibniz, at the same time, brought to light even more clearly than Descartes that, since finite and relative existences are such by the admixture of a passive element that is their matter, the true infinite, the absolute, was the wholly active existence that is mind.

Kant, further developing what Descartes, Pascal, and Leibniz had conceived, showed, better than anyone ever had, that in the freedom of the will there lies a special principle, wholly independent of the sequences of phenomena, a principle that alone constituted, beyond the conditions of material existence from which the intellect itself did not seem wholly exempt, what he called the supersensible, what we can call, with more familiar and synonymous terms, the supernatural or metaphysical. Persuaded that all experience is subject to the conditions of sensibility, it seemed to him that freedom was not an object of experience; he believed that we could only deduce it as a necessary consequence of the law of

---

[6] Blaise Pascal, *Pensées*, no. 793 in L. Brunschwicg's numbering. See Blaise Pascal, *Pensées and Other Writings*, trans. H. Levi (Oxford: Oxford University Press, 1995), p. 86.

duty, which implies power. Whatever the case may be, no one saw better the quite particular excellence of the will; no one did more to show that the infinite, the perfect, the absolute is spiritual freedom, and that the last word on everything is the moral principle.

Before philosophy came to find its definitive ground on the profound basis of this infinite or absolute, it had to, in departing from the point to which Descartes had led it, be put to the test and purified more than once.

Descartes had banned the abstract entities by means of which the Schools explained, as if by so many causes, the different phenomena; but it seemed that, beneath the two grand facts of extension and thought, he allowed to remain, as something different to these facts themselves, substances or beings.

However, when considered in abstraction from any way of being, could a substance be distinguished from any other? Extended substance and thinking substance, according to Spinoza, must be the same thing, and there was only, beneath different attributes, a single and unique substance. However, as Berkeley soon said, substance distinguished from any way of being is nothing. Substance, causes, power, being are incomplete ideas, the debris of scholasticism. To be is to be this or that. Pure and simple being, without anything else, is nothing; it is a mere conception, perhaps even a word wholly devoid of meaning. Moreover, whatever exists for us exists only in our perceptions. If therefore we seek what being really is, we will find that it is to be perceived, to exist in a mind as something that it thinks. Our first ideas are, Berkeley said, sensory ideas. They do not come from us; we do not produce them at will; it is therefore another mind who causes them in us. An infinite, superior spirit, God, in a word, provides to our minds their first ideas; on this basis, which is the whole of reality, our mind, by comparisons, abstractions, generalizations, establishes the multitude of relations that it all too often subsequently takes to be realities.

Berkeley thus sought to overturn the hypothesis of a substance placed outside any mind as a support that is not in itself perceptible, while its qualities are perceptible by the senses, a substance that materialism took, as he said, as an idol with which it replaced the true God. The cornerstone of atheism was, in his opinion, the idea of a stupid and unthinking substance able to exist by itself, from which everything was supposed to emerge with a necessity excluding all freedom and, thus, all morality. In withdrawing this cornerstone, the whole edifice of impiety would collapse. He aimed to maintain all the more Descartes's thinking things, finite minds and the infinite mind that illuminates them. At the same time, he involuntarily opened the path to scepticism, the path to scepticism that was going to affect ideas of mind also.

Descartes had distinguished three types of ideas: 'adventitious' are those that come to us from the outside by the senses; 'factitious' are those that we produce in operating on the former; 'innate' are those the mind finds in its self-consciousness with which it forms 'factitious' ideas. Malebranche already admitted that the mind has no idea of itself, holding that it only had a feeling of itself. Locke saw that beyond sensations there is in us reflexion, by which we are aware both of our sensations and of intellectual operations; but he failed to see in it—this was Leibniz's reproach—an original source of knowledge. Berkeley, at least in his first writings, i.e. those that preceded Hume's *Treatise of Human Nature*, recognized as true ideas only sensory ideas that, according to him, could be explained only by the immediate action of God, as we have just said. Of the operations of our mind and of our mind itself we have, as he thought then, only a deaf and obscure perception, which he proposed to give the name of *notion*.

Hume took a large step further.

These immaterial substances, saved by Berkeley, and to which he transferred everything real that he had taken away from matter, were eliminated by Hume; he put an end to the great exception in favour of minds. And, indeed, if we had of mind only such weak and obscure knowledge, was this really knowledge? Was it not rather a deeply ingrained prejudice, a final illusion?

According to Hume, this was one of the most important discoveries to enrich science: nothing real corresponds to abstract and general ideas. We just have to draw the consequences of this. Berkeley had accepted that genuine knowledge occurred through the senses; in pushing the analysis further along, says Hume, we find that our knowledge is composed of two elements: sensations or impressions, and ideas; ideas are only the traces that sensation leaves behind it; it is prolonged and weakened sensation. Impressions first of all, then ideas, which are like copies, echoes, and this is all we have within us, all that there is for us. To posit in addition, either outside of us or within us, substances to support them, causes or forces to produce them, is pure imagination, a mere reverie.

Berkeley had already noted that we perceive by the senses, the sole source from which we draw our ideas, nothing of what we name 'cause'; that we see facts, and in no way a tie that binds them, in no way a force that connects them to each other. Nature presents to us only phenomena accompanying or following each other with a certain constancy; these were actions of the supreme spirit, each independent of the other, and whose order he had decided as he pleased.

In us, however, it seemed that Berkeley still recognized some causality, although in vague and obscure terms. There is no more of it within us, according to Hume, than without us. All our ideas come to us from impressions. From what impression does the idea of cause come to us? Within us, just as without us, experience shows us certain facts that always accompany each other. Habituated to seeing them together, it becomes difficult for us to separate them; they seem to us necessarily connected; this is what we express, and nothing else, when we say that some are the causes of the others. That is true of our impressions; that is true of our ideas, which are only reflections of it. Our impressions, considered in themselves, independently of us, is what we call objects and the 'outside'; our ideas and our feelings constitute the inside, and this is what we call 'us'. Without and within us, and at bottom it is the same thing, there is nothing but successive phenomena, no necessary connection, no cause, no ground. No substance either; if we do not encounter causes in the field of experience, we do not, a fortiori, encounter substance there. Everything is therefore reduced to impressions and ideas that succeed each other in us. What could this supposed 'us' be, given that it is neither an impression nor an idea? It would be vain to posit that mind is something like the theatre where ideas come successively to appear. Let us not be led astray by the metaphor: it is the very succession of ideas that constitutes what we call mind, and we have no notion, even distant and confused, of a theatre where these scenes would be represented. We are for ourselves only a moving series of perceptions.

In order to represent Hume's world, we only have to picture impressions and ideas floating in series in the air and in a void.

For having wanted to abandon fictions, to go back to what is real in experience, to the positivity of facts, philosophy was limited to phenomena alone, multiple, diffuse, without connection or unity, to the scattered material of sensory appearances. This was, in a new form, the doctrine of the Sophists and Epicureans, and that we could call the doctrine of universal dissolution.

Without speaking of the contradiction Hume's theory involved, Reid opposed to it the beliefs that are natural to us and which such an explanation of our ideas does not account for, beliefs by which existences superior to physical and sensory things, the object of metaphysics, are guaranteed for us. The work of Reid and his school consisted in re-establishing, above the material order, the intellectual and moral order, but without bringing to light any necessary relation between the superior and the inferior.

In order to refute Hume, Kant did not content himself with showing what there is in our notions that sensation cannot explain. He showed that these notions are like forms in which the matter provided by experience gains consistency and shape, and that consequently they are the necessary conditions of sensation. As to these forms themselves, they are different applications of the action that is knowledge, action by which we gather into a unity the multiple and diffuse matter given through the senses.

Is the unifying operation, or, to employ Kant's own expression, the 'synthesis'—first of all imaginative, and then intellectual—of sensory diversity, a phenomenon like any other? No, since no conscious phenomenon is possible without it. To the maxim of vulgar scholasticism, repeated by Hobbes and Locke, that 'nothing is in the intellect that was not first in the senses', Leibniz added: 'except intellect itself'; and Kant: 'all the matter of knowledge is in the senses, but it is the intellect that gives it form'. The pure empiricist, we could add, is like a physiologist that explains nutrition by food alone, and who forgets what receives and transforms it, the stomach; he is like a physiologist who, forgetting the lungs, explains breathing merely by air.

Adopting Locke's system in France, Condillac had, like Hume, eliminated from it what threatened its homogeneity, namely the idea of reflexion or of consciousness that the mind has of its own operations. Like Hume, Condillac taught that our knowledge was only transformed sensations. However, neither he nor his principal disciple, Destutt de Tracy, concluded what Hume concluded from this, namely that there is nothing else for us and that we ourselves are nothing more than series of sensory phenomena. This is because, among the series of sensations to which intellect, reasoning, reason seemed capable of being reduced without too much difficulty, an element appeared, obscurely at first, but more and more clearly, which, beneath the mobile spectacle of wholly relative phenomena, beyond the perpetual change in sensory appearances, revealed something constant and absolute. This element, different to essentially passive and necessary sensation, was action, will.

How can we perceive anything beyond our sensations? 'This is', says Condillac, 'a problem that, in my first edition, I addressed badly.'[7] And he establishes, against his own system, that, by the resistance that we experience, we learn that outside of us there are bodies. But it is our own action, our motive action that makes us aware of this reaction on the outside. 'The principle of movement', as Destutt de Tracy almost immediately added, 'is the will, and the will is the person, the human being itself.'[8] In the torrent of sensations, there is nothing but appearances without either 'I' or 'non-I'; surfaces, so to speak, without an inside or outside. Through our awareness of our will, we learn at the same time about ourselves and about something other than ourselves; beneath, beyond sensation an interior world, and an external world, as two realities opposed to each other, but which, in the action where they meet, touch and interpenetrate.

To rediscover activity—beneath the passivity of sensations that, since Hume, seemed to explain everything—was to rediscover, beneath matter, mind itself. Strengthened by this discovery, philosophy was soon to free itself from physics, with which Locke, and Hume, and Condillac himself had somehow overwhelmed it. Two men helped in this task: Maine de Biran and Ampère.

The Scottish philosophers had emphasized the diversity, inexplicable by sensation alone, of our ideas and beliefs. Kant had shown that what there is in us that goes beyond sensations are the diverse ways of binding them, of synthesizing them, and that this is what constitutes knowledge. Maine de Biran noticed that the operation by which we know, which Kant attributed to what he called intellectual spontaneity, is activity, effort, will; Condillac and Destutt de Tracy had rediscovered the mind in the will. Our knowledge, our thoughts, according to Maine de Biran, are thus, like the movements that we enact in our limbs, effects of our will, as is

---

[7] See Etienne Bonnot de Condillac, 'Extrait Raisonné' in *Traité des sensations* (Geneva: Slatkine Reprints [from the Paris 1821–2 edition]), vol. 3.
[8] See Destutt de Tracy (1754–1836), *Mémoire sur la faculté de penser* (Paris: Fayard, 1993 [1794]).

everything that belongs to us. By this willing we constitute everything that belongs to us, and in this willing our own being can be found and recognized. Descartes had said: 'I think, therefore I am'; we can say, better still: I will, therefore I am. To will, indeed, is not merely to be like phenomena, which are born and die in the same instant. 'In each of my resolutions', remarked Maine de Biran, 'I know myself as a cause prior to its effect and that will outlast it; I see myself beneath, outside of the movement that I produce, and independent of time; and this is why, properly speaking, I do not become, but rather I exist really and absolutely.' It is in adopting this unique perspective of a free personality, beyond all the conditions of nature and of things, that Spinoza could have rightly said, as he did say: 'We feel, we experience that we are immortal.' 'And such is', added Maine de Biran, 'the model, the unique model according to which we conceive causes outside of us. We conceive of them as beings that are volitions. Being, acting, willing, by different names, is one and the same thing.'[9]

We will see what fruits these thoughts have produced or are near to producing.

Maine de Biran revealed the crucial fact that reveals us to ourselves as an existence situated beyond the course of nature—a fact that makes us understand that such is any veritable existence, and that the rest, which occupies space and time, is in comparison only appearance. At the same time, Ampère, a thinker who would later be celebrated for important discoveries in the sciences, but who was then occupied principally, with Maine de Biran, by psychological and logical research, and who exchanged ideas with him, illuminated in dissertations and letters that have been published only quite recently a part of our nature that had been left in the shadows by Condillac, attentive above all to sensations, and by Maine de Biran, occupied almost uniquely by the will. This was the faculty that applies the action of the will to the elements provided by the senses; this was the faculty of comparing, in which the simple terms that the faculties of intuition provide for us are reunited and connected to each other; this was, in other words, the faculty of reasoning and discourse, reason. Knowing, said Kant, is above all to unite; but the mind unites, said Maine de Biran, by an act, by the will; it unites, added Ampère, by means of a relation. Ampère evinced so much true genius in all sorts of sciences, but he has genius consist in the faculty of perceiving relations; 'one person sees numerous relations, while another sees none. The progress of the sciences in the last centuries is the fruit not so much of the discovery of new facts, but rather of the art of apprehending their relations with their consequences and causes.'[10] No one saw better or better revealed than he the importance of relations and the value of the role that belongs, in the formation of knowledge, to the faculty that

---

[9] Even with digital search tools, it is not possible to say which work of Maine de Biran Ravaisson is citing here, or how faithfully he is citing it.

[10] On André-Marie Ampère and Biran, see Maine de Biran, *Oeuvres*, vol. 13/1: *Correspondance philosophique Maine de Biran—Ampère*, ed. A. Robinet (Paris: Vrin, 1993).

discovers and combines them. This is the part that he attributed to himself in the task of philosophical regeneration for which he laboured with Maine de Biran: the latter had discovered the will; Ampère had discovered reason.

Although he remained in his analysis of will at particular manifestations of sensory experience as a whole, Maine de Biran nevertheless glimpsed and pointed to what there is in the latter that is independent of empirical and natural conditions. Ampère, in the analysis of reason, does not seem to have gone so far. In considering relations, he seems not to have tried to reduce them to primary and simpler elements, nor to have sought whether reason, in determining them, is referred to a unity that serves as their measure. This is a question that would perhaps have led him to the supersensory and truly metaphysical principle that his friend's thinking tended towards. On the contrary, to judge by his published writings, Ampère believed that he had to seek to prevent his friend from moving in this direction, and to keep him in the sphere of what can be called phenomenal and empirical consciousness. For the things of a metaphysical order, Ampère had faith only in reasoning.

These three elements of sensation, will, and reason, studied and developed principally by the three psychologists Condillac, Maine de Biran, and Ampère, were combined by Royer-Collard in a theory of knowledge inspired above all by the Scottish, and whose principal concern was to re-establish, against the scepticism to which pure empiricism had led, the beliefs that the common sense of humanity seems to guarantee. He briefly made of this theory a matter of public instruction, for a period long enough to bring to an end what had seemed for a while to be the almost absolute dominance of Ideology, which issued from Condillac's first theories. From this teaching emerged the doctrine that, ever since, has reigned almost exclusively in all our country's schools. This doctrine was proclaimed under the name of *eclecticism* by Royer-Collard's eminent successor in the chair of the history of philosophy.

II
Cousin and the Eclectic School

When Victor Cousin started out, Schelling's philosophy reigned in Germany; he had some knowledge of it, and was influenced by it above all in his early writings. Under this influence, he undertook, while still very young, the publication of unpublished works by Proclus, the last major representative of the Neoplatonic school whose doctrines offer some analogy with those constituting the German system of absolute Identity. Neoplatonism wanted to reconcile, in what it called an eclectic theory, the principal doctrines engendered by the Greek genius. It occurred to Cousin to reunite, in his own way, in a new eclecticism, all that was true in the different systems of different periods and different countries. For this, it was necessary, first of all, to rectify or complete the available knowledge of these systems. In addition to editing the works of Proclus and analysing the unpublished commentaries of his disciple Olympiodorus on some of Plato's dialogues, Cousin also produced a complete translation of Plato, editions of Descartes, of Abélard, and of several of Maine de Biran's works, a translation of Tennemann's *A Manual of the History of Philosophy*, etc.[1] Moreover, we owe to his advice and encouragement a great number of publications that have served to clarify many aspects of the history of knowledge, and that will remain one of the principal honourable distinctions of the modern philosophical period: for example, Jouffroy's translations of Thomas Reid and Dugald Stewart; translations of Mackintosh's *Dissertation on the Progress of Ethical Philosophy*[2] and Matthiae's manual of

---

[1] *Grundriß der Geschichte der Philosophie für den akademischen Unterricht* by Wilhelm Gottlieb Tennemann (1761–1819), professor at Jena and then Marburg, was first published in Leipzig in 1812, and then re-edited in 1815. Tennemann died while preparing a third edition, and afterwards the book became the basis of more collective, protean enterprises. The task of re-editing was taken up by Amadeus Wendt, professor at the University of Leipzig, who published third, fourth, and fifth editions in 1820, 1823, and 1825 respectively. Victor Cousin (1792–1867) published his French translation of this fifth edition while deleting some of Wendt's additions, which he thought to be too concise to be intelligible to a French public, in 1829: *Manuel de l'histoire de la philosophie*, tr. V. Cousin (Paris: Pichon et Didier). The 1825 edition was also translated into English in 1832 by Rev. Arthur Johnson, a translation that was updated in relation to later editions of the text and with some extra sections by J. R. Morell in 1852: W. G. Tennemann, *A Manual of the History of Philosophy*, tr. A. Johnson, ed. J. R. Morell (London: Bohn).

[2] *Histoire de la philosophie morale, particulièrement aux dix-septième et dix-huitième siecles* was a translation by Hector Poret (Paris: Levrault, 1834) of James Mackintosh's 1830 *Dissertation on the Progress of Ethical Philosophy, Chiefly during the Seventeenth and Eighteenth Centuries*, first published as part of the 1830 edition of the *Encyclopaedia Britannica*. Poret (1798–1864), a specialist in Scotttish philosophy, had been Ravaisson's school philosophy teacher in the early 1830s at the Collège Rollin, Paris, and Ravaisson became his son-in-law.

philosophy[3] by Hector Poret; translations of Aristotle by Barthélemy Saint-Hilaire, who, moreover, wrote knowledgeable essays on Indian philosophy and Buddhism; translations of Bacon and Plotinus by Bouillet; of Spinoza, by Emile Saisset;[4] of Kant by Tissot and Jules Barni;[5] Francisque Bouillier's history of Cartesianism;[6] those of the Alexandrian school by Jules Simon and Vacherot;[7] Paul Janet's studies of Plato's dialectic;[8] the works of Adolphe Franck on Jewish Kabbalah and the history of logic;[9] of Charles de Rémusat on Saint Anselm, on Abelard and on Bacon;[10] of Hauréau and Rousselot on the philosophy of the Middle Ages;[11] of Montet and Charles Jourdain on the philosophy of Thomas Aquinas;[12] of Nourisson on the philosophies of Leibniz and Bossuet;[13] of Chauvet on the

---

[3] The classicist August Matthiae (1769–1835) published a successful philosophy manual, *Lehrbuch für den ersten Unterricht in der Philosophie*, in 1823 (Leipzig; 3rd edition, 1833) that was translated by Poret as *Manuel de philosophie* in 1833.

[4] Emile Edmond Saisset (1814–63) belonged to Cousin's eclectic school and taught at Caen, at the École Normale in Paris and later at the Sorbonne. He published Spinoza, *Oeuvres*, 2 vols. (Paris: Charpentier) in 1842; an extended edition followed in 1860, and a third, after his death, in 1872.

[5] Claude Joseph Tissot (1801–76) translated many of Kant's works into French. Jules Barni (1818–78) translated Kant's writings on aesthetics and morality and wrote commentaries on his work before entering into politics as an exiled opponent of the French Second Empire and then as a deputy in the Third Republic.

[6] Francisque Bouillier (1813–99), *Histoire et critique de la revolution cartesienne* (Paris: 1842). Bouillier was professor at the Lyon Faculty of Humanities and then director of the Ecole Normale Supérieure in the last years of the Second French Empire.

[7] Jules Simon, *Histoire de l'école* d'Alexandrie, 2 vols. (Paris: 1884–5). Simon (1814–96), philosopher and moderate republican statesman, edited the works of Malebranche, Descartes, Bossuet, and Arnauld, and deputized for Cousin at the Sorbonne, before a long political career that was crowned by becoming Prime Minister of France in 1875. *Histoire critique de l'école d'Alexandrie* by Etienne Vacherot (1809–97), perhaps Cousin's most illustrious pupil, was published in three volumes between 1846 and 1851 (Paris: Ladrange).

[8] Paul Janet, *Essai sur la dialectique de Platon* (Joubert: 1848). Janet (1823–99) was a Cousinian appointed to a chair in philosophy at the Sorbonne in 1864.

[9] Adolphe Franck (1809–93) was a protegé of Victor Cousin, and the first French Jew to pass the *agrégation* in philosophy. Ravaisson is referring to his *La Kabbale: Ou la philosophie religieuse des Hébreux* (Paris: Hachette, 1843) and *Esquisse d'une histoire de la logique, précédée d'une analyse étendue de l'organum d'Aristote* (Paris: Hachette, 1838).

[10] By the politician and prolific writer Charles de Rémusat (1797–1895), Ravaisson is referring to: *Abélard*, 2 vols. (Paris: Ladrange, 1845); *Saint Anselme de Cantorbéry: Tableau de la vie monastique et de la lutte du pouvoir spirituel avec le pouvoir temperel au onzième siècle* (Paris: Didier, 1853); *Bacon, sa vie, son temps, sa philosophie et de son influence jusqu'à nos jours* (Paris: Didier, 1857).

[11] Barthélemy Hauréau, *Examen critique de la philosophie scolastique*, 2 vols. (1848), a work crowned the same year by the Academy of Moral and Political Sciences (Académie des sciences morales et politiques). Hauréau (1812–96) went on to publish a *Histoire de la philosophie scolastique* (1863–80) in three volumes. Xavier Rousselot (1805–95), teacher of philosophy at the Collège de Troyes (which became a lycée in 1853), published a three-volume study from 1840 to 1882: *Etudes sur la philosophie dans le moyen-âge* (Paris: Joubert).

[12] Léon Montet wrote a *Mémoire sur Thomas d'Aquin* (Paris: Firmin Didot, 1847) and seems to have published his secondary, Latin doctoral thesis the following year as *De principiis quibus constat Thomae Aquinatis Ethica commentatio* (Paris: Joubert, 1848). *La philosophie de Thomas d'Aquin* (Paris: Hachette) by Charles Jourdain (1817–86) appeared in 1858.

[13] *La philosophie de Leibniz* (Paris: Hachette, 1860) and *Essai sur la philosophie de Bossuet* (Paris: Martinet, 1852) by Jean-Félix Nourisson (1825–99), a prolific writer who held the chair of the history of modern philosophy at the Collège de France from 1874.

theories of human understanding in antiquity;[14] of Waddington on Aristotle's psychology;[15] of Ferraz on Augustin's psychology;[16] of Emile Charles on Roger Bacon,[17] etc. We should not forget numerous expert articles on all the periods of the history of philosophy in Adolphe Franck's *Dictionnaire des sciences philosophiques*.[18]

It remains the case, however, that Victor Cousin's proposal to select what is most true and the best in each philosophy was never actually realized. Not only did he seek to refute, under the name of sensualism, the philosophy of Locke and all those who in his footsteps attempted to explain all knowledge by sensations; also, in most other philosophies, from Aristotle to Leibniz and Kant, he signalled above all what he found to be errors. If he borrowed from Kant the most general outlines of his theory of morality, he otherwise fought against him in classifying him among the sceptics on almost every issue. If he was content to refer his own ideas to the principles of Platonism and Cartesianism, this was only in interpreting these principles according to Scottish empiricism. In his teaching of the general history of philosophy, Victor Cousin places all systems under four headings: sensualism, idealism, mysticism, and scepticism. What he understood by 'mystical systems', which included the whole of Christian theology, were those wherein direct communication between God and man is admitted, and he accuses them all of being chimerical. Of the four classes to which the diverse systems that have been produced, and that could ever be produced, are reducible, only one, in his eyes, contains a large share of truth: this is what he calls idealism, and to which he relates Plato and Descartes; but, once again, this is on condition of enclosing them in the limits traced out by Reid and Stewart. And as Victor Cousin advanced in his career, while bearing, as he put it, the flag of eclecticism, he was in fact increasingly reduced to a particular system whose basis was formed by the ideas of the Scottish philosophers together with a few of those of Maine de Biran and Ampère, and which can be defined as a brilliant development of the half-spiritualism inaugurated by Royer-Collard.

---

[14] Emmanuel Chauvet, *Théories de l'entendement humain dans l'antiquité* (Paris: A. Durand, 1855). Chauvet (1819–1910) taught at the Rennes Faculty of Humanities.

[15] Charles Waddington-Kastus, *De la psychologie d'Aristote* (Paris: Joubert, 1848). Charles Waddington (1819–1914) was born in Milan to English parents, studied at the Ecole Normale Supérieure in Paris and taught at the Sorbonne; his cousin William would become Prime Minister of France in 1875.

[16] *La psychologie de Saint Augustin* (Paris: Durand, 1862), by Marin Ferraz (1820–98), who taught at the Lyon Faculty of Humanities after teaching at the lycée de Strasbourg.

[17] Emile Charles, *Roger Bacon: Sa vie, ses ouvrages, ses doctrines* (Paris: 1861). Charles (1825–97) taught for some time at the lycée Descartes in Paris.

[18] *Dictionnaire des sciences philosophiques, par une société de professeurs de philosophie et de savants* (Paris: Hachette), edited by Adolphe Franck, was published in 1844–52. A second edition appeared in 1875, but it was superseded by the *Vocabulaire technique et critique de la philosophie*, a collective effort edited by André Lalande (1867–1964) that was first published in the *Bulletin de la société française de philosophie* between 1902 and 1923 and that is still in print (Paris: Presses universitaires de France, 2010).

Reid, Stewart, and Royer-Collard had not only adopted the principle that all knowledge derives, as from its source, from experience as a general principle of modern science; they admitted, with Locke and those of his school, that in philosophy just as in the other sciences, method consists in the observation and analysis of phenomena, in applying induction to them. In truth, and this is what sensualism was wrong to deny, we find in ourselves principles that authorize us to extend our beliefs beyond what we see, and to affirm, in perceiving phenomena, the existence of causes and substances—of, in a word, beings. But induction alone could not teach us what these beings, these substances, these causes were. Victor Cousin adopted these ideas. There was only, as he said in following the Scottish philosophers and Royer-Collard, one method, the one whose principle Bacon had pronounced and codified. It applied, however, to two broad classes of phenomena that were wholly different: on the one hand, external, physical, and physiological phenomena, the only ones, more or less, that Bacon had in view; on the other, inner phenomena. The true method of philosophy consisted, after having described and classified inner phenomena, in drawing from them the knowledge of what the soul must be, and then in going from the soul, along the path that Descartes had traced out, up to God. Victor Cousin named it the psychological method.

In other words, there are two entirely different orders of knowledge: perceptions and conceptions; perceptions, for phenomena, the only objects of experience; conceptions, for beings [*les êtres*]; for beings, and also for the true, the good, and the beautiful, for space and time, etc. Everything that goes beyond phenomena is available to us, said Victor Cousin, only by a sort of mysterious, inexplicable revelation, the work of what he called reason.

One particular circumstance, together with the influence of Scottish philosophy, had a large part in the founder of eclecticism's preoccupation with this distinction between objects of immediate knowledge and objects of pure conceptions, to which his whole philosophy can be reduced: this was the theory concerning art and beauty that predominated when Royer-Collard was teaching. According to this theory, which Winkelmann[19] had sketched during the kind of renaissance that marked the end of the eighteenth century, and from which Quatremère de Quincy established a system,[20] art had for its object the representation of beauty, not in natural forms that we might consider to be real, but in ways incompatible with reality. Reality is determinate, definite; the ideal, such as Winkelmann and Quatremère de Quincy defined it, was something general, and thus indeterminate. A figure whose beauty is worthy of the description 'ideal' must, in the absence of

---

[19] See J. J. Winkelmann, *History of the Art of Antiquity* (Los Angeles: Getty, 2006).
[20] Antoine-Crysostome Quatremère de Quincy (1755–1849) was a French historian, archaeologist, and art theorist whose theories concerning the Venus de Milo as originally belonging to an ensemble with Mars Ravaisson developed in his writings on the statue; see Ravaisson, 'The Venus de Milo', *Selected Essays*, pp. 189–228.

particularities, hold itself as if at a distance and above real and individual existence. This was to honour abstractions, those incomplete ideas whose insufficiency Aristotle, Berkeley, Leibniz had already demonstrated. The modern partisans of the ideal looked to Platonic theory, which seems to make of such ideas the supreme models of perfection. They relied above all on examples of classical art, which had become again the object of enthusiastic admiration, but which was known still only imperfectly, by works belonging for the most part to periods of relative decadence, when tradition and convention begin to replace the inspiration of greater epochs, and when general rules and abstract formula predominate.

However, the sculptures and the bas-reliefs that decorated the Parthenon were brought to our Occident. It was then recognized that the monuments of Greek literature should have been enough to teach us that if Greek art, at the time of its apogee, had perhaps not yet penetrated as far as possible into the depths of life, it had nevertheless impressed on all its works, with a higher beauty, a striking characteristic of life. Canova, a highly appreciated artist in a quite different genre much more in conformity with the theories of Quatremère de Quincy, who put him above the ancients, was still able to appreciate Phidias; he stated that the study of the grand tradition of Athenian statuary would one day produce a revolution in art. It has produced a notable change in ideas at least, and made the theory of abstract ideals lose all its credit. Victor Cousin, nevertheless, remained with this theory that had seduced him in his youth. In his 1818 dissertation, *Real Beauty and Ideal Beauty*, he writes: 'the ideal in beauty, as in everything, is the negation of the real. The idea is what is pure generality' etc.[21] In his lectures on beauty, and in the later revised and corrected editions of this work, just as much as in the earlier editions, ideal beauty is represented as a general quality, abstracted from all particularity and incompatible with real existence; it is the object, in a word, not of perception, but of simple conception. Certainly, in these same lectures Victor Cousin recognized that, if art is distinct from nature, it cannot be opposed to it, and that a work of art cannot be beautiful if it is not somehow alive. But to add, as he does immediately, that it is not real life that the work of art seems to animate, but an ideal life, is to return definitively to the theory that represents the ideal as irreconcilable with reality and as excluding existence. Thus Victor Cousin fought against, with Quatremère de Quincy, the idea that a work of art representing a living thing ought to present the appearance of real life, an idea supported by all the great masters, and that had even been adopted by the philosophy that eclecticism was so keen to attach itself, Socratic and Platonic philosophy. 'How do you go about producing', as Socrates asks a sculptor somewhere, 'this effect that touches us the most, that the statues seem to live?' And the sculptor answers: 'They have to be modelled on the living.' Pascal said in the same sense: 'The agreeable and the real are both necessary; but what is agreeable has to be true.'[22]

---

[21] Victor Cousin, 'Du beau reel et du beau idéal' in *Archives philosophiques, politiques et littéraires* III (Paris: Fournier, 1818).

[22] This is Pascal on eloquence, the art of persuasion: *Pensées*, §932 in Brunschwicg's numbering.

Victor Cousin, in his aesthetics, thus always remained faithful to the doctrine that makes abstract generalities, which should always guide art, float above the reality of individual things; and this doctrine was his whole philosophy.

In truth, concerning beauty itself, he did not entirely content himself with such a general and indeterminate notion of the ideal: with Reid, he saw in beauty the expression of moral perfection, the expression of the good. But what is the good? He did not try to define it. And there is nothing determinate to say, more generally, of the supersensory element that reason, in his theory, reveals to us on the occasion of particular and sensory perceptions, since we have of it, properly speaking, no knowledge, but only a conception. What goes for the good and the true, goes for the soul and God also. We judge of God through the soul; and of the soul itself, we judge of it only by the phenomena appearing at any given instant to consciousness. Whatever recourse one might have to induction, how to grasp what is absolute by what is relative, substance by what is relative, the supersensory by what is sensory? Is not saying that reason reveals to us a substance beneath the accidents, a cause beyond the effects, only to indicate, beyond the positivity of experience, a *je ne sais quoi* of which nothing can be affirmed apart from what is borrowed from this positivity itself? To have recourse, in order to account for the existence of particular human beings, to a general or ideal human being that would be their model would amount simply to duplicating what has to be explained. What are these entities, indefinable in themselves, of which we can say only that on the occasion of facts we conceive their ideas, if they are not a sort of reflection or calque of these facts in our understanding? We are led back to Hume's view, which summarizes sensualist empiricism, that ideas are nothing other than weakened copies of impressions.

The principle of this view is, indeed, the belief, essential to sensualist empiricism, that we have immediate knowledge only of phenomena.

In 1834 Victor Cousin edited a collection of several of Maine de Biran's works that had not yet been published. In studying more closely, on this occasion, his thought, which was not well known, he came to appreciate better its justice and depth, and, in the preface to the collection, he was evidently not far from admitting, with the author of the *New Considerations on the Relations of the Physical and the Moral*,[23] that the method of a science of mind, having for its basis not the knowledge of simple phenomena, but the immediate knowledge of their cause, could no longer be that whose rules Bacon had delineated.

A few years afterwards, the most eminent of Victor Cousin's pupils, Théodore Jouffoy, adopted a quite different doctrine to the one he had taught until then. For a long time he had attempted to apply all the resources of a naturally meditative and quite penetrating mind to the execution of the plan that his master had traced out, to gathering carefully what they both called psychological

---

[23] Maine de Biran, *Oeuvres*, vol. 9: *Nouvelles considérations sur les rapports du physique et du moral*, ed. B. Baertschi (Paris: Vrin, 1990).

or internal facts, to draw from them later, by means of induction, the solution to metaphysical questions, above all to the questions relating to the existence of the soul and of God.

Noticing, perhaps, the distinct lack of success of the enterprise, and perhaps under the influence of the ideas expressed by Maine de Biran, he came to recognize that the proposition that had until then formed the basis of all their work, namely that only phenomena can be an object of immediate knowledge, was more than a little dubious.

In his *Essay on the Legitimacy of the Distinction of Psychology and Physiology*, read to the Academy of Moral and Political Sciences, he claims in his own terms that the human being is conscious of something other than phenomena; that it reaches in itself the principle that produces them, which he calls the 'I'; that the soul feels itself as the cause of all of its acts, as well as the subject of each of its modifications, and he adds: 'It is necessary to erase from psychology this venerated proposition: the soul is known to us only through its acts and modifications.'[24]

The author, a stranger to the eclectic school, of an *Essay on the Metaphysics of Aristotle* (1837–40)[25]—in which he showed how the philosopher who named and first established the science of the supernatural, posited as the principle of this science, instead of number or the idea, which are equivocal entities, abstractions erected as realities, the intellect that, by an immediate experience, grasps in itself the absolute reality from which all other reality depends—published on the occasion of Louis Peisse's translation of a selection of Hamilton's work a study of 'Contemporary Philosophy',*[26] which highlighted the considerable difference separating the maxim proclaimed by the Scottish and Victor Cousin, according to which immediate knowledge is possible only of phenomena, and that which Maine de Biran established, which Victor Cousin seems no longer to reject and to which Jouffroy had officially adhered. Moreover, the author also sought to show that Maine de Biran, in situating the absolute of our substance beyond the active force of which we are conscious, had not yet reached the inner point of view whereby the soul apprehends itself in its own ground, which is wholly activity, without it being necessary or possible to imagine an inert substance that supports it. Whether or not this is exactly right, and even if we have to remain with Maine de Biran and Jouffroy, this was enough, the author remarked, to renounce the

---

[24] Théodore Jouffroy (1796–1842) presented his *Mémoire sur la légitimité de la distinction de la psychologie et de la physiologie* to the Academy of Moral and Political Sciences (Académie des sciences morales et politiques, one of the wings of the Institut de France that house philosophers) in September 1838 and it was reprinted in 1842 in Jouffroy, *Nouveau mélanges philosophiques* (Paris: Hachette). The passage cited is located on p. 276.

[25] See Ravaisson, *Essai sur la métaphysique d'Aristote* (Paris: Imprimerie Royale, 1837) and *Essai sur la Métaphysique d'Aristote*, vol. 2 (Paris: Joubert, 1845).

* *Revue des deux mondes*, 1840. [Ravaisson's footnote]

[26] See Ravaisson, 'Contemporary Philosophy', trans. J. Dunham in Ravaisson, *Selected Essays*, ed. M. Sinclair (London: Bloomsbury, 2016), pp. 59–84.

specious parallelism that one had sought to establish between the method of the physical sciences and that of philosophy.

If, in the sciences of nature, we proceed from effects to what we call causes, as one term to another in a wholly physical homogeneous series, this is because what we here call the 'cause' of a fact is nothing but this fact itself abstracted from accidental and indifferent circumstances, and reduced thus to a greater generality; it is only the circumstances, physical like the fact, to which it is connected. In psychology we can, perhaps, in studying the laws of inner phenomena in their simple relations of succession or simultaneity, proceed in a similar manner; but the true cause, that which produces the fact, which is somehow its soul, cannot be discovered by going about things in this way.

To consider what we call inner phenomena in abstraction from oneself in order to draw a conclusion from that abstraction is, in truth, to make external phenomena of them, on the basis of which we will never arrive at the self. 'How could I ever come back to myself', Jouffroy asked, 'from thoughts that I have without knowing that it is I who have them?' The true psychological method, the one that grounds what is called rational psychology or metaphysics, ought not, it would seem, be described as that which, from supposedly internal or conscious phenomena, moves inductively to their causes, but one through which we discern, in everything of which we are conscious, which from the outside is phenomenal and natural, what belongs to our actuality, what is genuinely internal, and what, in truth, as superior to all extended and even temporal conditions, is in its essence supernatural or metaphysical. The true psychological method is that which, from the fact of a particular sensation or perception, distinguishes, by a quite particular operation, what carries it out in making it one of our operations, which is nothing else than us. This operation is reflection: 'reflection', said Farcy in the preface to his anonymous translation of Dugald Stewart, 'folds the mind back onto itself and habituates it to grasping itself always in its living action instead of drawing conclusions from external effects'.[27]

After having discussed the visible change, probably under the influence of the ideas of Maine de Biran, in Jouffoy's views, and even in those of Victor Cousin, the aforementioned study added that the school formed by these illustrious masters would doubtless follow them along their new path.

Adolphe Garnier, well versed, like Jouffoy, in the study of the Scottish philosophers, devoted the most substantial of his works to the *Faculties of Mind*.[28] Attentive above all to differences in the phenomena that he studied, he discerned with finesse a great number of faculties; sometimes he perhaps took accidental differences for essential differences; he consequently, perhaps, considered as

---

[27] See Duguld Stewart, *Elémens de la philosphie de l'esprit humain*, trans. P. Prévost and J.-G. Farcy (Geneva: Pachoud, 1808–25).
[28] Adolphe Garnier (1801–64), *Traité des facultés de l'âme* (Paris: Hachette, 1852).

independent phenomena that are reducible to each other. It is also to be regretted that, with the psychologists of the Scottish school, he generally rested content, for any explanation of our nature, with reducing the different sorts of phenomena, after having described their circumstances, to a number of primitive faculties, and that he stopped at the first degree of the science of observation, namely classification. Nevertheless, Adolphe Garnier, in this same work, his last, approved the proposition that the human mind has an immediate knowledge of itself. If he had lived longer, in adopting this principle, he might have developed its consequences, and have arrived at a genuinely metaphysical perspective after beginning with a descriptive physics.

The same can be said of Emile Saisset, who was stopped, like Théodore Jouffoy and Adolphe Garnier, in the middle of his career by premature death.

Charles de Rémusat, without directly contradicting the opinions of the Scottish philosophers and of their French disciples on method, remarked in his *Essais* (1842) that the experimental method, such as it has been described and recommended, was not everything, and that something more was required for philosophy than observation and induction. And in his more recent work on Bacon (1857) he said: 'With the methods of Plato and Aristotle we go beyond physics to attain metaphysics, while, with Baconian induction, we go further than the final limits of phenomena on pain of attaining only pure idealities.'[29]

Adolphe Franck, Paul Janet, and Caro have adopted in its essential outlines the doctrine proclaimed, after Maine de Biran, by Jouffroy. In their teaching and their works tendencies are visible that, however diverse they may be, increasingly distance them all from the starting point of the eclectic school.

As for the leader of this school, though perturbed for a moment, he persisted with his original views. In what he published after 1840, and in the new editions of his old texts, we no longer find, it is true, the assimilation, which he had reproduced so often previously, of philosophical method to that of the natural sciences; but he maintained until the end that we know directly of ourselves only mere phenomena and not the substance.

How, indeed, to abandon a proposition so essential to a philosophy entirely founded on the absolute opposition between direct perception and conception, and, to employ Kant's terms, between the 'phenomena', objects of experience, and the 'noumena, intelligible things', objects of reason alone?

In 1840, a previously unknown writer who had acquired alone a great store of knowledge, in mathematics above all, and who added to that a powerful style, Bordas-Dumoulin, presented to the Academy of Moral and Political Sciences a noteworthy prize-winning dissertation, *Cartesianism*, which was published in

---

[29] De Rémusat, *Bacon, sa vie, son temps, sa philosophie et de son influence jusqu'à nos jours* (Paris: Didier, 1857), p. 366.

1843.[30] The author of this dissertation showed with force the immense value of the philosophical, mathematical, and physical discoveries made by Descartes. At the same time, he showed how they depended to a large degree on the way the author of this great dictum: *cogito ergo sum*, had, by the reflexion that it summarizes, 'recalled thought to itself'. Bordas-Dumoulin's work exalted, at the expense of the legislator of induction, the superior merits of the renovator of philosophy. He was not, it seems, without an influence on the apparent change in the ideas and the language of the inventor of modern eclecticism.

Since the publication of the essay 'Contemporary Philosophy' mentioned above, eclecticism almost entirely stopped relying on Bacon concerning the general question of method; after the publication of *Cartesianism*, it appealed to Descartes instead.

But the Descartes invoked by Victor Cousin is not the Descartes of Bordas-Dumoulin; nor is it the author of the *Geometry* and the *Dioptrics*, nor even that of the *Principles* or the *Meditations*. In the maxim that, as Descartes admitted, inspired all his work, and that Leibniz adopted, namely that 'all truths ought to be interconnected like those constituting the object of geometrical speculation are interconnected', Victor Cousin sees a disastrous error. 'The demon of geometry was', he says, 'Descartes's evil demon'; these expressions can be found in the work of Emile Saisset. From Cartesianism, eclecticism retains just this one principle: that philosophy begins by *I think*, from which it rises up to God. But Victor Cousin does not understand this principle as Descartes did. In the proposition by which the latter enunciated with a wholly new simplicity and clarity this great idea that our being is to be found and possessed wholly in thought, Victor Cousin only ever saw, despite some variations, the observation of facts of consciousness as pure phenomena, with the indeterminate notion of a being, of an unknown thing, to support them. This is Cartesianism without its breadth or depth: without the breadth of the notion of the rational connection of all things, from which reason gains its infinite import; without the depth of inner reflection, which attains alone, beyond whatever is relative in particular acts, the absolute of spiritual nature.

Eclecticism, in continuing to highlight the imperfections and errors contained in the systems explaining everything by the senses, and the moral, social, and aesthetic consequences deriving from them, and in exalting, on the contrary, the beauty of ideas and things of the rational order, increasingly contented itself with recommending—as capable of leading, necessarily by degrees, to that superior order of knowledge—the method that it named psychological, a method of observation and induction. Abstracted from all the other sciences, whether physical or mathematical, it increasingly confined itself, in relation to what concerns philosophy itself, in the circle that it had drawn of speculations relative to the classification of

---

[30] Jean-Baptiste Bordas-Dumoulin (1798–1859), *Le Cartésianisme ou la véritable renovation des sciences* (Paris: Hetzel, 1843).

intellectual and moral facts, speculations that were more logical, as Maine de Biran put it, than truly psychological. After having abandoned a few general propositions with which it had initially seemed to tend, following Schelling and Hegel, towards a sort of systematic pantheistic cosmology, and after having renounced any attempt to explain the things of the natural world, Victor Cousin had ended up almost entirely advising against, in the parts of philosophy dealing with the existence of the soul and of God, any regular procedure of reasoning, and by disapproving logic almost as much as geometry. In the end, his doctrine was reducible, or tended to be reducible, to mere generalities, forming a kind of introduction to the part of psychology that deals with the origin of ideas, generalities expressed by assertions expressing—with phrases that, as Schelling remarked, seemed to borrow from Jacobi's semi-mystical phraseology—Reid and Stewart's perspective: that experience brings us into contact only with phenomena, and that reason reveals to us, on their basis, by a singular procedure and as if by an inexplicable miracle, things of a quite different order, not of perception, but of pure conception.

Eclecticism, at the same time, kept its distance, not without scholastic aridity, from the things of the soul, of the heart, which also has, and perhaps even more than the soul, its own revelations. In recommending an accord between philosophy and religion, and even in proudly working towards it, it was to religion that, more often than not, eclecticism seemed to address its unfavourable descriptions of mysticism; all that was solid in religion seemed, in its eyes, to consist in the little that it gained from reason, and what it taught about justice to derive from the truth of charity.

After having won over many superior minds, through the always elevated tendency of his moral theories, or by the support he offered to the school of art that aspired to beauty, he ended up satisfying neither scientific minds nor religious souls. For a long time, in the general and figurative terms that it pleased him to use, it was thought that enough could be found to answer the principal questions of philosophy. It was recognized, in the end, that more often than not these terms did not contain what one wanted to know. Eclecticism had announced and promised much, and the prestige gained by the eloquence of its author served to form great expectations for it. One increasingly had to recognize, in a philosopher having given rise to so much hope, merely an orator for whom what is merely apparent, in the absence of truth, sufficed, as it suffices for orators in general, if Aristotle is to be believed. People had thought they were convinced, but they had often simply been seduced—a seduction that was perhaps more powerful at the time when eclecticism emerged—by language and style. Times have changed: henceforth people have come to seek, in less brilliant forms should that be necessary, a richer base, with less literature perhaps, and more doctrine.

By all these diverse causes and by others still, eclecticism has come to lose much of its credit and influence, even though it remains almost everywhere in possession of public instruction.

III
Lamennais's Metaphysics and Theology

Lamennais was one of those unsatisfied by eclecticism. In its general presentations, almost entirely concerned with the question of the origin of knowledge, he saw almost nothing that corresponded to his idea of philosophy. Far from having to accept confinement in what he calls the 'solitary I', philosophy seemed to him to have to aim at universal explanation. In a substantial work, *Sketch of a Philosophy*, for which he had prepared by long studies of many sciences and arts, he attempted, as had in Germany the authors of the most recent systems, to show how, in the physical and moral orders, everything was composed, though in different proportions, of identical principles, which were nothing other than the necessary elements of a first and universal principle, of an absolute and infinite being.[1]

Lamennais said that the most general idea that we can reach, an idea without which understanding is impossible, and that can be denied only verbally, is the idea of being, being independent of any specification, of any limitation, the infinite being that is named God. Absolute being is not only the ground of thought, it is also the ground of existence; it is existence before any and every limitation. However, in order to exist, according to Lamennais, properties are necessary: there must be within it, beyond the radical unity of its substance, an energy that realizes it; there must be something within it that impresses a form on this realization; there must, finally, be something else that brings the energy deployed in the form back to radical unity; this something is life. Force, form, life, or, from an inner perspective, spirit, power, intellect with love, such are the three essential elements integral to the divine essence; these are the elements of the Christian Trinity.

The divine essence is therefore not solely unitary; there is within it a principle of distinction and plurality. Infinite, the finite has its root within it; whence the possibility of three different elements in the simplicity of its substance. Similarly, in the second of these elements, in the one through which substance, in determining itself, takes form, an infinity of differences is possible, those by which all the forms, all the ideas that the intellect can contain, in which the principle of form can realize itself, are distinct. It is this world of intelligibles that Platonism and Christian theology showed to be enclosed in the unity of the Verb.

The distinction is realized, the differences are decided in passing from the possible to the real by means of creation. 'Creation', as the profound mystic Olier said,

---

[1] Félicité Robert Lamennais (1782–1854), *Esquisse d'une philosophie*, 4 vols. (Paris: Pagnerre, 1840).

'is God rendered physically present [*sensible*]'. For Lamennais, creation is the successive manifestation, in space and time, of everything that is in God. It is the unity of God projected by a sort of immolation or sacrifice into the diffusion of extension, where then, by the development of divine powers, in the successive orders where complexity and unity increase hand in hand, first inorganic things, then organized beings, and finally free and intelligent beings come back and bring everything back to themselves. In all the degrees of this progressive development, in each thing can be found the two opposed elements contained by the absolute essence. Everything belongs to the finite by what brings it to its completion, and to the infinite in the ground of being.

As Plato, Plotinus, and Leibniz thought, it is matter, which we understand only by the negation of its opposite, that limits, that is itself the limit in introducing division and multiplicity everywhere; what it stops and interrupts, and which, in itself, is unlimited, infinite, is thought, intellect, mind. Mind and matter compose everything that exists. In the inferior degrees of creation matter predominates, and, with it, necessity; in the superior degrees, it is mind, and with mind, freedom. From these two elements, combined in different proportions, arise the different reproductions, increasingly complete, of the three divine powers in the progress of creation, in such a way that in each being there is something of everything that God is.

The essential properties of matter are, first, to occupy space, and this is what is called impenetrability; second, to occupy space in a figure, whatever it may be; third, to have its parts connected and reunited by attraction, since without some degree of cohesion, no figure is possible. Impenetrability is the realization in the physical order of force; figure, that of form or intellect; attraction, that of life and love.

Kant, in his *Metaphysical Foundations of Natural Science*,[2] reasserting and expressing with a new precision ideas that were present at the origin of philosophy, had proposed a general explanation of the constitution of bodies and of natural phenomena by two antagonistic forces such as the projective force of stars and their centralizing forces, namely a force of expansion producing space, impenetrability, elasticity, and an attractive force, a principle of cohesion first of all, and then of all sorts of affinities. De Rémusat, in a chapter of his *Essays*, adopted these ideas and gave a lucid presentation of them. It is these ideas that Lamennais developed, but in relating them, as to their first principles, to the ideas of the fundamental properties of being.

In moving from the metaphysics of nature to nature itself, we find ether, according to Lamennais, as the primary matter of which all bodies are composed. At the beginning of things, there exists an ocean of ether without limits. At the

---

[2] Immanuel Kant, *Metaphysical Foundations of Natural Science*, ed. M. Friedman (Cambridge: Cambridge University Press, 2004).

heart of ethereal substance, a triple action represents and reproduces the mutual action of three primary principles: this triple action is that of electricity, light, and heat. From the ethereal substance, worked upon by these three agents, are formed elementary gases whose condensations and different combinations have engendered all bodies; first of all, the nebulous ones, as we still see them now in some astral regions; a denser core is produced, the analogue of the core of the cell, the primitive element of any organic body; surrounding it, an atmosphere limited by an external envelope. Worlds are born thus, worlds unfolding by degrees, within increasingly vast spaces, within interminable immensity; in this way are produced all the orders of creatures that develop in their richer and more complete constitutions the inexhaustible infinity of being; and each new order involves a new degree, a higher degree of the radical powers, representations of the primordial elements of the absolute. While within inorganic things composing the mineral order there is only assemblage of homogeneous parts without true unity or any awareness, organized beings form individuals, with some knowledge of what relates to them and a certain obscure awareness of themselves; intelligent and free beings, with the knowledge of what they are, and of their relation to the absolute, form persons in the image of the absolute itself.

In inorganic things it is the inferior principle of limit or matter, and thus of division, that is dominant; in free and intelligent beings, it is, with unity victorious over the most diverse multiplicity, the infinite. And if, in things without life, it is the first of the three powers of the absolute essence, namely force, that predominates, so too in beings that think and feel, in persons, it is the third and highest power, love, that predominates.

The absolute being gives birth to things in lowering itself in some way to the conditions of finite existence and as if by a perpetual sacrifice. Creation is but a perpetual giving of Himself, and the end of each of his creations is to dissolve itself in order to serve a new creation; so that everyone can live, each has to die. But it belongs to the intelligent and free creature, it is its most perfect destiny, to immolate itself for the purposes of creation as a whole and, in the final analysis, for the infinite. The cycle opened by love is thus closed by love. God created the world in giving of himself, in communicating himself. On the model of the creator, everything communicates with everything. Everything lives from other things and, in turn, serves other lives. Creation is like a banquet where everyone gives himself as food to all, and, since all substance comes from God, everyone in the end lives and is nourished in God. But to intellect and to will alone, free in themselves of the limitations and the imperfections of matter, is communicated in a direct and immediate way the immaterial essence that is infinity and perfection, and it is of the intelligent and free soul that we can say, without any restriction, that it is nourished by God.

In moving from the consideration of existences to that of knowledge, we find the same order, the same progress. We know by the senses the reality of particular, variable, and limited things. By the intellect alone we know the true, the invariable, the necessary, in a word, the infinite and the absolute; the infinite, the absolute, in other words, the cause, the reason for all the rest. Particular things, objects of the senses, are only, indeed, applications of intelligible models, objects of reason, which, in the end, can be reduced to the manifold possible combinations of the properties of the infinite and absolute Being, and thus to the primordial properties and to the Being that grounds them. 'To conceive, to know', says Lamennais, 'is to penetrate beyond the phenomena to the ground of phenomena and to embrace them with a single regard: the perception of the infinite or the direct vision of the single Being who includes in itself, with the eternal exemplars of things, their law, their reason, their substantial cause', belongs therefore to the intellect. In this way the fact is completed by the idea, observation by thought, experience by theory, science by philosophy.

So too, finally, the human being, in the exercise of its active faculties, begins with the work required by the satisfaction of its material needs, the needs of the inferior elements of its being: this is the work that is named industry; to industry is added art, to utility is added beauty. Beauty is the infinite manifested in the finite, the absolute in the relative, the spiritual in the material, and thus the revelation, in things that are the object of our senses and by forms of differing perfection and value, of intelligible powers constituting the very nature of being.

With these ideas, applied to the principal spheres of science as well as to the principal branches of art, Lamennais gathers together, with often luminous generalities, and almost always with elegant forms and lively colouring, a number of particular theorems, and the general philosophy of the sciences and the arts will owe something to him on more than a few points.

One regrettable aspect of the *Sketch of a Philosophy* is that the principles on which all the rest depend or ought to depend are perhaps not drawn from their true source, nor scientifically deduced; to this the continual repetitions can be attributed, as the result of irregular work that was ceaselessly recommenced.

In his first and celebrated work, *Indifference*,[3] which opposed the uncertainties of philosophy to the certitudes of religion, Lamennais had expressed the view, common to many writers at the time, that by reason, which he called individual reason, nothing could be established; that we can draw fundamental truths, on which all the truths of the moral order depend, only from the universal tradition, the source of which was a primitive revelation whose depositary was the Church itself, which had been instituted to keep it for ever intact. This is the doctrine that, after having been in great favour among the theologians, was finally rejected and condemned by the Church itself, under the name of traditionalism, as

---

[3] Lamennais, *Essay on Indifference in Matters of Religion*, trans. Lord Stanley of Alderley (London: Macqueen, 1895); originally published as *Essai sur l'indifférence en matière de religion* (Paris: Tournachon Molin, 1818–23).

undermining the necessary rights of reason. In the first pages of his *Sketch*, which were doubtless written not long after the *Essay on Indifference*, Lamennais repeats that, given over to his individual perspective, the philosopher is unable to go beyond arbitrary hypotheses and paralogisms, that he ought to ask for his principles from universal beliefs, and that Catholic theology is the only authentic tradition of the latter. Consequently, it is in theological doctrine about God, in the dogma of the Trinity that the author of the *Sketch of a Philosophy* draws the elements that seem to him to be those of a universal explanation, the elements of divine nature. He submitted these primary ideas imposed by faith only to superficial analysis, to a rapid and insufficient critique. With the principles imperfectly defined, all the applications and all the consequences have the same character and remain in the same indetermination; whence the lack of scientific rigour and, instead of a chain of reasons, a series of analogies that are sometimes specious. If Lamennais had taken his work further, if to the study of the physical world, which forms its principal object, he had added special and profound study of the intellectual and moral world that he considers anterior to the other, he would perhaps have recognized the primary origin of the principles that first he thought it necessary to draw from tradition and theology; perhaps these principles would have shown themselves to him in a brighter light and in more precise forms, and perhaps he would have deduced from them more rigorous and more tightly bound consequences.

In the fourth and last volume of the *Sketch*, which was published only in 1846, at a time when, wholly separated from any religious communion, Lamennais had to attach himself all the more narrowly to philosophy, he no longer appeals to tradition and theology; he provides conceptions of mind with a criterion in natural phenomena, and phenomena with a criterion in the conceptions of mind. True science, he says, is thereby neither the knowledge of simple phenomena, a pure materialism reducible to sensations forming no science, nor the knowledge of essences or absolute causes, a pure spiritualism that would involve only non-verified logical hypotheses; it is rather a natural and spiritual science all at once. And from this still uncertain and even contradictory doctrine, whereby, with a manifest diallel, the idea is the proof of the fact and the fact the proof of the idea, he subsequently moves to another doctrine whereby, in the two elements between which his thought floated, the one that he names the spiritual element wins out in the end, a doctrine according to which the highest certainty derives immediately from reason.

Finally, if in the first volumes of the *Sketch* divine nature seems sometimes to be conceived and defined as being in general, which is not really distinct from particular beings, just as Rosmini understood it;[4] and if, moreover, what is called

---

[4] The reference here is to Italian liberal Catholic theologian Antonio Francesco Davide Ambrogio Rosmini-Serbati (1797–1855).

finite within them, what particular beings consist of, is sometimes presented as a necessary principle that is the equal of the infinite, which is universal and absolute being; and if, consequently, it was possible to accuse the doctrine contained in these volumes of following the path that Spinozism had cleared, and to lead to the identification of creation and creator, in the later books Lamennais shows more clearly that, in his eyes, although the principle of distinction and limitation is inherent to the divine nature, it is only by an act of the divine will that this principle moves from ideality to reality, actuality, and that creation begins; that to the infinite, to the absolute alone belongs necessary existence; and that veritable infinity, in implying the plenitude of being, implies intellect, will, personality. How could intellect and will come into the world if they were not born from the infinite? This entails, in the end, that if creation is subject in its development to necessary laws that spring from the very laws of divine nature, it is no less a free process, and that—given that God, like any intelligent being, does nothing without a goal—the final cause or the good is, as Plato and Aristotle said, the ultimate reason for things.

IV
Socialism
Saint-Simon, Fourier, Proudhon

Lamennais wanted to replace the psychology, which was for him entirely sterile, of the eclectic school, with a metaphysics giving rise to the laws of general physics, a physics whose highest goal was to demonstrate the metaphysics. A quite different movement returned to the scene, though in new forms, in the philosophy that the work of Maine de Biran, Ampère, and the teaching of Royer-Collard and Victor Cousin had marginalized, which Lamennais had rejected with them: the philosophy that explains everything by the senses and that reduces everything, in the final analysis, to physics. The origin of this movement is to be found in the systems by which one attempted, among the ruins of the Middle Ages, upturned by the Revolution, to establish the bases of a new social constitution, systems that consequently have been designated by the name 'socialist'.

Under the preponderant influence of the dogmas that Christianity had originally opposed to the corruption of a later, degenerated antiquity, the Middle Ages had been constantly dominated by the preoccupation with a kingdom above to which the kingdom below, the world, was almost always opposed, and, consequently, the general characteristic of the theories relative to the moral order had been a mysticism disdaining, often to excess, the things of this world. In contrast, the dominant, even exclusive preoccupation of socialism was to realize here below the perfect and felicitous order that the Middle Ages reserved for a wholly supernatural existence: instead of heaven, earth.

A principal characteristic of the philosophy of our time has often been seen in the idea of universal progress, and Condorcet was celebrated for it. It is true, however, that this honour should be accorded to thinkers of a more elevated order, to Pascal and to Leibniz. Pascal said that humanity should be considered as a subsisting person who continually learns.[1] Leibniz, expressing an even more extensive view, said: 'What completes the beauty and the perfection of divine productions is that the universe advances endlessly, and from the freest movement towards a more and more complete order.' He saw movement and progress even in celestial beatitude: 'Our happiness will never consist, and must never consist, in complete joy, wherein nothing is left to desire, and which would dull our mind,

---

[1] See 'Preface to the Treatise on Vacuum' in Pascal, *Minor Works*, translated by O. W. Wright (New York: P. F. Collier & Son, 1914).

but must consist in a perpetual progress towards new pleasures and new perfections.'[2] In presenting the idea of universal progress, all Condorcet did, imbued with the principles of a half-materialist philosophy, was to limit it to the conditions of natural and terrestrial existence. So did the socialists, and primarily the earliest of those of our epoch, namely Henri de Saint-Simon.

According to Saint-Simon, Christianity, in the name of a wholly spiritual God, had made an anathema of the flesh; the Middle Ages had disdained and oppressed it; the modern age had to rehabilitate it. For that it was necessary to see that God was both body and spirit. Disdaining the flesh, matter, the Middle Ages had looked down on those in society who were principally occupied by material and carnal matters, in other words the people, and glorified those occupied by matters of spirit. Modernity had to rehabilitate the people; its task was, according to a formula that Saint-Simon borrowed from Condorcet, to work to better the fate of the most numerous and poorest class. Such were the generalities, of a vaguely philosophical character, that served as principles for the doctrine that was called, by its author, Saint-Simonianism. Enfantin added further developments in which we find often shocking signs of a cult of the functions by which the human being is the least distant from animals. But Saint-Simonianism was first and foremost, as is known, a system of general politics and political economy, where philosophy had not much of a place.

Charles Fourier's goal, with his phalansterian system, was the same as that of Saint-Simon: to establish for everybody on this earth the felicity that Christianity reserved for the chosen ones in another life. However, what Saint-Simon expects, to this effect, from a more or less absolute authority, Fourier expects from the absolute freedom of all, with freedom meaning, on his account, satisfaction without constraint of all the passions. Given that the physical world, says Fourier, has been explained, after Newton, by the mutual attraction of all the parts of matter, the moral world must be explained by what can be called 'passionate attraction', which brings together and associates the individuals shaped by analogous and harmonious inclinations. All miseries, all ills result from frustrated passions. If we grant free reign to all the passions, just as the molecules composing the physical world harmoniously come together according to their affinities, all the individuals forming the molecules constitutive of the social world will harmonize in grouping together, according to Fourier's favourite expression, in free phalanges, in pacific and happy phalansteries.

This notion supposed more or less new and quite particular views on the nature of the passions and, more generally, on human nature; this is what Fourierism contributes to the philosophical work of the period in which it appeared. But it

---

[2] The second citation is the concluding sentence of Leibniz's 'Principles of Nature and Grace, Based on Reason' in Leibniz, *Philosophical Papers and Letters*, ed. Loemker (Dordrecht: Springer, 1989), pp. 636–40, but the first proved unlocatable.

was marginal; Fourierism distinguished itself by hypotheses concerning the future of the world and humanity that were as strange as they were unjustified, rather than by just and useful observations.

This is also the verdict that posterity, in all probability, will offer concerning the ideas of Pierre-Joseph Proudhon.

Proudhon will doubtless always hold a distinguished position among the writers of our time, but not, perhaps, among the thinkers. 'Being able to articulate everything that one wants is not', as said Swedenborg, a better judge in matters of science and thought than he is generally considered to be, 'a proof of understanding; instead, being able to discern that what is true is true, and that what is false is false, is the mark and defining characteristic of intelligence.'[3] Besides, for philosophy, in its most general meaning, intellect does not suffice: the type of intellect that manifests itself in the consistency and development of ideas is required, and this is not what we find in Proudhon. Moreover, although he approached philosophical matters in more than one of his works, it is not possible to say that he ever presented or even suggested anything like a philosophy. In sum, although the audacity of the paradoxes by which he made himself known, joined to his literary talent, earned him great notoriety, science owed him little, and it is doubtful that he had ever sought to serve it.

---

[3] Ravaisson is referring to the eighteenth-century Swedish scientist and then mystical theosophist Emmanuel Swedenborg.

V
Socialist Philosophy
Leroux and Reynaud

In the work of Pierre Leroux and Jean Reynaud, who also belong to the socialist schools, we see the signs of a sincere pursuit of philosophical truth.

Saint-Simon had wanted to reconstitute society on a triple basis: the three classes of industrialists, artists, and scholars, which for him corresponded to the three principal applications and, consequently, to the principal faculties of the human mind. Pierre Leroux apprehended, after him, that there were good grounds to distinguish in human nature three great parts corresponding to industry, art, and science: sensation, feeling, knowledge. The development of this idea filled to a large degree his *Refutation of Eclecticism*.[1]

In *Of Humanity* he attempted, moreover, to demonstrate that if the human being, with these three great principal faculties, supposing also that it is perfectible and infinitely so, is to attain felicity, not, as Christianity taught, in a wholly supernatural celestial life, but, as Saint-Simon said, in the conditions in which we find ourselves, on this earth, this could only be within an eternity of successive existences. 'You are,' he said, 'therefore you will be; for to be is to participate in eternal and infinite being', but for that it is as little necessary as it is possible to abandon our conditions of existence, essential to humanity. Immortality could thus consist only in being reborn after death, in surviving, the same and different at once, in the successive generations that will forever occupy this earth. To the objection that we have no memories of previous lives, and that immortality, for an intelligent and moral being, seems inseparable from memory, Pierre Leroux answered: 'Is not to live to change? To change, for the mind, is this not necessarily to forget?'[2] And he thought he found in Leibniz, as in all the greatest of philosophers and theologians, thoughts that confirmed his own.

Perhaps, on the contrary, Leibniz thought, as did Plato, Aristotle, Plotinus, and Descartes, that rather than living and changing being the same, living is to triumph over change, and at every moment to reclaim oneself from death; that living, for spirit, is therefore to rediscover itself and to recognize oneself is always, always and eternally, to remember.

---

[1] Pierre Leroux (1797–1871), *Réfutation de l'éclecticisme* (Paris: Gosselin, 1839).
[2] The two quotations: Leroux, *De l'humanité* (Paris: Perrotin, 1840), pp. 244 and 245.

What will remain from Pierre Leroux's speculations is the idea, more strongly expressed than it had been since at least Joseph de Maistre, who deduced it from the dogma of reversibility, that humanity forms a real, substantial unity, from which it follows that all its members are bound together by an intimate solidarity. But in this unity as Pierre Leroux describes it, we see nothing different from the phenomenal existences whose relations it was supposed to explain, and thus perhaps only one of the purely nominal entities whose emptiness thinkers such as Aristotle, Leibniz, and Berkeley brought to light, and which only have the meaning that the mind itself gives to them in producing them, even unknowingly. If there is something in which we all agree, despite our dissidences, something in which, as different as we are, we are still identical, then what Victor Cousin called impersonal reason is not enough to account for it: this something that is deeper than any human personality can be only a higher and more complete personality. 'I am the vine', said Jesus, 'and you are the branches; I am the head, and you are the members.'—'In every conversation', said one of our contemporaries, the profound thinker Emerson, 'the interlocutors tacitly refer to a third person, which is our common nature, and this third person is God. The one who has made both everything and everyone is always there, behind us, and what fills both ourselves and things is his formidable omniscience.'[3]

Pierre Leroux wanted, he said, to make the difference, so pronounced in Christianity, between heaven and earth disappear; and this was, in his view, to uncover the genuine sense of Christianity. This was also the thought of Jean Reynaud. However, Pierre Leroux wanted to reduce heaven, the site of a future existence, to earth, whereas Jean Reynaud wanted instead to extend earth to heaven. Pierre Leroux believed in a future existence consisting in an indefinite repetition, without personal identity and without memory, of terrestrial existence; Jean Reynaud imagined, after this life on this globe, a succession of other lives on other globes, infinitely, without personality and without memory ever being lost.

The idea that inspired Jean Reynaud was that of universal perfectibility in its application to human destiny. In studying, in order to compose the Zoroaster entry in the *Universal Encylopaedia*,[4] the relics of the religion of the Mages, which Eugène Burnouf had started to interpret, he was struck by the resemblances between this religion and Christianity. Moreover, the Mazdean faith in the ultimate victory of the good seemed to him closer to the idea of universal progress than what Christian theology teaches about hell and eternal damnation. At the same time, he found in what we know of the ancient beliefs of Gaul, in the dogma,

---

[3] Ralph Waldo Emerson, 'The Over-Soul' in *Nature and Selected Essays*, ed. L. Ziff (Penguin: London, 2003), pp. 205–24, p. 213.
[4] Although he writes '*Encyclopédie universelle*', it seems that Ravaisson is referring to Leroux and Reynaud's 1834–47 *Encyclopédie nouvelle: dictionnaire philosophique, scientifique, littéraire et industriel, offrant le tableau des connaissances humaines au XIXe siècle* (Paris: Gosselin et Furne).

essential to them, of the perpetual existence and activity of souls, material to enlarge and complete Christian dogmatics.

Such were, joined to the deep faith in the law of the continual progress in all things that science seems increasingly to confirm, the elements that Jean Reynaud put to work in the composition of his dialogues between a theologian and a philosopher that he entitled *Earth and Heaven*.[5]

According to this book, this earth is only the site of one of the existences, of an indefinite number, that we have to traverse successively. We have already existed, when we live here below; we will exist again, and always as more and more perfect, in the different worlds, of an indefinite number, that populate space. We will not pass in an instant from a corporeal state to a spiritual state: there are no pure spirits, lacking any body, such as the majority of theologians have imagined the angels; there is no life, even in God, that is, rigorously speaking, immaterial. Immortality consists in an indefinite progress from one existence to other existences that are, at bottom, similar, through which one is increasingly purified. To adopt the style of theology, there is no more paradise, no more hell, but only an eternal purgatory.

The Périgueux council of 1857 hardly approved of the improvements that the author of *Earth and Heaven* thought he had brought to Christianity; it saw in it only renewed errors from past heresies, and it declared it to be anathema contrary to the Catholic faith.

Without entering into discussion of theology or history, and in remaining with a philosophical perspective, it is possible to wonder if understanding heaven, following Jean Reynaud, by assimilating it, almost entirely, to earth is not to deny it; if denying the terminus of progress is not to suppress progress itself; if denying absolute perfection is not to reject any idea of improvement.

What has always been understood by heaven, when it was a matter of a future life, whether or not this was clearly recognized, is not a particular place more or less distant from where we are now, but a life exempt from the miseries of life here below, a life wholly different from our life of phenomena and movement. In one of Plato's dialogues, and this is a passage that Pierre Leroux has cited, one of Socrates's interlocutors defined astronomy as a science that leads the mind from things here below to those up above: 'It seems to me,' says Socrates, 'given this way of understanding astronomy, in wanting to make of it philosophy itself, we are made to look down. Do we believe therefore, he added, that looking with one's head tilted back at the paintings on a ceiling is to consider with thought and not with the eyes? To my mind, no study is capable of making the soul look on high other than the one related to the infinite and to the invisible.' In the same way, it can be said, talking of a life similar to ours is hardly to talk of a celestial life, in whatever constellation it is situated, even if one adds, with Jean Reynaud, that this existence up above will be much superior to our existence here below, and will

---

[5] Jean Reynaud (1806–63), *Philosophie religieuse: terre et ciel* (Paris: Furne, 1854).

continue to perfect itself indefinitely. In order to respond to what our heart demands, to what our reason requires, we need a perfect life, one to be found only above everything sensory, beyond space, beyond time also, there where God lives, in the ultra-stellar as well as ultra-terrestrial region of pure spirit.

'Everywhere', as Swedenborg said, 'where the Lord is known and loved is heaven.' And, before Swedenborg, the Gospel: 'The kingdom of heaven lies within you.' Already in this life, on this earth, we can, by soul, by spirit, be inhabitants of heaven. The true question of immortality is one of knowing, while in an indefinite future we will always have to depend for our existence on material and sensory conditions, whether our destiny is to be, more than we presently are, in the wholly internal home of glory and eternal beatitude, whether our destiny is to live in God and with God.

Subtracting the supernatural, subtracting metaphysics, is therefore here to reject any thought of heaven, and to reduce everything to earth.

Of Jean Reynaud's book one thing at least seems to endure: this is—without speaking of the feelings of generous goodness and sweet sympathy with which, while combatting a particular article of theology, he is never very far from the spirit of Jesus—the general idea that inspires him, although he takes it in a sense that is perhaps too narrow. This is the idea that, like the rest of the world, the human soul, and it above all, is active [*en marche*], in progress, and, from the most tenebrous depths of embryonic existence, always moves, despite a thousand deviations, closer to God. This idea, verified by every progression in the sciences, will be accepted, perhaps, by theology one day. The one by whom the 'good news', which others wanted to retain within a small corner of the universe, became the good news of the entire earth said: 'Every creature longs for the Lord.' And if it is true, as he also said, that 'it is the spirit itself of the Lord who prays in us with ineffable groans', can there be a 'longing for the Lord' that will be answered?

VI
Iatromechanism and Phrenology
Broussais and Gall

The renaissance of the philosophy opposed to all metaphysics, of the philosophy of the senses and body, could not be limited to systems relating to morality, politics, public economy; it had to happen, as it normally does, that this philosophy regained life and force from the philosophical and medical theories that reduce life to a pure mechanism. It had, in the middle of the present century, two famous promoters in Broussais and Gall.

Author of a theory of pathology explaining all illnesses, including mental illnesses, by the phenomenon of irritation alone, Broussais aimed more generally, following the likes of Lamettrie and Cabanis, to explain the human being as a whole solely by means of its corporeal organization. His own doctrine provided him with no argument to add to those of his predecessors, but phrenology arrived, which aimed to destroy spiritualism in its foundations. Materialist physiology had already sought to demonstrate, by all the facts that show the dependence of mind [le moral] on the physiological, that intellect can be explained by matter alone. Gall came, in addition, to retract from mind what had always been claimed for it as its exclusive characteristic, namely simplicity and unity. He aimed to show that what we call mind is an assemblage of absolutely distinct and independent faculties, products of different parts of the brain. Inspection of the skull, cranioscopy, in comparison to the acts manifesting aptitudes and dispositions, was supposed to prove this. Broussais thought that here a definitive proof of materialism could be found: he adopted cranioscopy. Despite the talent and the credit of such a powerful auxiliary, despite Gall's and also Spurzheim's undeniable knowledge, the new science did not have a long career. Not only was psychology able to show that our faculties, though diverse in their applications, possess no less a radical unity, but also physiology, in the works of many of its most eminent representatives—Flourens, Longet, Lélut, Parchappe, Camille Dareste, Vulpian, Gratiolet, and still others—demonstrated many times over that the supposed anatomical or physiological facts that cranioscopy relied on were simply not real. Many of those who believed for some time in phrenology, Littré among others, have now entirely abandoned it.

VII
Comte's Positivism

The doctrine founded by Auguste Comte with the name *positive philosophy* or *positivism* had a double origin in the theories of Saint-Simon and those of the phrenologists, particularly Broussais. Auguste Comte's principal goal, with Saint-Simon, was to discover the best social order, the constitution of which he called sociology. At the same time, he wanted to ground his sociological system in a universal scientific system, barely different in its principles from that of Broussais, although the latter, in this essential respect inconsistent with his principles, continued to admit a first cause of nature, while the principal purpose of the author of positivism was to abolish any idea of a first cause.

Auguste Comte, still young, began by associating himself to Saint-Simon's project of founding, on the ruins of a society deriving from the Middle Ages, a new society, whose basis would be industry, and whose unique goal would be felicity on this earth. In 1825 he worked with him on the publication of *The Catechism of the Industrialists*.[1] But the disciple, an excellent mathematician, came to distinguish himself from the master in that instead of privileging the class of producers of the material order he claimed the first rank for science.

Saint-Simon, in his system, granted a role to feeling, to which he related religion. On this point also, Comte did not follow him. The master, in praising the work that Comte had published in *The Catechism of the Industrialists* under the heading of *System of positive politics*, found it necessary to say that its author expressed the point of view of the physical and mathematical sciences. He reproached him not only for having failed to attribute to industrial capacity all the importance that he attributed to it, but also for recommending, in the order of science, 'the direction that Aristotle represents, at the expense of the one represented by Plato'; and he says, in sum, that 'the pupil has examined only the scientific part of our system, but he has not presented its sentimental and religious part'.[2] In other words, Auguste Comte's ideas seemed to him to constitute an explanatory system whose perspective was too narrowly logically and geometrical, from which the soul was unduly excluded, and that ended up with a 'dry atheism'. Such was, indeed, the true character of Auguste Comte's philosophy at the beginning.

---

[1] See Henri de Saint-Simon (1760–1825), *The Catechism of the Industrialists* in *The Political Thought of Saint-Simon*, ed. G. Ionescu (London: Oxford, 1976).
[2] Saint-Simon, 'Catéchisme des industriels' in *Oeuvres*, vol. 4 (Paris: Anthropos), pp. 1–207, pp. 4–5.

Saint-Simon professed a great aversion to metaphysics. Instead of these vain speculations, we need, as he often repeated, positive knowledge. This was Auguste Comte's starting point. For him, as for his master, only the positive or real can be the object of science. By 'positive' he means the facts that we know from experience; and these facts in the end are, in his view, wholly relative things. Metaphysics claims to know things existing by themselves, independently of any relation, in other words, existing in an absolute manner: it is, consequently, an illusory science. 'There is only one absolute maxim and this is that there is nothing absolute.'

The fundamental maxim that there is nothing, or that we can know nothing, that is not relative is not specific to Auguste Comte. Without speaking of the ancient Greek sophists, whose philosophy the maxim summarizes, it is also the foundation of Hume's philosophy; it was adopted by Hamilton, Brown's eminent successor in Reid's and Stewart's chair, and by Mansel, his pupil; it is, at this very moment, the first principle of the systems promoted by several distinguished philosophers and scholars in England, by Herbert Spencer, Alexander Bain, Samuel Bailey, Stuart Mill, and George Lewes.

This maxim, as Stuart Mill has remarked, has for those who support it more than one meaning: for the most part it means either that we can know an object only in opposing it to another object or to ourselves, or that everything known by us thereby depends on our faculties themselves, on our means of knowing. It is in this way that it was understood, after Kant, by Hamilton, and Mansel, Bain, Bailey, Herbert Spencer, and Stuart Mill still understand it thus. As for Auguste Comte, the theory of knowledge never occupied him much, and he was thinking more about the things themselves than their relations to our faculties of knowledge. Without, perhaps, having sought to define with sufficient precision the sense that he attached to the word 'relative', it is clear that by it he generally understood what exists only on condition of something else and in a certain proportion with it. The absolute would, on the contrary, be what is sufficient unto itself, that whose idea, as Spinoza said of substance, would need the idea of nothing else. Such would be a cause that did not require another cause; this is what we call a primary cause. But, rigorously speaking, a first cause and a cause is the same thing. By this maxim, according to which we can know only what is relative, Auguste Comte meant that we cannot know causes, but only facts in relations to other facts, and so on infinitely; facts, and that is to say, the phenomena revealed to us by our senses.

We should add that, under the heading of causes, he not only proscribed forces or powers that we represent to ourselves more or less, as the School did, by way of souls and minds; he also proscribed the type of active properties that the physiologists call vital properties, the affinities of the chemists, and the imponderable fluids of the physicists, their electrical and magnetic fluids, their ether—all vain hypotheses, residues of scholasticism, constructions invented to explain conveniently the facts, but that serve in reality only to hide our ignorance concerning the physical antecedents of particular facts, and which, consequently, prevent us searching for and discovering them.

Positive science limits itself to observing the sensory facts that precede, follow, or accompany other sensory facts, and the relations they have with each other in space and time.

In order to understand this mode of explanation, we have to compare it to other customary modes. There are two, according to Auguste Comte: the theological and the metaphysical.

In the beginning, natural phenomena were explained by means of voluntary phenomena. Facts were conceived as the appearance of spontaneous determinations; agents similar to human beings were held to be their causes. Moreover, natural phenomena seemed to emanate from powers, superior to human power, that lay beyond direct acquaintance, and that are all the greater in our eyes due to the obscurity enveloping them; it is not to beings similar to the human being that these powers are attributed, but to divine beings, to gods. This is first philosophy, which is not distinct from religion: it is philosophical theology.

It was next seen that phenomena have a constancy that does not accord with the arbitrariness of will; the powers ascribed to them as causes are then conceived as each limited to a certain type of effect: for movement, a motive force; for vegetation, a vegetative force. It is recognized that we know not what these powers are in themselves; they are mysterious, occult virtues or qualities, which are defined only by their effects, which are only, in truth, abstract and collective expressions of phenomena, and even just words that serve to order them in memory. This is what Auguste Comte calls 'metaphysical entities', and which numerous metaphysicians introduce, but which it would be more exact, since they are symbols that subsist only in our thought, to consider as wholly logical entities. These are the notions whose emptiness was seen and shown so well by Berkeley among the moderns, and to which, in antiquity, the founder of metaphysics, Aristotle, opposed already a truly supernatural principle, intelligible and real at the same time.

Positivism is essentially expressed in what Auguste Comte calls the 'law of three stages', of, that is to say, the three epochs of thinking and science, a law that his disciples thought to be his most important discovery.

Saint-Simon had already opposed to the fictions of theology and metaphysics positive knowledge; and he owed this idea perhaps to the doctor Burdin, one of his friends. In an 1815 conversation with Saint-Simon, related by the latter in his *Memoir on the Science of Man*,[3] Burdin, speaking in a way that has since become familiar, said that all the sciences began as conjectural, and that they would all end by becoming positive. Astronomy, he said, had begun as astrology; chemistry was originally only alchemy; physiology was only just beginning to establish itself

---

[3] Saint-Simon, *Memoir on the Science of Man*, ed. K. Taylor (Abingdon: Routledge, 1975).

on observable and discussed facts; psychology had only just begun to take physiology as its basis and to rid itself of the religious prejudices on which it had been founded. He added, and this is the principle of the whole of Auguste Comte's doctrine concerning the comparative history of the sciences, that certain sciences became positive sooner than others, those in which facts were considered in their most simple and least numerous relations. Astronomy, consequently, had arrived the first at the positive stage; physics and chemistry next, and then physiology; general philosophy was to reach it last.

But in order to find the real origin of these ideas, we have to go back to one of the philosophers that Auguste Comte, Saint-Simon, and Burdin considered as dreamers, to the one who, in the famous *Existence* entry in the *Encyclopaedia*,[4] began to re-establish, on the basis provided by Descartes, high philosophy. 'Before knowing the connection of physical effects with each other', said Turgot in his *History of the Progress of the Human Mind*, 'there was nothing more natural than to suppose that they were produced by invisible intelligent beings similar to us. For what else could they have resembled? Everything that happened without the human being having a role in it had its own god... When the philosophers recognized the absurdity of these fables, but without having acquired true enlightenment about natural history, they thought they explained the causes of phenomena by abstract expressions, as essences or faculties, expressions that, however, explained nothing, and about which one reasoned as if they were beings, new divinities replacing the old... It was only much later, in observing the mechanical action that bodies have on each other that other hypotheses were drawn from this mechanics, hypotheses that mathematics could develop and experience verify.'[5]

Thought, says Auguste Comte, passes through three successive stages: the first, in which things are explained by a will superior to nature but similar to human will, and having generally the human being for its object; the second, in which things are explained by entities of a poorly determined nature, which are the weak copies of the supernatural causes of the first ages; the third, which is concerned to determine only how facts accompany and follow each other. The first of these three epochs is the religious period; the second, the metaphysical period; the third, the scientific period. In this last period, instead of having recourse, in order to explain phenomena, to the unknown causes that were imagined as separate entities acting without measures or determinable rules, a notion destructive of all idea of natural law and consequently of science, we are limited to seeking the physical and observable circumstances in which phenomena are produced and to which they are relative.

---

[4] On Turgot's (Anne Robert Jacques Turgot, 1712–81) 'Existence' entry in Diderot and d'Alembert's *Encyclopédie*, see G. Cavanaugh, 'Turgot and the *Encyclopédie*', *Diderot Studies* 10 (1968), pp. 23–33.
[5] Although he writes '*Histoire des progrès de l'esprit humain*', Ravaisson seems to be referring to Turgot's 1750 *Tableau philosophique des progrès de l'esprit humain*, now available in Turgot, *Oeuvres*, ed. Schelle, vol. 1 (Paris: Alcan, 1913–23).

The purpose of science, indeed, following Auguste Comte, and as Bacon said, is to make us masters of nature, or to make us independent of it at least. It ought to allow us to modify as we wish the things that depend on us; and it should teach us to foresee the things that in no way depend on us, so that we can consequently alter our conduct. But, for this double goal, it is enough that we know the only thing that it is in our power to know: the circumstances in which each phenomenon occurs. The fact that, with one thing occurring, another thing occurs also, is what is named, by means of a figurative expression, a law of nature, and which Stuart Mill, in order to reject any idea of necessary dependence, in order to remain more closely to the facts, names 'natural uniformities'. The union of natural laws constitutes for each type of object a particular science: it is possible, moreover, to establish, between the most general laws of each science, relations constituting still more general laws. This, according to Auguste Comte, is the work of philosophy. Since, in his eyes, there is no reality beyond sensory phenomena, since any possible existence beyond these phenomena, whether it is called matter or spirit, is a pure chimera, since the words soul or God, in particular, are words without meaning, there is no philosophy that would have, like any other science, a special object; philosophy can be nothing else than the collection of the most general truths established by the particular sciences.

The highest goal of positivism is thus to determine the most general relations of the objects of the different sciences. Now almost entirely preoccupied by the mathematical point of view, which is that of quantity, as Auguste Comte remarks, the differences of the relations come back, in the final analysis, to differences of simplicity and complexity, and to simplicity is tied generality. The most general properties, those belonging to the most objects, are necessarily the simplest; generality decreases therefore as complexity increases; generality and complexity exist in a proportionate and inverse relation to each other.

This law that Auguste Comte believed himself to be the first to demonstrate is the one according to which a property extends over more species the fewer elements it includes, a law that is the basis of logic, and that logicians call the law of the inverse relation of the extension and of the comprehension of ideas. Aristotle was the first to apply this on a grand scale to nature, in showing that each order of existence comprehends within itself all the inferior and simpler orders of existence. But at each degree Aristotle also conceived, in order to explain the combination of the inferior elements in a new and more complex order, a special active cause, or, better, a special manifestation of the universal cause. Auguste Comte, at least in the first part of his career, saw no other differences between the inferior and the superior than those of the very elements that they contained. From other principles, he admitted only the simple elements that mathematics considers: all the rest, in his eyes, consisted only in arrangements of these elements, and in arrangements of these arrangements; whence it followed that each species could be explained solely by the simpler principles that it contained. Everything that has vital properties has physical and chemical properties, but the inverse is not true; everything with physical and chemical properties has mathematical properties, is shaped, extended, and the inverse is not true. Mathematics, consequently, explains physics, physics explains chemistry, chemistry explains life. The progress of science consists in reducing every complexity, by a graduated analysis, to the simplest and most general elements.

If we look through the different sciences, we see, says Auguste Comte, that they are naturally classified in an order wherein complexity increases, and, to the same degree, extension, generality diminishes. At the first degree, mathematics; at the last and highest degree, sociology, the science of human society. Number, extension, shape, indeed, are the simplest of what nature offers to us; whence the precision, the exactitude, the relative ease of mathematics. The relations of men to each other are, on the contrary, the most complex of all, since everything included in nature contributes to them; whence the difficulty of discovering the laws of these relations. Already in astronomy, we encounter phenomena whose elements are too diverse for it to be easy to estimate their relations exactly, to define them, and consequently to calculate them. How much is that not more difficult in chemistry, in biology, in sociology, whose elements are more numerous and even more variable! It is no less certain that, following August Comte, just as any geometrical proposition can be translated, as Descartes showed, into an algebraic proposition, so too any truth must be resolvable into geometry, into arithmetic, into algebra, and every quality into quantity alone. However distant science still remains and even must always remain from perfect analysis, the phenomena must be considered as all being transformations of primordial mathematical elements. The facts presented to us by living bodies are not, as Auguste Comte said in summarizing his doctrine, of another nature than the simplest phenomena of inert bodies. This is why mathematical science is universal, and forms the unique basis of all natural philosophy.

In sum, philosophy is nothing other than mathematics.

It is, in addition, in exact proportion to their simplicity that the different sciences pass from the primitive state to the final state, from the theological phase to the positive phase. Mathematics has, since time immemorial, been an almost entirely positive science; Lagrange dispelled the last remnants of metaphysics from it. Metaphysical hypotheses still play a role in vulgar physics and chemistry, as various supposedly special forces, and above all, under the heading of vital forces or properties, in physiology, where the science of man is still adulterated not only with metaphysical but also religious hypotheses. The ultimate triumph of science will consist in bringing sociology to a positive state, to reduce everything within it to simple relations of phenomena, and all the phenomena to the simplest among them.

This doctrine, exposed in the voluminous *Course of Positive Philosophy* published between 1830 and 1842, found in France adherents of whom many were physiologists and doctors. Although its author had declared that, since it is not an object of experience, positivism did not have to bother itself with what is called matter, and although he described the materialists as anti-scientific, most of his followers understood the doctrine as a materialist system. Perhaps, indeed, what we call materialism consists not so much in explaining things by matter, with this term designating some kind of indefinable support of sensory phenomena, a theory that would imply a belief in an existence imperceptible to the senses, and which consequently would be a sort of metaphysics, but rather in reducing everything to sensory phenomena and the latter to simple mechanical elements.

Littré, the wise translator of Hippocrates, who contributed more than any other to the favourable reception of positivism, advocates, as he puts it, a perfect disinterest concerning the choice between materialism and spiritualism. However, it cannot be denied that in his edition, with Robin, of Nysten's *Dictionary of Medicine*,[6] he expressed himself on the soul, on life, on organization, on matter, in terms identical to those employed by all the materialists. But, for him, saying that the substance of the nerves thinks would amount to a materialist proposition only if one added that it thinks by virtue of a particular arrangement of molecules, if, perhaps, it were explained not by a special property of a particular material, but by a purely mechanical disposition of universal matter. Comte advanced in this direction by assimilating, as we have seen, supposedly vital properties, which Littré preserves, to the occult qualities of the scholastics, and by considering the vital as being, at bottom, reducible to physics, and physics to geometry; and this is doubtless the most consistent and complete materialism. But it is still materialist, though perhaps without being sufficiently clear about it, to explain thought by a property of matter, to make of it, in whatever way, a function of the body. Besides, Littré supplied a preface to Leblais's 1865 *Materialism and Spiritualism: A Study in Positive Philosophy*. The author of the book says: 'I declare myself frankly to be a materialist', and the author of the preface adds that he wants, over a few pages, 'to defend what this book defends, to combat what this book combats'.[7]

---

[6] P. H. Nysten, *Dictionnaire de médecine, de chirurgie, de pharmacie, des sciences accessoires et de l'art vétérinaire*, ed. Littré and C. Robin (Paris: Baillière, 1854).

[7] Alphonse Leblais (1820–90), *Matérialisme et spiritualisme: étude de philosophie positive* (Paris: Germer Baillière, 1865).

VIII
Positivism in Britain

Positivism found even more favour in England than in France; it was brought there principally by George Lewes. Stuart Mill adopted its principles, and they can be found in the works of Bain, Bailey, Herbert Spencer. In a letter to Stuart Mill, on 4 March 1842, Auguste Comte expressed the hope that his philosophy would receive a better welcome in England than it had in France; he found, he said, more 'positivity' in the English thinkers than in his compatriots. And often, indeed, modern philosophers from Great Britain have expressed ideas very close to those familiar to positivism. Without going back to Bacon and Locke, Bentham is not far from positivist ideas. Macaulay said: 'The glory of modern philosophy consists in that it aims for what is useful and avoids ideas.' 'Our own philosophers have been,' says Bailey, 'in the main, disposed to conform their researches to the methods employed in physical inquiry; and although their scientific success has not been great, owing to the many traditional prejudices under which they have entered upon the subject, and also to their not perhaps seeing clearly how to follow the line of inductive investigation pointed out to them by physical science, they have usually felt both the desire and the necessity of speaking plainly to the practical understandings of their audience. Hence they have given us much good sense, if not more precise thinking, and at the same time comparatively little mysticism.'[1]

'Whether in the Vedes, in the Platonists, or in the Hegelians,' as Stuart Mill says in a passage related by Bailey, 'mysticism is neither more nor less than ascribing objective existence to the subjective creations of the mind's own faculties, to mere ideas of the intellect.'[2]

As is clear, Mill and Bailey recognize as sound philosophy only the one promoted by the 'sons of the earth', as Plato says, 'who want to hold as existent only what they see with their eyes and touch with their hands'. Beyond the philosophy of the senses, they seem to acknowledge only that which takes 'subjective creations of the mind' as realities, without examining the philosophy founded by a 'positive' Aristotle, which Descartes and Leibniz developed, and which takes as a principle, not the creations of the mind, but the mind itself in the most immediate and the most positive of experiences.

---

[1] Samuel Bailey, *Letters on the Human Mind: Second Series* (Longman: London, 1858), pp. 131–2. Ravaisson is translating the English original; the text had not already been translated into French.
[2] Ibid., p. 164.

Bain, Bailey, Stuart Mill, Spencer sought to construct a positive psychology and logic.

For these philosophers, constructing a positive psychology amounts, in renouncing inquiry into the supposed faculties or powers from which feelings and ideas derive, to limiting oneself to these feelings and ideas themselves; it is to limit oneself, with Hume, to determining, just as physicists do with physical and external things, how internal phenomena accompany and succeed each other. It is, consequently, to restrict oneself to what Hume called the laws of the association of ideas. In psychology thus conceived, metaphysical entities or realized abstractions—against which Berkeley, after Hume, had led such a campaign—are eliminated, as is the thinking subject, the soul, the very principle of psychological phenomena.

Establishing a positivist logic was the task that Stuart Mill set himself. As he understood it, and as he presented it in the grand work that Louis Peisse has just translated into French, this logic can be summarized in the principle, already familiar to Locke and Hobbes, that ideas cannot be deduced from each other, as ordinary logic teaches, in such a way that from something known, we could, without the aid of experience, draw another thing known; that, having between themselves relations of mere concomitance rather than dependence, they can be added to each other either by experience or by that extension of experience that is the inference from the similar to the similar that is named induction. Hence the new theories, or rather the renewed theories of Hobbes and Hume, on all the parts of logic, on all the intellectual operations. Definition, for example, does not consist, according to Stuart Mill, in characterizing an object by the essential properties from which derive all the others that it possesses, but solely in stating that with one property, another one, in fact, is to be found: it is a pure description. Reasoning does not consist, according to Stuart Mill, in drawing one thing from another but simply in recalling how with one thing another is encountered, in reproducing, in another order, the result of the observation of induction. Induction itself, to which all reasoning is reducible, consists only in adding mechanically to the series of facts offered by experience other similar series. To this it will be objected that, by virtue of some principle that authorizes us to do so, we establish between the analogous things a connection, if not necessary, then at least probable—in no way, says Stuart Mill; this supposed principle arrives only after the fact. Induction is an instinctive operation through which from a particular fact we pass to another, without this requiring any sort of reason.

Just as we can ask of positivism how it is, if mathematical notions come to us only from experience, that from these notions is it possible to draw so many consequences that experience always verifies, so too we can ask of it how it is, if induction is a mechanism without reason, that the facts so often confirm it. Is it enough, besides, to prove that we carry out inductions without having a reason for it, to claim that we do not perceive that we have one? Did the author of the

New Essays on Human Understanding not answer rightly to an equivalent assertion by Locke that we often reason according to principles that we do not apprehend, or at least, of which we have only a confused and obscure awareness: 'We know many things', as he said after Plato, 'about which we seldom think.' 'Thus there are in us instinctive truths which are innate principles that we sense and approve, even when we have no proof of them—though we get one when we *explain* the instinct in question. This is how we employ the laws of inference, being guided by a confused knowledge of them, as if by instinct, though the logicians demonstrate the reasons for them; as mathematicians explain what we do unthinkingly when we walk or jump.'[3] 'The truths that we start by being aware of are indeed particular ones, just as we start with the coarsest and most composite ideas. But that does not alter the fact that *in the order of nature*—as distinct from the chronological order of our thoughts—the simplest comes first, and that the reasons for particular truths rest entirely on the more general ones of which they are mere instances. And when we want to consider what is virtually in us before any apperception, we are right to start by what is the simplest. General principles enter into our thoughts, serving as their inner core and as their mortar. Even if we give no thought to them, they are necessary for thought, as muscles and tendons are for walking. The mind relies on these principles constantly; but it doesn't find it so easy to sort them out and to command a distinct view of each one separately, for that requires great attention to what it is doing, and the not very thoughtful majority of people are hardly capable of that. The Chinese have articulate sounds, just as we do, so they have the basis for an alphabet like ours. But they have adopted a different system of writing, and it hasn't yet occurred to them to make an alphabet. It is in that way that many things are possessed without the possessors knowing it.'[4] And when asked about these innate principles with which, without thinking about them, we govern our thoughts and actions, he answered that 'they are primary truths that form the very foundation of reason'.

In the opinion of Stuart Mill, which, besides, is only the boldly deduced consequence of the principles of positivism, given that experience offers only facts in relation to each other, and everything is known only by experience, there is no reason, and thus no necessity whatsoever, no absolute or relative, logical or moral necessity. It could have been the case that the sciences had quite different relations to each other than those presented by Auguste Comte; they might have had no relation to each other. It is possible that, on other planets or in still unknown parts of our own, there be a different physics, a different geometry, a different logic. And in the regions of our planet that we do know, who can say what physics, geometry, and logic will become tomorrow? And who knows if tomorrow,

---

[3] Ravaisson is paraphrasing here Leibniz, *New Essays on Human Understanding*, I, i, §19, p. 83.
[4] Leibniz, *New Essays on Human Understanding*, I, i, §20.

whether in a short while, there will be some kind of science, whether there will be two similar things, whether there will be anything at all?

If the theological or scholastic causes that positivism has eliminated really were distinct from ideas of law and natural science, it can be even less a question, with the hypothesis whereby phenomena follow each other without reason, of invariable laws, of an assured order, of scientific certainty.

Thus, at the same time as the disciples of Auguste Comte in France drew materialism from positivism as its consequence, the most eminent of his disciples in England deduced scepticism from it, no less rightly.

IX
Auguste Comte's Later Philosophy

Auguste Comte, however, began to take a quite different path from the one that Littré and Mill had taken after him; from his original positivism he moved by degrees to a metaphysics and religion.

One of the most important scholars in England who adhered to positivist principles, Herbert Spencer, expressed a reservation concerning the grand maxim according to which 'we know only that which is relative'. The very idea of the relative, he remarks, cannot be understood without its opposite. And we can conceive, indeed, beyond all the relations of phenomena, the absolute: this is situated beyond any science, and is the object of religion, but it is something mysterious, obscure, on which, according to Spencer, no light can be shed.

How the absolute, to which corresponds, as its opposite, the relative, lies at the heart of all knowledge was established more than twenty centuries ago against the ruling doctrine of universal relativity and mobility by Platonic dialectic, which opened the path to metaphysics. It did more: it showed that relations are intelligible only through this absolute, because it is the measure by which we judge them. Metaphysics, in the hands of its immortal founder, went further still: it showed that this absolute, by which the intellect measures the relative, is the intellect itself. This is what Leibniz repeated when, to the assertion retrieved from scholasticism by Locke that there is nothing in the intellect that has not first been in the senses, he responded: 'except the intellect', and when, with Aristotle, he showed in the intellect the higher measure of sense.

In our time, one woman has had a profound feeling for this doctrine, a woman of great learning and penetrating spirit. Sophie Germain not only gained the admiration of Gauss and Lagrange for her original work on the theory of number and on the calculation of surfaces; in the 1833 *General Considerations on the State of the Sciences, of Letters, and of the Arts in the Different Stages of their Development*,[1] published after her death, she signalled, with a remarkable precision in thought and expression, a point of view at which Herbert Spencer had not yet arrived, but from which it is possible to explain both how originally we had to envisage things, and how ultimately they should be understood.

---

[1] Sophie Germain, *Considérations générales sur l'état des sciences, des lettres et des arts aux différentes époques de leur culture* (Paris: Lachevardière, 1833). Ravaisson refers also to Germain's *Recherches sur la théorie des surfaces élastiques* (Paris: Courcier, 1821). For Germain's contributions to the theory of numbers, see J. H. Sampson, 'Sophie Germain and the Theory of Numbers', *Archive for History of Exact Sciences* 41/2 (1990), pp. 157–61.

'There exists in us', says Sophie Germain, 'a profound feeling of unity, order, and proportion that guides all our judgments. Within it we find in things of the moral order, the rule of the good; in intellectual things, knowledge of the truth; in things purely of pleasure, the characteristic of beauty.' And, after having indicated what is contradictory in the theories according to which only relative truths exist, she shows that there is necessarily a type [*type*] according to which we judge, compare, measure, and that this type is to be found in the awareness that we have of our own being. 'Can we doubt that the type of being has an absolute reality when we see the language of calculation bring forth from a single reality that it has followed all the realities bound to that first reality by a common essence?' The progress of science consists in reducing, by observation and calculation, everything to the unity of this type, 'which has its model in the feeling of our own existence. Being belongs to us, it penetrates our intellect and illuminates it with the torch of truth. The ideas of beauty, of the good are more complicated: we owe them to the comparison between acquired knowledge and our interior model.' And again: 'It is to the uniformity of the conditions of being that we have to relate the feeling for analogy that directs all the operations of our understanding. Now that different branches of physics have entered into the domain of the mathematical sciences, we see with admiration the same integrals, with the aid of constants provided by several genres of phenomena, represent facts between which the slightest analogy would never have been suspected. Their resemblance is thus evident; it is intellectual; it derives from the laws of being; and the identity of relations of order and proportion in the most diverse existences, which was previously the dream of an intrepid imagination still uncertain about the forms that it dared to adopt, appears to the eyes as well as to thought, with the evidence that belongs to the exact sciences.'[2]

Auguste Comte did not go so far. Never did he want to admit that the intellect had any sort of immediate knowledge of itself. Consequently, it never occurred to him that the intellect could find within itself the measure of the true, the good, and the beautiful, the absolute by which the relative is judged. He did not even see, or he did not see clearly like Herbert Spencer, that an absolute always and necessarily responds to a relative.

From the beginning, however, obeying a tendency whose principle escaped him, he aspired to unity in everything. D'Alembert said: 'The universe, for whoever knows to embrace it as a whole, would be a single fact, a great truth.'[3] Sophie Germain added that this unique fact has to be necessary. Without going that far, for this would have been to betray positivism as a whole, Auguste Comte tended, with all the effort of his thinking, to understand things as forming a whole. Stuart

---

[2] The three passages can be found on pp. 18, 56, and 62 respectively of Germain's *Considérations générales*.

[3] Germain cites this dictum of D'Alembert on p. 57 of the *Considérations générales*.

Mill, more faithful, in this regard, to the positivist principle of remaining with facts alone, pointed out and emphatically criticized in Auguste Comte this constant preoccupation that was betrayed by the constant use of the words *system*, *systematize, systemization*, and others of the same ilk. He was astonished by it, and sees in it the effect of a natural inclination of the French mind, always a friend of order and unity. This need for order and unity that Mill explains in Auguste Comte by a national character trait, Sophie Germain had remarked that it is to be found in all superior minds.

'Pure empiricism is sterile', as Comte says somewhere. And he added that, in order to orient oneself among the multitude and infinite diversity of facts, some kind of guiding conception is required, be it a pure hypothesis, and that it falls to the imagination to make a path for observation. This is an idea analogous to Descartes's idea that, even when things appear to be without any order, it is necessary, in order to come to know them, to suppose that they have one.

Auguste Comte also said: 'Any science consists in the co-ordination of the facts. It can even be said generally that science is essentially destined to dispense with direct observation, as much as the diverse phenomena involve it, in making it possible to deduce from the smallest possible number of immediate data the greatest possible number of results. Is this not, indeed, the real use, in either speculation or action, of the laws that we manage to discover between natural phenomena?'

Thus, according to the disciple of Bacon and Hume, in agreement, on this essential point, with Descartes and Leibniz, by means of a provisional order, thought traces out a path for experience, and it is the very goal of science to dispense with observation, by a definitive order, and ultimately to replace experience by reasoning.

When Auguste Comte, following his encyclopaedic work on the generalities underlying all the sciences, passed from considering inorganic things to things belonging to the vital order, he made a great leap forward, or, rather, he saw open up before him a wholly new path that was to lead him to a point of view almost entirely opposed to the one on which he found himself first of all, and to make him move by degrees from a geometrical materialism to a sort of mysticism.

Particular circumstances of his life contributed to this, indeed, and movements of his heart influenced those of his mind; but they only precipitated a revolution that was bound to be produced in him, as his studies advanced, by the development of the feeling that was natural to him of the necessity, in all things, of some principle of order and unity.

Even when it is a question just of inorganic things, it is not enough for science, in the terms of positivism itself, which defines science by prediction, to ascertain solely for each phenomenon the phenomena that experience has always shown to precede or accompany it. Who says to us that necessarily, that probably even, the same will occur in the future? Evidently, and whatever efforts have been made by

Mill (and with him, Bain, Bailey, Spencer, Littré), in forgetting the sceptical consequences that he rightly draws from his own principles, to show that observation and accumulation of phenomena suffice to explain the prediction of their return, here experience, understood in a narrow sense, clearly does not suffice.

If we believe with an assured and reflective belief that what has been will be, this is only in the case where we judge that there is a reason for it. In this way, intelligent expectation in man essentially differs from the mechanical expectation of the animal.

'The shadow of reason which can be seen in beasts is merely an expectation of a similar issue in a case which appears to resemble the past, with no knowledge of whether the same reason obtains. And this is just how men behave too, in cases where they are merely empirics.'[4] And elsewhere: 'beasts pass from one imagining to another by means of a link between them which they have previously experienced. For instance, when his master picks up a stick the dog anticipates being beaten. In many cases children, and for that matter grown men, move from thought to thought in no other way but that. This could be called "inference" or "reasoning" in a very broad sense. But I prefer to keep to accepted usage, reserving these words for men and restricting them to the knowledge of some *reason* for perceptions being linked together. Mere sensations cannot provide this: all they do is to cause one naturally to expect once more that same linking which has been observed previously, even though the reasons may no longer be the same. Hence those who are guided only by their senses are frequently confused.'[5]—'That is what makes it so easy for men to ensnare beasts, and so easy for simple empirics to make mistakes.'[6] And elsewhere again: 'However often one experienced instances of a universal truth, it would not be possible to know inductively that it would always hold unless one knew through reason that it was necessary.'[7] This is not to say that the number of experiences is good for nothing; it means only that it is insufficient, however large it may be, without knowledge of the reasons for the connections of things, in order to guarantee that it will always take place. 'And given that we are often ignorant of the reasons, we have to pay attention to examples insofar as they are frequent; for then it is reasonable to anticipate or recall one perception upon the occurrence of another which is ordinarily linked with it, especially when it is a matter of taking precautions.'[8] But it belongs to the reason for facts, when it can be known, to dispense with so many experiences and to replace them with something more in providing, instead of more or less probability, necessity and perfect certitude. 'Demonstration spares us from having to make these tests, which one might continue endlessly without ever being perfectly certain. And it is precisely this—namely the imperfection of inductions—that can be verified

---

[4] Leibniz, *New Essays*, IV, xvii, §3, p. 475. [5] Ibid., II, xi, §11, p. 143.
[6] Ibid., preface, p. 50.   [7] Ibid., I, i, §10, p. 80.   [8] Ibid., II, xxxiii, §18, p. 271.

through the trying out of particular cases. For there are progressions that can be followed a very long way before the changes, and the laws that they involve, are grasped.'[9]

It can be said that induction is grounded on the assumption, by analogy, of necessitating reasons, the knowledge of which is the complete knowledge that is called science.

In the development of the doctrine that shapes the whole of positivist logic, according to which we know nothing of things other than that they follow each other, even Stuart Mill found himself obliged, in order to justify prediction, to add to the idea of simple succession a quite different element. 'It is not enough', he said, 'to have observed that things have always been thus, we have to show that they will be thus.'[10] We arrive at this, he claims, by remarking that a particular event has an antecedent that it cannot not follow, after which we have good grounds to expect the event; this is an antecedent that admits between it and the event no other event, and that we can consequently call an unconditional antecedent. Evidently, this is to bring back, under a new name, the idea of something that necessitates, i.e. a cause. But at the same time this is to look for a cause in a material fact, in a pure phenomenon, in opposition to what Berkeley, Hume after him, and then the founder of positivism himself had previously established.

How can we perceive reasons between things? Leibniz again tells us: in the light of necessary truths, eternal principles, of which they are the application: 'The knowledge of necessary and eternal truths is what distinguishes us from animals and allows us to have reason and the sciences.'[11]

Reason teaches us that everything appearing in space and time is only, for that reason, an effect: this is what is called the principle or axiom of causality. Reason, carrying within itself the idea of the absolute or perfection, sees that at bottom nothing can exist that is not absolute or perfect, if not in itself then at least, and this is the case for any phenomenon, by something else whose plenitude makes up for its insufficiency.

Spinoza said that reason can grasp something only under the form of eternity; Hamilton said that, if we seek a cause for a fact, it is because, unable to comprehend a beginning, we relate what seems to begin to an antecedent existence. He saw therein an application of his favourite principle that we know nothing without condition or nothing absolute, but we have to see therein above all the greater principle that we understand the necessity of going back, from condition to condition, to the absolute, to what is, in other words, complete.

---

[9] Ibid., I, i, §24, p. 85.

[10] This seems to be a loose paraphrase of, in particular, chapter 3, §2 of J. S. Mill's *A System of Logic, Ratiocinative and Inductive* (London: Parker, 1843).

[11] Leibniz, *Monadology* (see Leibniz, *Philosophical Essays*, ed. D. Garber and R. Ariew (Indianapolis: Hackett, 1989), §29).

This is what Sophie Germain expressed even better in saying that what leads us to seek a cause for every fact is that a fact always appears to us as a fraction or part for which we require the whole.

Thus, from action to action, from power to power, reason obliges us to go back to a power that is finally sufficient unto itself, to a primary cause, that evidently can be only a perfect spontaneity.

Even had we not this awareness of the necessity of going back, from any given phenomenon, to a primary cause, not even the awareness of the necessity of going back from any given phenomenon to an immediate cause that accounts for it, it would be no less true that in any reasoning consisting in concluding, by analogy, from one particular assemblage of phenomena to another, it is in virtue of the principle, implicit or explicit, of a causality linking phenomena that are always found together, it is by virtue of this principle alone that we reason, and that the axiom of causality, regardless of the phenomena at issue, is the hidden nerve of all induction.

Reason teaches us that there is necessarily a cause; induction only isolates among the facts, in the light of analogy, which phenomenon is, for a given phenomenon, the one that is the means or the condition of the action of causality.

Given that a true cause, the one that is being itself and the substance of the fact, is an action that does not fall under space or time, a phenomenon cannot be, properly speaking, the cause of another phenomenon: this is the true sense of what Berkeley said in this connection, reserving causality for will alone, and that Hume repeated after him. Nevertheless, it does not follow that every phenomenon provides the active cause with only an occasion, according to Berkeley's ideas and Malebranche's words, rather than a reason. 'Nothing without reason', Leibniz says here and everywhere. A phenomenon, without being the real cause of another phenomenon, can be a condition, a means for the action of the cause, in the way that an initial state, a primary degree, is necessary for establishing, by a creative power, of a higher degree, a higher state; in the way that a sketch exists relatively to the finished work.

Now, since it is a matter only of phenomena linked to each other according to simple mechanical and physical laws, it might not be clear how the one serves the other and prepares for it. Causality, in not being made manifest by the evident relations of subordination between phenomena, remains unperceived. Thus, for as long as we remain with mechanics, with physics and even with chemistry, we are often inclined to limit science to the enumeration of series of facts presented by experience, and to deny any necessary connection and any reason. In this way is formed the materialist and, consequently, sceptical doctrine advanced by Auguste Comte, and which is still that of most of his disciples.

When we come to consider living beings, things are no longer quite the same. In the living being, certain phenomena possess the characteristic of determining other phenomena of which they are the goal: the phenomena of movement and sensation, for example, seem to determine, to command phenomena of a lower order, without which they cannot be realized. With this characteristic, higher phenomena such as those of movement appear as analogous to what are in us the ends that we propose to ourselves, which all our powers serve.

In the living being, therefore, there is manifest a general cause determining a multitude of effects; even the most superficial examination of the living being discovers in it something similar in this way to what thinks, something that gives existence and form, through what is active and unified within it, to what is multiple and passive within it.

In the presence of life, materialist theory evidently becomes inadequate.

When Berkeley, who, in his first works, occupied himself only with mechanical phenomena, came in his profound and ingenious *Siris* to consider those of vegetation and, more generally, of life, he understood better the general character of nature: that things are linked together according to harmonic progressions (whence, above all, the very title of *Siris*: a series or chain). In this way, in the latter part of his career, he passed from his first theory of the universe envisaged as a pile of detached facts, under the arbitrary power of God, to the notion of a universal chain, suspended from the absolute good, consisting of more and more perfect forms.

Auguste Comte also, in the second period of his philosophy, when he arrived at organized beings on the way to what was always his goal, namely the social world, passed from a first theory of the world, understood as a simple conglomeration of more and more complicated facts, without Berkeley's supreme regulator, to a quite different theory of progressive order and universal harmony. In the presence of life he understood that it was not enough, as he thought it was in the sphere of mechanical and physical things, to consider phenomena successively or contiguously, and that it was necessary, above all, to take into account order and the whole.

'In the presence of organized beings, we see', he said, 'that the detail of phenomena, whatever more or less sufficient explanation we might give of them, is neither the whole nor the principal element; that the principle, and we could say almost everything, is the ensemble in space, progress in time, and that explaining a living being would be to show the reason of this whole and of the progress that is life itself.'[12]

At the end of the last volume of his *Course*, while continuing to condemn 'chimerical research into essential causes and the intimate nature of phenomena', Auguste Comte expressed the thought that, if the spirit of detail can suffice for the geometer, and even for the physicist and chemist, the true physiologist requires

---

[12] This seems to be a paraphrase rather than a direct citation of Comte. The style of the passage is not Comtian, but the ideas resemble in particular a passage of the *Système de politique positive* (Paris: Mathias, 1851), pp. 641–2.

conceptions of the whole. 'Even in chemistry', he said, 'we witness an increase in the inner natural solidarity proper to the whole of the subject, which was so insufficient in physics and even, at bottom, in mathematics.'

'The sciences of inorganic things', as he said again, 'proceed by deduction of details from the totality [*le tout*]; in the sciences of organized beings, it is from the whole that is drawn, by deduction, true knowledge of the parts.'

Moreover, now in agreement with Plato, Aristotle, and Leibniz, he declared that—the whole being the result and the expression of a certain unity towards which everything conspires, for which everything is co-ordinated, and which is the goal toward which everything advances—the secret of the organism lies in this unity, in the goal, the end, or the final cause.

On 16 July 1843, writing to Stuart Mill, he expressed the opinion that were Mill not to follow him on the broader paths that he would henceforth take, this would be because, well versed in the mathematical and physical sciences, he was not sufficiently familiar with the phenomena of life.[13] Had he been more advanced in biological science, Mill would have understood better how something beyond the detail of the facts is required, something that dominates them, that combines and co-ordinates them.

According to this quite particular characteristic, it was necessary to recognize that organisms are not simply, as the founder of positivism had previously said, complications of separate elements in an inferior order of existence, and that these elements, however necessary they may be to their constitution, are insufficient to explain them.

After having said, in the first volume of his *Course*, that the phenomena presented by organized beings were simple modifications of inorganic phenomena, from the second volume, published in 1838, if he accepted this for vegetative life, he denied it for animal life; he denied that either sensibility or muscular contractility could be reduced to physical or chemical facts. So many vain attempts to explain, for example, perception by physics were, he added, 'a proof that physiology was still in a state of infancy'. Later still, in the sixth volume of the same work, published in 1842, and then much more sharply and strongly several years afterwards, in the *Positive Polity*, he profoundly separated vital phenomena, of any level, from physical and chemical phenomena.[14] Here he gave expression to the important proposition that in biology, where all phenomena are characterized, as Cuvier had said, by an inner and continuous solidarity, the method for bringing us into possession of what is essential is no longer analysis, but rather synthesis, which aims at the totality, and that, consequently,

---

[13] See, in this connection, *The Correspondence of J. S. Mill and Auguste Comte*, trans. O. Haac (Abingdon: Routledge, 1995).
[14] Ravaisson is referring to Comte's *Système de politique positive* (Paris: Carillan Gueury, 1851-4); see Comte, *System of Positive Polity* (London: Longmans, 1877).

'an analytical operation can only ever be conceived as the more or less necessary preamble to an ultimately synthetic determination'.

Now, in leaving behind general and abstract terms, what is the unity to which we must, in order to explain the order and the whole of the phenomena, relate them by synthesis? It is that of an idea, a thought. The highest synthetic determination that dominates and explains biology as a whole is therefore, says Auguste Comte, that of human nature, such as it results not, in truth, from the direct study of the soul, which until the end he persisted in believing to be sterile and even impossible, but from study of the human race in history.

The whole dominating the parts, and the whole itself as dominated by what can be properly called the human element, is what the arts present to us. And this did not escape Auguste Comte: 'The universal preponderance of the human point of view and the corresponding ascendancy of the spirit of the whole', as he said in the last pages of his *Course*, 'are profoundly favourable to the general rise of aesthetic dispositions.' And given that he was then much preoccupied by poetry and music, art helped him indeed to see science from a higher vantage point than his mathematical studies had ever led him before.

From this perspective, Auguste Comte discovered that no science can be explained by inferior sciences. 'Physics must defend itself against the usurpation of mathematics; chemistry, from that of physics; finally sociology, from that of biology.' Each order of existence, as Aristotle had shown long before, is for the higher order a matter to which it gives form. This entails, says Auguste Comte, that reducing a thing, in order to account for it, to something of a less elevated order, is to explain it by its matter; materialism, therefore, is the explanation of the superior by the inferior.

This is a profound formula that will remain for its author one of his honourable distinctions as a philosopher. But there is more. To this maxim is to be added, according to Auguste Comte, a second: that it is the superior that explains the inferior. In other words, it is in humanity that we can find an explanation of nature. In the last volume of his *Course on Positive Philosophy*, he had already said: 'The study of man and humanity is the principal science, the one that ought above all to attract the attention of great intellects and the continual solicitude of public reason. The simply preliminary purpose of preceding speculations is even so clearly felt that together they have been able to be described only with the aid of purely negative expressions: inorganic, inert, etc., which defines them only by their contrast with this ultimate study, the preponderant object of all our direct contemplations. Sociological science, the moral science of humanity, is the ultimate science of which biology itself is simply the last preamble.'

To the moral science of humanity belongs therefore 'scientific supremacy, philosophical presidency'. It is not to mathematics but rather to ethics that 'universal domination' belongs.

At several points of the *Positive Polity*, Auguste Comte signals in inorganic phenomena sketches of vital phenomena: in inertia, for example, which is the first law of mechanics, the sketch of the persistence in action that will be called habit in living beings; in the sociability of certain animal species, the sketch of human sociability. 'Organic progression in general', as he says, 'can be defined well only when its last term is known'; 'the whole of animal life would be unintelligible without the superior attributes that only sociology can appreciate.' 'The supreme form' in the end 'constitutes the exclusive principle of biological unity, and each animal species can be reduced, at bottom, to a more or less aborted human being'. This is a proposition that can be found, in almost identical terms, in the *History of Animals* and in the *Metaphysics*, in the work of the philosopher who was the first to find in intellect, which is the essence of humanity, the final cause by which all of nature can be explained.

To listen to Auguste Comte, however, this is not to invoke the final causes that he had previously proscribed, and he in no way deviates thus from his principles. On the contrary, he has done nothing more than develop them, in applying them to the objects that, from the beginning, he had principally in view. If he has managed, in his words, to guarantee the rightful preponderance, which is just as much logical and scientific as it is political and moral, of the social point of view, this is by extending to the highest speculations, instead of the religious or metaphysical spirit, which reigned within them until recently, what he calls 'rational positivity'. This consists in revealing in the facts of the moral order, just as in those of the physical order, relations subject to observable laws. Just as biology consists in the knowledge of the mutual action and reaction of organisms with their physical milieux, philosophical history is the knowledge of the mutual action and reaction of organism and social milieux, from which result the formation and the evolution of the nature that is wholly relative to humanity. Relativity and positivity of human nature, such is the dual discovery by which Auguste Comte aims to crown, in the *Positive Polity*, the edifice whose solid foundations he laid in his *Course*.

In other words, instead of explaining humanity and its history either, following the theologians, by an arbitrary action of a supernatural power, or, following the metaphysicians, by a cause conceived as something entirely separate from phenomena, and as an independent entity that would determine them in some way from without, without being bound to them at all, it is still by phenomena that here the founder of positivism wants to account for phenomena.

Stuart Mill, in rejecting final causes with Auguste Comte, also represented them as existences of a special order that can be imagined only outside of reality, outside of its relations and laws.

This is perhaps the notion of it provided by the vulgar theory of an 'ideal' considered as the cause of the movements of nature; but it is not what the founder of metaphysics, or what those of his interpreters who had most penetrated his thought, had in mind.

Aristotle did not believe that a man was formed, for example, as the Platonists might have thought, under the inexplicable influence of an idea: 'It is a man', he says, 'who begets a man.' A complete man, by the perfection he carries within him, sets in motion the imperfect germ and brings it to its form. This perfection is an action, and it is this action which, in the form, to which it is limited, of this or that phenomenon, is at the same time the goal and the source of a particular movement.

If we take for a cause an ideal completely outside of reality, we have nothing sufficient to explain nature. It is this idealism against which positivism has risen, not without reason. However, if we recognize nothing real but the phenomena alone, how are we to find within them, following positivism, any causality, any explanation of any other phenomenon? To consider the phenomenon of a higher order as the reason for the inferior phenomenon, precisely because it presents the perfection of that of which the inferior phenomenon possesses only the beginnings, is necessarily, although perhaps unknowingly, to imply within perfection an effective action, and Auguste Comte's theory, in its final form, explains the conception of the final cause, if not such as it is exposed by ordinary idealism, which represents nature on the model of human art, then at least such as one finds it in what one can call the realism or metaphysical positivism that Aristotle founded, by providing a basis for it in the at once experimental and supra-sensible idea of action.

Auguste Comte remained faithful to the initial idea of positivism in that he always seeks within facts the explanation for facts. But from a positivism that could see no other explanation for a fact than the simple pre-existence, in any case inexplicable, of some quite different fact, he arrived at a quite different positivism, according to which a fact is explained by a fact of a higher order, whose perfection is its reason, whose action is its cause. From a superficial physical positivism, he arrived at a moral positivism.

In his *Positive Polity*, published from 1851 to 1854, Auguste Comte went even further in this direction. This time it was no longer bare life that he had to study, but moral life, that of the intellect and the heart.

He came to think that everything in the human being could be explained by what leads it to goodness—by, in a word, love.

Now he not only understood that matter cannot explain everything in the human being, and that it is intellect, on the contrary, which, to a large degree at least, accounts for matter; like Pascal, he placed above the intellect itself—which is still, in certain respects, what is physical in the mind—what within it is moral *par excellence*, the moral faculties properly so called, the affective faculties. The human being appeared to him as having to explain itself by its heart. The intellect is made, he said, to be used, the heart to be the master. The intellect exists only to serve the ends of our affections. These ends are summed up in one thing: the good, the object of love. Love is the word, the secret of human nature. That is not all: it is the secret of the world. It is what Auguste Comte expressed by saying that everything had to be explained, in the end, by the subjective method.

He had once said that, in contrast to metaphysics and religion, which explained the universe through man by making man the goal for which the universe had been formed, it was through the universe that positivism had to explain both man and all things: this was what he called the 'objective method', a method which proceeded from the objects of thought to the subject who thinks them. Now he came to admit that it was to this subject that everything had to be related; that through it everything could be explained, and that everything tended and had to tend towards it. He went so far down this new road as to proscribe all scientific research beyond what was not of direct use to the human being.

The last work of his life was the 1854 *Subjective Synthesis of Mathematics*,[15] in which he tried to develop even the science of quantity, the furthest of all the sciences from the sphere of the affections, by subordinating it to the special ends, to the moral and social ends of humanity.

It should not be forgotten here that Auguste Comte had had some years previously serious disagreements with geometers, disputes which perhaps brought him to realize, better than he had done before, either what is lacking in mathematical notions in order to explain everything, or, and consequently, what is disadvantageous in the mathematical spirit when it becomes exclusive or merely dominant. And, on the other hand, an ardent affection, taking hold of him, disposed him to grant to affective life a great preponderance, even over the most intellectual life, a great preponderance, and to seek the last word of science itself in love. We can add that his reason, fatigued either by the extraordinary tension of incessant work, or by the storms of his life, seems to have left a course always freer to the sometimes impetuous and disordered movements of an increasingly ardent imagination, of an increasingly tender and enthusiastic soul.

In his last years, he turned away from the labours of composition only to read Italian and Spanish poets, to the *Imitation of Jesus Christ*,[16] and to music. To live for others had become his motto; the chivalry of the Middle Ages, his ideal.

Little by little his philosophy changed into a religion, one close to the primitive belief in which he had seen only a dream of human infancy. The first men had conceived everything in the image of man, had given everything a soul, had seen in every movement an act of will: this was fetishism, which had been succeeded gradually, as nature came to be understood as more independent of the will, by polytheism at first and then by monotheism. What was necessary now, said

---

[15] See Comte, *Synthèse subjective, ou Système universel des conceptions propres à l'état normal de l'humanité. Par Auguste Comte. Tome Premier, contenant le Système de logique positive ou Traité de philosophique mathématique* (Paris: Chez l'auteur, 1856).
[16] Ravaisson is referring to Thomas à Kempis's 1418–27 *De imitatione Christi*.

Auguste Comte, was a new fetishism: it was necessary again to adore in things, everywhere present, everywhere active, the will and love.

In Auguste Comte's religion, there is no God, there is no soul either, at least no immortal soul: this is how, after so many changes, he remained the same. The Supreme Being, for him as for Pierre Leroux and many of our contemporaries, is humanity. He calls it the 'great Being'.

The great Being has for its origin the earth, the common source of all beings, mother of all particular fetishes, and that can be called 'the great Fetish'. The earth is in space, whose laws are the primary conditions of all existence, and to which the name 'great Milieu' is appropriate. Great Milieu, great Fetish, great Being, such is the trinity that the positivist cult honours. The great Milieu first saw the great Fetish produced in it, whose members were originally superior in vitality, in power, to what they are today; the great Fetish, in order to give rise to the advent of the great Being, reduced, lowered, and sacrificed itself. This sacrifice deserves our grateful veneration on earth; but it is in humanity itself that humanity honours supreme perfection, for which the great Fetish immolated itself; and in humanity the most perfect form, because it is the one in which the affective faculties predominate, is woman. But since humanity exists only in the succession of ephemeral individuals, what cult should be paid to it? The cult that Auguste Comte called the subjective cult, and which was none other than a pious commemoration of the dead. It is, according to him, in remembrance among the living, of the individuals worthy of existing, of above all the women who nobly realized the ideal of devotion and tenderness for which they were made, and in this remembrance alone that immortality, the crowning of life, consists.

In this metamorphosis of positivism, what becomes of the maxim on which it was founded, namely that, given that in the whole of nature generality is linked to simplicity, generality diminishes as complexity increases? Auguste Comte did not explain himself in this respect, but it is perhaps not impossible to make up for his silence. Obviously, we must now add, first, that with complexity a certain simplicity increases: with the complexity of the elements, the simple unity, which makes a whole of them; second, that with this unity there also increases, as a necessary consequence, a certain generality. This is a remark whose basis belongs to the author of the *Metaphysics*. The inferior elements, very simple in their poverty, are by that very fact in everything, as the matter of the superior principles. The supreme principle is in turn in everything, in the sense that in different degrees and in different forms it acts everywhere, it does everything. As the author of *Siris* says: 'In all that exists, there is life; in all that lives, feeling; in all that feels, thought.' Each cause is thus found in the order of things where it is all that it can be, and in all the lower orders which, in different proportions, receive its influence and participate in it. The soul, in a sense, is in everything; and, even more than the soul, God, in this sense also, is the universal being. It is not that God is everything, like a matter of which everything is composed, as the doctrine called pantheism understands it; it is rather that, as the supreme cause, He is consequently what is real and true in everything. 'In Him we live, in Him we are.'

Auguste Comte, in one of his last works, the 1852 *Positivist Catechism*, still calls Hume his main philosophical precursor.[17] At that time, however, he was very close to what we have called a spiritual or metaphysical positivism. He never abandoned the proposition that for us there is only the relative. Nor did he ever place himself, or even admit that one could place oneself, at the point of view from which, in the cause that we are, there appears the absolute against which, in the end, everything relative is measured, a point of view which is that of self-reflection. By observation alone, or supposedly alone, of external things, which are illuminated by our interior light and that present to us, though altered, our own image, he came, after having for a long time put aside any idea of causality, to accord more and more importance to causality, and to causality understood as purposive, intentional. It remained, in order to know the true character of such an idea, to recognize its true origin. The assiduous reader of the *Imitation of Jesus Christ* and of the mystics of the fifteenth century, the apostle of altruism, would have doubtless come to this point if time had not prevented him from doing so.

---

[17] Comte, *Catéchisme positiviste ou sommaire exposition de la religion universelle en treize entretiens systématiques entre une femme et un prêtre de l'humanité*, translated as *The Catechism of Positive Religion* (London: Chapman, 1858).

X
Littré and Philosophy

Littré, as we have seen, did not follow Auguste Comte in the second part of his career; he wanted to remain at the point that the latter had surpassed, and to maintain even more strictly than Stuart Mill the terms of primitive positivism. But even he did not succeed in remaining within them.

We have seen that Herbert Spencer, while advocating the great maxim of positivism that we know nothing but the relative, admits beyond the relative some absolute existence of which we have, if not veritable knowledge, at least an obscure conception; an idea with which he returns, more or less, to the systems of the Scottish school, of Kant, of the eclectics. In his 1865 *Auguste Comte and Positivism*,[1] Stuart Mill reproaches Auguste Comte for going beyond experience by negation, instead of remaining with experience alone as positivism prescribes, when he declares that any conception of an origin of things and of a first cause is impossible. Stuart Mill would like us, while following the positive method for the study of this world, while limiting ourselves to considering nature as a compound of phenomena that follow or accompany each other, to admit as possible some supernatural principle, a universal antecedent of which the whole of the natural world would be the consequence and the effect; he would like us to admit as possible that such a principle be an intellect; in a word, that we admit, if not the reality, at least the possibility of a God.

The second reproach that Stuart Mill makes to Auguste Comte is that he never wanted to admit any psychology apart from physiology, that he never wanted to admit any direct study of feelings, ideas, and volitions, which constitute what the positivist school, with a term borrowed from German philosophy, ordinarily calls the 'subjective'.

Of these two criticisms, Littré admits neither the first nor the second. To the first he replied* that one cannot, if one admits the principles of positivism, consider as an open question, as Mill puts it, the question of the existence of a first cause, of a creative and directive intellect, of God, of providence.

As for the second point, Littré agrees that feelings, ideas, volitions can be the object of detailed study and provide the subject matter for particular sciences. He maintains that they are cerebral phenomena, and that, as such, they belong to physiology, but given that subjective phenomena are the objects of a very

---

[1] J. S. Mill, *Auguste Comte and Positivism* (London: Trübner, 1866 [1st edition 1865]).
* *Revue des deux mondes*, 1866. [Ravaisson's footnote]

particular mode of knowledge, which is consciousness properly so called, it is evident that modifications of the brain, which are known by sight and touch, do not constitute them entirely, and are only its conditions or means. Now, to explain facts entirely by what is merely their condition is to explain the superior by the inferior; it is, according to Auguste Comte's profound phrase, regardless of one's opinion concerning matter, and even if one does not admit the notion of it, to provide an entirely material, and therefore insufficient, explanation of things.

Are atheism and materialism then, as has been said, the whole of Littré's doctrine?

We have seen that when he encountered organism and life, the founder of positivism recognized, in more or less explicit terms, the reality of causes, and of the final cause; Littré, in different terms, made the same admission.

It is the ordinary maxim of materialism, since Epicurus, that wings were not made to fly, as those who find in nature evidence of design say, but that birds fly because they have wings; in other words, that it is not the functions that account for the organs, but the organs, on the contrary, that account for the functions.

Littré had belonged to those who refused to admit that organs were made for functions; and he had published, in the *Revue des deux mondes*, a work composed expressly against the doctrine of final causes. At that time, he did not yet belong to positive philosophy. At first, it could only strengthen his aversion to a doctrine whose overthrow was the primary aim of positivism. Since then, perhaps under the influence of some of the ideas which filled the second part of Auguste Comte's career, but perhaps also as a result of his own reflections, he arrived at a different point of view. Looking closely at that organ of ours which, by the complication and at the same time by the unity of its structure, has always provided the partisans of final causes with the most arguments, that is to say, the eye, he recognized that there was in this organ an undeniable appropriation of a set of means to an end. He recognized something similar, as more or less manifest, in the whole of the organism; and the doctrine of universal finality, which he had formerly fought against, both on his own and in the name of positivism, became his own.

However, in adopting it, Littré did not intend to be unfaithful to positive philosophy, as Paul Janet supposed he was in the pages of *The Philosophical Crisis* (1865) that he devoted to him.[2] 'It would be so', says Littré, 'if the appropriation of the means to the end were explained either by a soul or providence, or by a general property of matter, but to say that organized matter adjusts itself to ends is to state a fact without seeking the cause; it is to remain with the primitive phenomenon'. We are familiar with the facts, says Littré, that living tissue has the property of growing, muscular tissue that of contracting; that organized matter has the property of accommodating itself to ends is one more fact to be added to those of

---

[2] Paul Janet, *La crise philosphique: MM Taine, Renan, Littré et Vacherot* (Paris: Germer Baillière, 1865).

which physiology is already in possession. But we may notice that if the contraction of a muscle, the growth of an organ, are facts of experience attested to by the senses, perhaps it is not the same for the appropriation of material parts to an end. The senses attest to the fact that particular organs take particular forms, a particular situation; but that it be 'for an end' is a judgement of our mind, and this judgement implies that there is in the body a feeling or a conception, however obscure we wish to suppose it, of a purpose of its movements. 'For an end' and 'with a view to an end' are synonymous expressions, of which the first only envelops under an abstract and equivocal term what the second expresses more clearly. To say, as Littré does in his preface to Leblais's book, that 'the organs are not born otherwise than by or for an accommodation of organized nature to its ends', is thus, it seems, to attribute intentional movements to living nature, it is to admit that any phenomena of life reveals thought.

Undoubtedly an intellect immersed in matter, as Cudworth and Leibniz put it, is not sufficient to itself; though it be a sufficient cause, perhaps, of vital phenomena, it is doubtless necessary to seek, with the metaphysicians, with Aristotle particularly, a superior cause within an intellect in full possession of itself. According to the expression employed, in a public lesson (1864) on the proofs for the existence of God, by a young teacher responsible for a part of the philosophy teaching at the École normale (Lachelier), it is necessary to say that nature is like a thought that does not think about itself, suspended from a thought that thinks about itself. But, without going that far, or even as far as Auguste Comte went, it is far from the starting point of positivism to recognize that nothing in living nature can be understood without design, and, consequently, without thought. It is assuredly to re-establish, though perhaps not to re-establish in all its rights, the superior element that primitive positivism, instead of studying and deepening its idea, aimed to eliminate.

It is difficult to believe that the learned Littré will go no further in the direction in which the one he admits to be his master went before him, in which the most eminent among Comte's other disciples are following him more or less closely, and in which he himself has already taken such a decisive step.

XI
The Philosophy of Taine

In an 1857 work entitled *French Philosophers of the 19th Century*,[1] Taine undertook, in occupying terrain not so far from that of positivism, to demolish the dominant position that the eclectic school then occupied.

Auguste Comte had limited himself to reproaching this school in general terms for withdrawing into sterile considerations on what it called the facts of consciousness and the psychological method, and into logical inquiries that were useless because they concerned completely abstract generalities rather than precise applications to the objects of the different sciences.

Taine sought to demonstrate, by examining the doctrines and works of Royer-Collard, Victor Cousin, Jouffroy, to which he joined Maine de Biran, that the philosophy which at the time reigned almost exclusively in public instruction, and which still holds the greatest place in it, had no scientific merit; that, under literary forms possessing, in various respects, eminent merits, it explained nothing, gave an account of nothing; and at the same time he tried to indicate, at least in their general traits, the theories and methods that he believed should replace the theories and methods of this philosophy.

We have seen that, after Berkeley had shown what is incomplete and empty in those ideas of faculties, powers, causes, substances, by which vulgar philosophy attempted to explain phenomena, and after Hume had concluded that sensory phenomena alone formed all that was real, the Scottish school—although it felt that the ideas that had been thus proscribed, and whose proscription left the field free to scepticism, answered to important truths, objects of legitimate beliefs—did not go much further than this. Moreover, the French school, by which the Scottish school was continued among us, also did little more than restitute, as unknown objects or necessary conceptions, the purely rational entities whose defect Berkeley had made clear.

The main aim of Taine's criticism is to demonstrate the absolute inanity of the principles that Royer-Gollard, Victor Cousin, Jouffroy, Damiron, and their successors wanted to re-establish above, as it were, sensible phenomena. In 'these little spiritual beings hidden beneath the phenomena as if by clothes', he sees, and tries to make us see, pure fictions, or at least simple abstractions taken for things. And on more than one point he makes manifest the insufficiency of the

---

[1] Hyppolyte Taine (1828–93), *Les philosophes français du XIXe siècle* (Paris: Hachette, 1857).

psychology and of the psychological method that has been so highly commended, but which ends, after not particularly fruitful observations concerning our psychological states and interior operations, in a simple enumeration of faculties or forces of the same name.

It is odd that Taine includes among the partisans of abstract entities that he attacks, a thinker who, on the contrary, repudiated such entities, who detected better than anyone the error contained in the method, called 'psychological', that leads to them, and who, by his meditations, prepared a quite different method for the science of inner man. Maine de Biran may have left a lot to do for the analysis of the empirical conditions of psychological phenomena, but at least he did not stop, in order to explain them, at faculties and powers, invisible and indeterminate objects of conceptions and beliefs. On the contrary, in advancing further along the path that the founder of metaphysics was the first to trace with precision, and on which Plotinus, Saint Augustine, Descartes, Leibniz advanced after him, he relates psychological facts, as to their immediate principle, to an action of which we are aware by the most intimate experience, and which nothing, consequently, surpasses or even equals in positive reality. Is this to do what he himself condemned, to take abstract generalities for actual beings, and words for things?

Of the principal philosophers of the nineteenth century, the one who finds the most favour with Taine is one of the earliest, Laromiguière.[2] Taine approves of him as a continuator in several respects of the philosophy of the preceding century, the declared advocate of the method which Condillac set forth in his *Logic*, his *Grammar*, his *Language of Calculation*:[3] a method that does not consist, like the one whose principle eclecticism borrowed from the Scottish school, in relying for a moment on a few facts, the choice of which is almost indifferent, only to move on immediately to principles of another order—which could never produce, according to Fichte's expression, a philosophy of one piece—, but rather in breaking down our knowledge, in reducing it by successive abstractions to its simplest parts and to the relations of these parts, and thus in breaking down all our ideas into combinations of a few elements realized by means of successive equations.

This method, called 'the analysis of ideas', is, according to Taine, the basis of what was called in France, at the beginning of the century, Ideology. In his opinion, it would be the only one in conformity with our national genius.

Analysis, according to the author of the *French Philosophers of the 19th Century*, is not only the method to be used in the study of our intellect: it is also a

---

[2] Ravaisson is referring to Pierre Laromiguière, a philosopher who inspired Victor Cousin's move against the then dominant, Condillac-inspired Ideological school and who was thus important in the development of early nineteenth-century French philosophy.

[3] Etienne Bonnot de Condillac's *Grammaire* appeared as the first volume of his *Cours d'étude pour l'instruction du Prince de Parme*, while the *Logique* (1781) and the unfinished *Langue des calculs* (1798) were first published posthumously. See *Oeuvres philosophiques de Condillac*, ed. Georges le Roy (Paris: Press universitaires de France, 1947–51).

method for knowing things. This is what positivism does not seem to him to have sufficiently understood, and it is an idea with which he seeks to complete it.

In 1835, Taine published in the *Revue des deux mondes* a work entitled 'English Positivism: A Study of Stuart Mill'. In this work, he presents and approves the theories that form the basis of positivism, at least of the version of it that Auguste Comte first exposed. At the same time, he adds to them, and, by what he adds, he changes everything.

Taine admits with Stuart Mill the principle—advanced, as we have seen, by Berkeley, but which Hume took for the unique foundation of his philosophy—that substance, force, and all the so-called metaphysical entities of the moderns are an idle remainder of the wholly logical entities of the Schools. He admits with him that there is nothing real but the facts such as they offer themselves to our senses with their order of time and place, which facts are nothing else, in the end, than our very sensations. This entails that science consists only in the knowledge that particular sensible facts, that particular sensations follow or accompany each other.

And yet Stuart Mill's logic seems incomplete to Taine.

We have not only, he remarks, the faculty of adding, we also have that of subtracting; mathematics does not consist in addition only—subtraction plays its part. We not only assemble parts into wholes, we decompose wholes into their parts. This second operation, the opposite of the first, Taine calls abstraction; it is by it, he claims, that we deduce from a truth a host of other truths, from a principle an infinity of consequences; it is by it that all sciences are formed. Thus he calls the faculty of abstraction or subtraction a 'magnificent faculty, the source of language, the interpreter of nature, the mother of religions and philosophy, the only true distinction that separates man from brute and great men from small ones'.[4]

Stuart Mill also had to admit that, once the elementary facts are found by observation and induction, consequences can be drawn from them; but, for him, deductions are still merely disguised or rather inverted inductions. In drawing consequences from propositions formed by induction, we would be doing nothing else, in his opinion, than withdrawing from these propositions, part by part, what we had first put into them. According to Taine, at least as far as it is possible to grasp his thought beneath the figures with which he likes to adorn it, to deduce is not only to work out in particular propositions what we had gathered at first in a general proposition; it is to draw from a single proposition other propositions which might not have contributed at all to its formation; it is, for example, to draw from a property of the circle different properties which, until then, had been ignored.—But how is such a deduction possible, a deduction that from one idea

---

[4] Hyppolyte Taine, 'Le positivisme anglais: étude sur M. Stuart Mill' was published as a book the following year, and translated into English in 1870: *English Positivism: A Study on John Stuart Mill*, trans. T. D. Haye (London: Simpkin, Marshall).

draws another idea, if not on condition of conceiving that the second was enclosed in the first, that it was contained in it as the part is contained in the whole? This is a relation that is no longer one of simple proximity, but rather of measure; it is a conception of relations or reasons which is no longer a passive fact of sensation, but the result of an action of comparing, of evaluating, something of a completely different order, and which we call reason. By abstraction with all its effects, the last of which is reasoning, what Taine has in view is, at bottom, the operation, proper to the human being, by which, rising above the purely sensory state, it calculates relations, measuring relative terms to others, and all of them, more or less explicitly and forcibly, to some unitary absolute.

To speak as Taine does of abstraction and analysis is thus to re-establish, above pure experience, which is all that Stuart Mill and Hume admit, the rights of reason.

That is not all: while Stuart Mill's dominant thought is to banish everywhere the idea of cause to leave in its place only the simple succession or juxtaposition of phenomena, Taine invokes as universal what he calls the axiom of causes, and which is usually called the principle of causality. Everything, according to him, has a cause, and that is why everything must be able to be proved.

Taine, it is true, rejects causes such as the Scottish and eclectic school, he says, imagines them to be, distinct from all facts and like hidden beings lying behind them. The causes of facts are, for him, as for Auguste Comte, only other facts. But although he affirms that causality resides in the phenomena themselves and not elsewhere, he aspires no less to re-establish it, like reason, in all its rights and all its force.

According to vulgar positivism, instead of looking for the mysterious causes of facts with which metaphysics preoccupies itself, we need only look for the facts with which they are ordinarily preceded. Groups of inseparable facts being thus formed, according to Taine it is also necessary to find a simpler fact to which they can be reduced. This simpler fact is what we call the cause. Do we not say that the fall of heavy bodies, the rise of vapours, the equilibrium of liquids, have gravity as their common cause? Vulgar positivism limits itself to bringing together, by a work of assembly or synthesis, the phenomena that experience provides; it is also necessary, by the operation of abstraction or analysis that separates from these facts their accidental and variable circumstances, to reduce them to their greatest simplicity and, consequently, to the greatest possible generality. This is the condition and at the same time the terminus of science. Particular facts of a certain kind reduced to a single fact, that is what we call science; general facts reduced, in turn, if possible, to a single fact, is what would be universal science.

'The progress of science', says Taine, 'consists in explaining a set of facts, not by a supposed cause, outside of all experience, but by a superior fact that engenders them. By rising in this way from a higher fact to a still higher fact, we will arrive for each kind of object at a single fact, which is the universal cause. The different sciences are thereby condensed into a number of definitions from which all the truths of which they are composed can be derived. Then the moment comes when we dare to do more: considering that these definitions are several and that they are facts like the others, we see within them and extract from them, by the same method as with the others, the primitive and unique fact from which they are deduced and which generates them. We discover the unity of the universe, and we understand what produces it. It does not derive from something external to the world, nor from something mysterious, hidden in the world. It derives from a general fact similar to the others, a generative law from which the others are deduced, just as from the law of attraction derive all the phenomena of gravity, just as from the law of undulations derive all the phenomena of light, just as from the existence of the type derive all the functions of the animal, just as from the governing faculty of a people derive all the parts of its institutions and all the events of its history. The ultimate object of science is this supreme law; and he who could throw himself into its bosom, would see there, as from a single source, the eternal torrent of events and the infinite sea of things, flowing out through distinct and ramified channels. It is at this moment that one feels the birth in itself of the notion of Nature. By this hierarchy of necessities, the world forms a unique, indivisible being, of which all beings are members.'[5]

Does Taine mean by this that, as our knowledge progresses, the properties of one order of things must be reduced to the simpler properties of a lower order, and finally those of the various orders of the lowest degree, where there is still some diversity, to common properties, the most elementary ones that exist? That would be, in Auguste Comte's judgement, to explain each thing by what constitutes its matter; consequently, analysis thus applied by leading science, degree by degree, to a pretended first cause—that would amount, in the end, only to the simplest and most abstract of facts—would be merely to reduce science to pure materialism.

It remains to explain, and this is what Taine does not seem to have attempted so far, how it is possible to conceive that the simplest and most abstract fact—as, for example, gravity—could have produced, only by way of increasing complication, all the facts of a higher order: chemical combinations, organization, life, thought. It would remain also to be seen whether the most elementary and simple fact of movement, whether even extension can be understood without anything more than matter, without some principle of form and union. These are difficulties that up to now no materialist doctrine has been able to solve.

But it would be a mistake to believe, from the passage we have just quoted and from other similar ones, that Taine has stuck to materialism as the last word in philosophy. Far from it: what happened to Auguste Comte happened to him. In the presence of organized nature, of life, it appeared to him, too, that among the

---

[5] Taine, *Les philosophes français du XIXe siècle*, pp. 359–60.

facts that always follow or accompany each other, there are some that require others and command them. When they are simplified by analysis, freed from accidental and variable circumstances, it is even more evident that, in animate beings, such facts, given that they exist in a relation to others of completion to beginning, of perfection to imperfection, require them and oblige them to be. Nutrition requires for digestion, for swallowing, for chewing, for grasping, that there be particular organs, built in such and such a way. But nutrition itself is necessitated by loss [*déperdition*], and something makes loss necessary, namely the conservation of the species: the conservation of the species is the main fact, the dominating fact on which all the others depend, which commands them all.

To arrive at this thought is no longer to limit an idea of cause to that of a physical antecedent, as vulgar positivism does, nor even to limit it to that of a simple fact into which analysis resolves a complex fact. It is to re-establish, perhaps not without contradiction, in matter, in the body, the complete causality that positivism had to banish, active intentional causality. To consider that perfection, in precisely this way, commands and necessitates is obviously to consider that it produces desire and, through desire, movement. To express oneself as Taine does, is to say, though in terms that require clarification, that what determines things, what founds their being, is not, as more vulgar scholars persuade themselves it is, their matter alone, but what it tends towards, which is the perfection for which it is apt.

Divided between the opposite directions in which the two different orders of knowledge embraced by the extent of his studies incline us, between the one leading to materialism, the direction in which mathematics and physics lead, and the one advancing towards spiritualism, that in which biology and especially moral and aesthetic sciences lead us, Taine, with his high intellect sensitive to all kinds of beauty, will in all likelihood pronounce more and more in favour of the latter.

XII
Renan and Philosophy

Ernest Renan, one of our most renowned scholars and one of our most brilliant writers, does not profess to be a philosopher and has not dealt with it anywhere methodically and in detail. It is nevertheless true that from his writings one can extract many traits which, when brought together, form the elements of a philosophical doctrine.

Renan's first studies concerned theology. One idea struck him in the course of his studies, and became, it seems, his constant preoccupation: this was the difficulty of reconciling the results of the natural or historical sciences, which increasingly show us constant laws in everything with the theological opinion according to which a power superior to nature intervenes in it by particular determinations, thus interrupting its course in such a way as to disconcert any prediction. The primary aim of his very diverse works, whether they relate to religions, to history, to languages, or to philosophy itself, is to show that phenomena are explained by natural laws whose regularity excludes any exceptional and superior intervention or, in a word, any miracle.

Moreover, not limiting himself to rejecting the idea of a supernatural being as consisting of an omnipotent will suspending natural laws by arbitrary decisions, Renan usually seemed inclined to reject a broader sense of the supernatural as designating an existence superior to the conditions of physical and sensory existence, and therefore to deny any metaphysics. Thus, he was often reproached for expressing himself, concerning the ideas of the human soul and its destiny, of Divinity and its providence, in terms incompatible with the moral beliefs tightly bound to these ideas.

And, indeed, although he has never formally adhered to what are called the positivist doctrines, he is very close, by his most familiar assertions, to the schools which profess these doctrines. He often repeats that there is no absolute science, that our ideas are all relative. Without attempting to draw in the way of a logician all the consequences of these principles, he seems at least to accept the scepticism that is so easy to deduce from them. He said that truth and falsity differ only in nuance; he spoke of substituting for philosophy a form of pure criticism that would examine and compare without pronouncing.

However, it is hard to believe that this was the last word of the writer who claimed in such dignified terms, in a rightly still-famous newspaper article concerning the 1855 Universal Exhibition, the rights of the moral order, the pre-eminence of intellect against the ascendancy of matter, and who, in several of his works, has expressed so many elevated thoughts about the mind.

In 1865, Renan expressed views, in a letter addressed to the eminent chemist Berthelot,* on the future of science and metaphysics; he sketches the past and future story, as it appears to him, of nature and mankind. Two ideas dominate it: that of the continuous progress of things and that of a cause of this progress.

Taine expressed very well the idea that science, as it advances, interposes, between two facts depending on each other, an increasing number of intermediary facts. By this intercalation of middle terms, science will always establish between the extreme terms, which are one to the other in a relation of cause to effect, a more perfect continuity. Through continuity, we see disappear, either in the sequence of facts, or in that of forms, the gaps, the hiatuses which seem to require, in order to be filled, the intervention of some foreign power. It is by the insensible passage from a modification to a very close modification that Darwin, in his famous treatise *On the Origin of Species*, sought to show how the passage from an elementary organic form to quite different organic forms could have been carried out over time. And this is the thought that Grove, the learned author of the treatise *On the Correlation of Physical Forces*, expressed in its generality as providing a key to the explanation of all natural phenomena in the *Discourse of Continuity* that he pronounced in 1866 in a meeting of the British Association.[1] Let us recall in passing, without going all the way back to Aristotle, that the first philosopher after him, the profound thinker Leibniz, the worthy inheritor of so many great ideas from the author of the *Metaphysics*, stated as a universal law the law of continuity and clarified its use in mathematics and in all the other sciences.

Darwin's book had made a strong impression on Renan's mind. It was a considerable document in support of his favourite thought that everything in the world is explained merely by the development of cosmic laws. What the English naturalist had wanted to do in detail for the organic kingdom, he then tried to do in general and summary terms for the whole of things. He tried to show how it can be understood that over a long period of time the world has passed, by a continuous series of transformations, from a primitive state where there would have been only atoms with purely mechanical properties, to the present state, where life has risen at last, from form to form of increasing complexity, to that point of perfection which is on our planet the present condition of the best part of mankind, and of which intellect, together with self-consciousness, is the most eminent character. 'For this', says Renan, 'it was not necessary to have successive creations proceeding, as it were, by jerks. The slow action of ordinary causes accounts for all the phenomena that were formerly explained by extraordinary causes.' He adds: 'Time was the agent *par excellence*.'

---

* *Revue des deux mondes*, 15 October. [Ravaisson's footnote]

[1] Ravaisson is referring here to the British Association for the Advancement of Science, which became in 2009 the British Science Association. William Grove's 22 August 1866 presidential *Address to the British Association for the Advancement of Science* was published the same year (London: Longmans, Green, and Co.).

Does this mean that, for the matter of simple atoms to acquire physical and chemical properties, and then vital, and finally intellectual and moral properties, a great length of time is sufficient? That such an assertion, without any correction, was untenable and even meaningless, is what could not escape Renan's penetrating intellect. Lamennais had spoken of an internal solicitation that pushes the development of natural beings. Renan adds to time, this 'universal coefficient', a second factor, which he calls the tendency to progress. 'A sort of inner spring, pushing everything to life, and to a more and more developed life—that is', he says, 'a necessary hypothesis.' 'It is necessary to admit in the universe', he adds, 'what can be noticed in the plant and in the animal, an intimate force which carries the germ to fill a frame traced in advance. —'There is', he also says, 'an obscure conscience of the universe that strives to realize itself, a secret spring which pushes the possible to exist'; then, with more precision: 'The universe is an immense struggle where victory goes to what is possible, flexible, harmonious. The organ makes the need; but it is also the result of the need. In any case, the need itself, what is it if not the divine conscience that betrays itself in animal instinct, in the innate tendencies of man, in the dictates of conscience, in this supreme harmony according to which all is full of number, weight, and measure? Nothing is but what has its reason to be; but one can add that everything that has its reason to be has been or will be.'

What does this mean, if not, as Auguste Comte, Littré, and Taine have glimpsed and more or less expressed, that the universal cause is an ideal to which things aspire, and that the great spring of the world is thought?

Renan does not, no more than Taine, no more than Littré and Auguste Comte, give himself up entirely to metaphysics for all that. For him, metaphysics is almost like mathematics and logic. Mathematics allows us to know, by means of its formula, which are those of the transformations of quantity by the simple development of the principle of identity, not what beings are, but the conditions to which they will necessarily be subject, the categories in which they will necessarily be included, if they ever are. So it is with logic, so with metaphysics. 'They are not separate and progressive sciences: they are only sets of immutable notions; they teach nothing, but they make us analyse what we know. Let us not deny that there are sciences of the eternal and the immutable; but let us place them clearly beyond all reality.' According to these expressions, the object of metaphysics that is named the perfect, the absolute, the ideal is thus something, and not a vain and empty word, as vulgar positivism believes; it is something on which all reality depends, but which is nothing real. This is an opinion intermediate between positivist empiricism and metaphysics, but which, deepened, will have to fall under the consequent theory that the ideal, cause of reality, can itself be only the absolute perfect reality.

Renan, already, has said in his most recent publications that the ideal alone is the true reality, and that the rest has only the appearance of being.

XIII
Renouvier's Neo-Criticism

Charles Renouvier proposed, like Renan, to replace what is generally called philosophy by what he called 'critique' or 'criticism': this is the object of his *Essays of General Critique*, the first volume of which was published in 1854, the second in 1859, the third and the fourth in 1864.[1]

Renouvier proposed to continue the enterprise of the famous author of the *Critique of Pure Reason*. He admits with Kant the maxim of all the schools that can be called empirical: that our knowledge does not go beyond phenomena. Any existence that we imagine in a sphere other than that of sensible experience is in his eyes a pure chimera. Things existing in themselves, outside the relations which our senses make known to us,—substances as they are conceived or thought to be conceived by most metaphysicians, substances such as they imagine God and souls to be—are nothing but vain idols, and metaphysics is nothing but 'idolology'. In the conception of something perfect, something complete, an infinite, a pure unity, a self-regarding intellect, and even of a universal order or science, he sees nothing but contradiction and absurdity; the pursuit of an absolute, whatever it may be, leads, for him, only to an abyss of error or rather nonsense. These ideas have been expressed, in barely different if not identical terms, by Hamilton, and especially Auguste Comte, Littré, Bain, Stuart Mill, Taine, and all those who have declared war, like Renouvier, on metaphysics.

Renouvier does not adhere to the doctrine known as 'positivist': he reproaches it for its 'sensualism, assumed everywhere, nowhere demonstrated'; this sensualism seems 'crude' to him. It is backward, in his opinion, to take no account of what Kant has acquired for science: that the sensory is only one element in phenomena, in what appears to us, and that there is another without which it cannot appear, namely the forms by which we grasp it and which belong to us, those ways of understanding that Kant, after Aristotle, called categories. Positivism, like materialist doctrines in general, takes phenomena outside our consciousness as self-sufficient, without considering what form and unity we give them. Renouvier notes, in contrast, with Kant, that the phenomenon is what it is for us only in the representation that we have of it; and, moreover, that we represent this representation to ourselves by becoming aware of it. Two factors can therefore be distinguished in it, the represented and the representing or, as Renouvier names

---

[1] Charles Renouvier (1815–1903), *Essais de critique générale* (Paris: Ladrange, 1854–64).

it, the 'representative'; in other words, the object and the subject of representation. These are two distinct terms, opposed from one point of view, but from another point of view, symmetrical to the first, each has the very characteristic of its counterpart. The subject, in fact, is in consciousness, at least when it rises to reflection, an object for itself; and the object being in consciousness a representation, an idea that does not really differ from the thought considering it, and consequently from the thinking person, the object is subject, and anything represented, as Renouvier puts it, is also a representative. The two elements of representation are thus only two inseparable sides of the same fact, two terms of a relation. From this observation, the author of the *Essays of General Critique* concludes that materialist realism, which sees only the represented, apart from what the representative joins to it, and spiritualist idealism, which considers only the representative, are two equally false theories: the true doctrine, according to him, will place reality in the conjunction, in the relationship of the two terms.

This is more or less how, between the materialism of the Epicureans and the spiritualism of Plato and Aristotle, a middle doctrine intervened, that of the Stoics, which made the passive principle and the active principle two equally necessary parts of an indivisible whole.

Renouvier easily refutes materialist realism. Perhaps it is not quite the same with the opposed doctrine. If the material element cannot obviously do without that which gives it form and unity, it is perhaps not as obvious that the latter cannot absolutely suffice for itself. A multitude cannot be conceived without some unity which makes it a number; unity, on the contrary, can be conceived by itself. What is true of the negative, which in itself is nothing, is not therefore true of the positive.

Representation is possible, remarks Renouvier, after Kant, only under the condition of those modes of representation which we call categories; and he takes up, after Kant, the difficult task of enumerating and classifying them. In his opinion, everything in representation is relative, and he places in the first rank, as dominating all the other categories, the category of relation; there then follow those of number, extension, time, and quality, which determine the characteristics under which phenomenal relations are presented in our experience; finally, those which the positivists, and which Kant himself, claim to eliminate or reduce to the first, the ideas of cause, end, and that of personality, which implies both. We cannot, in fact, conceive that a cause determines a movement without conceiving that it proposes an end; and to propose an end, to will, if we look at it carefully, belongs only to what, like us, says or can say 'I'—and this is what is called 'I'; this is what we call a person.

The analysis that Renouvier undertakes leads him to the result that if, in a given representation, this or that category dominates, there is nevertheless no single representation in which all the categories do not contribute, not a single thing represented which they do not help to determine. Renouvier, therefore, remarks importantly that everything is subject to the higher categories; that nothing falls within our knowledge in which we do not find both force and final causality, in which we do not find something, in some degree, of personality; that is to say, we can only represent nature under the conditions of mind. This is an original and very important result of his laborious inquiries. As for the corresponding and inverse proposition, that we represent nothing to ourselves except under the physical categories or conditions of representation, perhaps, in accordance with the observation we have just made on the independence of the higher principle, there is reason to remark that, while admitting that our representations, in general, are indeed subject to the categories of nature, there is one, however, which is exempt from them, namely the idea of the very activity by which we form these representations, an activity which is none other than ourselves.

According to Renouvier, enemy of all absolutes, of all perfect unity, to be a thinking being is, as Taine usually puts it, only to be a group or a series of thoughts that succeed one another; a proposition with which, incidentally, neither personal identity nor memory can easily be reconciled. For Renouvier, therefore, personality, like everything else, is only relation; but, for him, and with this proposition he places himself far above materialist positivism, relation is thought, it is will, it is personality.

This means that the soul finds the soul everywhere, at least in its provisional forms, and cannot conceive anything except in conformity with the type it carries and perceives in itself.

In studying this type more closely, and this is the subject of the second of his essays, the author of the *General Critique*, following in the footsteps of the immortal author of the *Critique of Pure Reason*, recognizes freedom as its characteristic, essential, dominating trait. For him, freedom is the essence of man; it is not only the principle of our actions, it is the very principle of our convictions.

Evidence, said Descartes, is the foundation of all certainty; evidence belongs, according to Renouvier, only to the simple perception of simple phenomena. For everything else, to be certain, according to him, is to believe; and the basis of belief is, among all desires, free choice. What we are certain of is, in essence, what we approve of as being in accordance with our moral destination, and this approval is an act of freedom. Will it be said that such certainty is not without a great deal of uncertainty? Renouvier agrees: 'It is', he says, 'the characteristic of the fool to doubt rarely, of the madman to doubt never: the man of good sense can be recognized by the fact that he doubts a great deal.'[2]

However these ideas may be criticized in the form that Renouvier has lent to them, the theory establishing between certainty and belief, between belief and will, an intimate connection certainly merits consideration. If, as Plato said, it is

---

[2] Renouvier, *Essais de critique générale*, vol. 2, p. 366.

the good that is the first principle and the last reason, the good is ultimately the supreme rule of truth. But what is the judge of the good, if not what is made for it, if not the heart? And why, therefore, would we not say, with Pascal, that it is the heart that judges principles? But the heart is love, and are not true love and true freedom the same thing? 'Spirit is love', says Christianity; and elsewhere: 'Spirit blows where it wills.'

It should be added here that some of Renouvier's ideas on liberty were shared with another thinker who was his friend, Jules Lequier, several of whose posthumous writings he published with reverent care.

When man is found to be free, and his liberty is maintained among the movements of natural things, which he bends to his own destiny, a question arises: is this destiny limited in time? Should it, on the contrary, extend into infinity? This is the question of immortality.

Without claiming to demonstrate this, Renouvier believes that legitimate inductions guarantee us an indefinite life. These inductions are derived both from the analogy of nature, where nothing perishes, where everything lasts while being transformed, and above all from the conventions, the analogies of the moral order. Consciousnesses destined to last forever, and no doubt to become more and more luminous, are like so many gods; and why, thinks Renouvier, should there not still be many existences of a higher order than our own, to which the present phenomena would be related as to their principles? Gods, then, and perhaps also some superior god governing them all; but a God such as Christianity and metaphysics understand it, a God without limits and without defects, an infinite of power, wisdom, and love, is what Renouvier cannot admit. Like another distinguished writer of our time, Louis Ménard, Renouvier seems to be led by the cherished ideas of democratic politics to similar ideas in theology. Although all metaphysicians have believed, in considering the harmonies of nature or in following the demands of the moral order, that one is necessarily led, in the search for principles, to unity, according to Louis Ménard and Renouvier, if one does not hold to plurality, one will fall into all the disadvantages that despotism and tyranny entail for a human society.—It may, however, be sufficient to avoid them by conceiving of divine unity, not as Spinoza conceived it, from a point of view that is basically physical, as a kind of universal matter of which individuals are only necessary modifications, but as conceived by metaphysics worthy of the name, as an absolute Beauty that is the cause of things only by the love it puts into them, and which, consequently, by the very way it determines them, makes them independent and free. Pascal said: 'The multitude that is not unity is anarchy; the unity that is not multitude is tyranny.' And the Greek poet: 'To show how everything is one, and how nevertheless each thing is a part, that is the question.'

Renouvier dislikes pantheism, which confuses everything in the unity of a supposed God. Rather than being drawn towards it, he would have gladly leaned towards atheism. In his first volume he went so far as to say, in a sort of emulation of Proudhon's supreme paradox, that atheism was the true scientific method. In the following volumes he softened, as Leibniz said somewhere of Spinoza, and did not want to be included among the atheists. Still, he remains the declared opponent of any theology or philosophy that concludes with unity, with infinity, and with perfection.

It is true to say, however, that from what might be called the decided phenomenism or representationalism of the first part of his *Essays*, Renouvier, in the following parts, seems to return on more than one point to ideas less remote from those of the metaphysicians.

Having arrived, in the study of the different parts of nature, particularly of humanity, at the recognition that 'all beings obviously have a destiny, that a general law of finality is an essential part of the order of the world', that consequently 'all the individuals of which it is composed have to perfect themselves by an unending progress',—assertions which go beyond what should be expected from the principles with which his research began—Renouvier recognizes that, in order to ensure the means of realizing particular ends, in order to constitute and maintain the moral order of the world, it is necessary to come at last to a belief in a real, supreme God, with whom all good ends, to a belief 'in the existence and reign of God'.—'Theism and the absolute itself thus reappear', he adds, 'in the ideal of moral perfection, in the affirmation of the Good as the law of the world, and of a moral order which envelops and dominates experience.' He immediately adds, it is true, that of this absolute we know nothing outside the relations which are the conditions of our consciousness; that it is, consequently, only a kind of relative absolute, and that, in this very expression, absolute means only negation, indeterminacy, ignorance. This is more or less, with a more pronounced moral character, the language of Herbert Spencer, concerning that great unknown whose existence, he claimed, as we have seen above, must be admitted beyond the horizon of the sensory phenomena in which materialist positivism tries to enclose itself. But, known or not, or, to put it better, more or less known (for how can one have the slightest suspicion of what would be entirely unknown and indeterminate?), it is towards an absolute, an infinite, towards an absolute in possession of moral perfection that the speculations of Auguste Comte and Herbert Spencer, like those of Taine and Renan, like those of Renouvier, tend, and at which they will inevitably end.

XIV
The Philosophy of Vacherot

Vacherot began with an edition of Victor Cousin's lectures on morality and natural law.[1] He became known soon afterwards for a thesis on Aristotle's theory of first principles, and then for a history of the School of Alexandria, which we have already mentioned, and to which the Academy of Moral and Political Sciences awarded a prize. In his thesis, in his history, he was already announcing opinions which differed to some extent from those of the school to which he belonged.

In the extensive work which he has since published under the title *Metaphysics and Science*,[2] Vacherot has arrived at a system in which we find what the theories of Taine, Renan, and Renouvier have in common. It may be said that Taine, Renan, Renouvier, and Vacherot aimed to reform, in different respects and from different points of view to a certain extent, the idea that theologians and metaphysicians have generally had of Divinity as an infinite and perfect being, an omnipotent will and a personality in full possession of itself. If Renan believed that he had to reject the idea of a will that is master of nature and capable of changing its course at will, and Renouvier the idea of an infinite and perfect substance, Vacherot, in agreement with Taine, holds the idea of a perfect personality to be particularly untenable. What characterizes his approach is above all the idea that perfection is, in his eyes, incompatible with infinity, and at the same time with reality.

'The two great objects of metaphysics', says Vacherot in the foreword to the second edition of *Metaphysics and Science* (1863),[3] 'are God and the world. The world is reality, the object of the senses, which is infinite; God is perfection, an object of the intelligence, the ideal.'—'The idea of this book', he adds, 'is the profound distinction between the perfect and the incomplete, the one being conceived as the supreme ideal, the other as the universal reality.' What he sets out to demonstrate, either by analysing the main philosophical systems of all times, or by analysing the intellect and by critically examining our knowledge, is that, if there is an idea of perfection demanded by everything, to which everything leads, an idea represented by the name of God, then this idea excludes by itself that of

---

[1] Victor Cousin, *Cours d'histoire de la philosophie morale au XVIIIe siècle*, ed. Vacherot (Paris: Ladrange, 1839).
[2] Etienne Vacherot, *La métaphysique et la science* (Paris: Chamerot, 1858).
[3] Vacherot, *La métaphysique et la science* (Paris: Chamerot, 1863, 2nd edition).

real existence. All real existence is therefore limited to the world. The world is all reality; God is the ideal.

'The real is known', says Vacherot, 'the ideal is conceived.' Knowing and conceiving; the whole future of philosophy lies, in his opinion, in this distinction.

This distinction between what is perceived and what is conceived was, as we have seen, established above all by the Scottish school, and from it emerged, under the influence of the aesthetic theories then dominant, the eclectic doctrine of the ideal considered as incompatible with reality. Only Victor Cousin made an exception, as it were, for God: in God, he claimed, the ideal was realized. Vacherot eliminates the exception by a more rigorous application of the general principle that reality alone is known, and that what is conceived is only an ideal without reality, and he thus comes closer to the doctrine common to the empirical schools.

According to Vacherot, given that the idea of the void is a contradictory idea, reality forms a continuous and infinite whole. This cosmological proposition is, he says, the main conclusion of his book. And, indeed, as infinite and universal, the world holds in this system the place occupied in many others by the Divine: God is left with, in addition to perfection, merely a purely ideal existence. Thus Vacherot, while distinguishing God from the world, often gives the world as he conceives it the great name of 'God'. Vacherot approves of Renan for having said that God is the category of the ideal; he criticizes him for leaving it in doubt whether God, while being an ideal for thought, would not still be in himself something real.

Bossuet, summing up the doctrine of all the great metaphysicians, his contemporaries or predecessors, addressed the following words to those who, in his time, proposed the opinion renewed by Vacherot today: 'They say: the perfect is not; the perfect is only an idea of our mind rising from the imperfect, which we see with our eyes, up to a perfection that has no reality except in our thoughts. It is not seen that what is perfect is first in itself and in our ideas, and that the imperfect, in all ways, is only a degradation of it.'[4] And elsewhere: 'The perfect is earlier than the imperfect, and the imperfect supposes it.'[5] And elsewhere again: 'Why should the imperfect be and the perfect not be? Is it because it is perfect? And is perfection an obstacle to being? On the contrary, perfection is the reason for being.'[6] Similarly, the author of the *Monadology* says: 'Perfection is nothing other than the greatness of positive reality taken precisely, setting aside the limits or boundaries in things that have them, so that where there are no boundaries, that is, in God, perfection is absolutely infinite'; and again: 'Every possible has a right to existence precisely in proportion to the perfection it envelops.'[7]

---

[4] *Oeuvres complètes de Bossuet*, vol. 3 (Paris: Lefevre, 1836), p. 5.
[5] *Oeuvres complètes de Bossuet*, vol. 10 (Paris: Lefevre, 1836), p. 83.
[6] *Oeuvres complètes de Bossuet*, vol. 8 (Paris: Lefevre, 1836), p. 390.
[7] Leibniz, *Monadology*, §41 (see Leibniz, *Philosophical Essays*, ed. D. Garber and R. Ariew (Indianapolis: Hackett, 1989)).

In these profound sentences, Vacherot sees nothing solid, and he has not even deemed it useful to refute them, so obvious does their absurdity seem to him. In this connection, in his *Philosophical Crisis* Paul Janet said: 'Vacherot assumes everywhere, as a self-evident postulate, that the perfect cannot exist, for the reason that the ideal cannot be real. It was possible to contest the Cartesian claim that existence was a perfection: it would be strange, however, if it were an imperfection. To be is better, after all, than not to be.'[8]

Vacherot's thought seems to be, not absolutely that it is an imperfection to exist, but that real existence has conditions that imply imperfection. He supposes that there is nothing real other than what the experiences of the senses make known to us; and, as Caro has remarked in *The Idea of God and its New Critics*,[9] as well as Paul Janet in his *Philosophical Crisis*, this supposition is the underlying principle of his whole philosophy.

'What Vacherot's demonstration supposes', says Caro, 'is that all existence is mobile, that it develops in time and space, that it occurs only within nature or history.' To which he adds: 'It is exclusively empirical definitions that create this alleged incompatibility between perfection and reality, definitions such as these: All reality is a passing phenomenon.' Similarly, Paul Janet says: 'I can see that the reality which falls under my senses, which is in contact with my own imperfect existence, is itself imperfect; but why conclude that all reality, that is to say all existence, is necessarily imperfect?'

To these remarks, we should, perhaps, add only that if Vacherot, instead of admitting material and sensory phenomena and others that are not material or sensory, recognized that all phenomena, without excepting those that the eclectic school calls psychological, are in some respects sensory and material, then we can only praise him for this, and that, consequently, concerning the principle of Scottish philosophy and eclecticism that only phenomena are perceptible and immediately perceptible, he was right to conclude from it that all reality is enclosed in sensory phenomena; and that under the relative terms of ideality and perfection—with which eclectic philosophy is perhaps too easily satisfied when it tries to characterize what, in its opinion, goes beyond phenomena—it is difficult to see, indeed, anything positive, anything real, anything other than an abstract and general concept, the result of some comparison of our mind. This ideal, this perfection, this completion, what is it in itself? This is what is left too much in the dark; at least the senses offer us something real and determinate; we should not be surprised if it is on their side that all reality seems to lie. It is therefore, it seems, only natural to see

---

[8] Paul Janet, *La crise philosophique*. There does not seem to be a sentence closely corresponding to Ravaisson's citation in the chapter of Janet's work on Vacherot.
[9] Elme Marie Caro (1826–87), *L'idée de Dieu et ses nouveaux critiques* (Paris: Hachette, 1864).

emerge on the trunk of eclecticism, which disavows it, the outgrowth that is Vacherot's philosophy.

If, with Aristotle, with Leibniz, we define perfection by action, action itself by the will, which is not an object of mere conception, but of inner awareness, then Vacherot's objections to the real existence of perfection fall away; we have the principle of a philosophy with which he himself is perhaps not far from accepting today. Does he not say, in a recent *Essay on Psychology*,[10] that we have in ourselves the immediate experience of an action which is not only a reality like sensations, but what is most real in them? But this philosophy is not the one that fills *Metaphysics and Science*.

According to Vacherot's approach in that work, the only real objects are the objects of the senses.

We should, it seems, conclude that for him there is nothing, strictly speaking, but the various phenomena of which the sensory world is composed.

However, he does not see in the universe, like the positivists, merely a multiplicity of phenomena. Beneath this multiplicity, which is the object of science, there is, for him, a unity, which is the object of metaphysics. There is no emptiness either outside or inside things; existence forms a continuum which nothing interrupts and nothing ends, nothing in space, nothing in time; the world is infinite, eternal, necessary. By the harmony of all things in space and time, it is manifest, moreover, that at the base of all things lies a unity. Not only are phenomena not everything, but everything is only one being, without limits, whose phenomena are only its modifications.

There is more, and the reality whose unique and infinite being is totality requires yet another principle, which is the object of theology. The harmony of things is not invariable, immobile; everything in this world necessarily changes and tends, in changing, to pass from the worst to the best, from confusion to order, and from one order to a higher order. The world is in progress, in perpetual progress. This progress needs a cause: this cause is perfection. Each order of things is not, as materialism imagines, a mere complication of elements from the lower orders, but a new state to which the universal and infinite Being rises by virtue of its constant tendency to perfection.

The idea of infinite being is thus completed by that of perfection which attracts it, and thus metaphysics is completed by theology.

Vacherot recognized, by taking up, as Auguste Comte said, the point of view of the whole, that to the particular things that form, so to speak, the detail of the universe, a God must be added. He divides this God, of which is he loath to make an individual, a person, into two: on the one hand, above things, perfection,

---

[10] Vacherot, *Mémoire sur la psychologie*. This was first published as 'La psychologie contemporaine' in *Revue des deux mondes* (1869), pp. 709–29.

which is the final cause, and on the other, at the bottom of things, absolute existence, which is the efficient cause, and which the final cause calls to itself.

De Rémusat, in a very recent publication concerning Grote's work on Plato,[11] has expressed the opinion that the Platonists of the school of Plotinus, if not Plato himself, had attributed to their 'ideas' a very particular existence, quite different from that of realities. And he shows himself willing to admit this kind of existence not only for the ideas or types of things, but 'for the idea of ideas', in Plato's language, i.e. for God. 'Do we not recognize', he says, 'that motives, which are ideas, have a force, exercise a power? This is to recognize that they act; and therefore it must be admitted that, although they are not beings, they exist.' To this we may reply that action, like existence, is attributed to ideas only in a roundabout and figurative sense, and that this is only a proof of the vagueness and ambiguity of the abstract terms action and existence. It is in order to dispel this vagueness and ambiguity—which indeed led certain Platonists, if not Plato himself, to consider qualities, quantities, and relationships as existing at least on a par with real beings—that Aristotle distinguished, as we have already said, in his *Categories*, what is really and truly, substance, and what exists only in it and through it. And how do we recognize substances? Through their action. But how to recognize action itself, given that it can still be metaphorically attributed to an idea, to a motive? By effort, by the will, added Leibniz. This is what finally answers de Rémusat's doubt, and gives the notion of existence its final and necessary precision. One will doubtless not go so far as to attribute effort and will to ideas without making them real in a mind.

The opinion proposed by de Rémusat is perhaps the most rigorous expression of the theory which, instead of reducing ideas, the ideal, to operations of the intellect, wants to put them outside of all reality; and it constitutes the idealism that is the most consistent with itself.

On the contrary, with Descartes, Leibniz, Bossuet, and many others, among whom we must perhaps also include—contrary to the opinion of de Rémusat—Plato and Plotinus especially, Vacherot thought that ideas could subsist only in some intellect, and refusing to admit with these metaphysicians the reality of divine existence and intellect, he could locate them only in human intellect. If, according to the whole of the *Metaphysics of Science*, the ideal explains, as a final cause, the life and movement of nature, from several formal passages it follows that it exists only in the human mind, which entails that it is contingent like the human being and perishable with it. 'If we eliminate man,' says Vacherot, 'God no longer exists; no humanity, then no thought, no ideal, no God, since God exists only for the thinking being. The universal being, the *real* God, if we may speak in this way, would always exist, since being is necessary, and the thinking

---

[11] *Revue des deux mondes*, January 1868. [Ravaisson's footnote]

being is only a contingent form of it, however superior it may be; but the *true* God would have ceased to exist.'

Without mentioning many other objections that could be raised against this doctrine, one wonders how, if the ideal exists only in our mind, it can act on nature, and especially how it could have acted on it before humans existed. In any case, if it is Vacherot's express opinion that the ideal exists only in the mind of man, his doctrine would seem to be, consequently, that nature, strictly speaking, is self-sufficient, and that the real God, as he calls him, is the sole and total cause of his own movement. But if we now ask what, for him, the existence of universal being consists of, we find that it is reduced to a virtuality of which particular things are the different realizations. One might wonder here how a virtual existence can, by itself, become reality. One might wonder what it is to be merely virtual, and whether it is to be. Finally, one might wonder whether Vacherot's infinite being, in whom he wishes to place all the effective force that he denies to his God, whether this being, reduced to virtuality, is not, like this God, a pure conception, entirely similar, in this respect, to all those substances of vulgar metaphysics for which it is supposed to act as a substitute, and whether, in the end, it is anything more than, as Lachelier said in an article in the *Revue de l'instruction publique* (25 June 1864), which we have already quoted, 'the abstraction of being in general, that is to say, the emptiest of all abstractions'.

If this is true, one may think that Vacherot, in the further development of his philosophy, abandoning these two halves of divine nature, in which he already sees only objects of mere conception, will be led to reduce everything, with the materialists, to sensible phenomena, to the detail of the physical world.

But if we consider that he is far from materialist explanations of natural phenomena and that the very purpose of his work is to prove the necessity of supplementing positive knowledge by metaphysics, at the same time as providing the means which he believes to be suitable for this purpose; if we consider how forcefully he brings out how nothing limited and imperfect can be understood without infinity and without perfection; if we consider that, in his last work, in his *Essay on Psychology*, he shows himself inclined, as we have just remarked, to attribute to action, which is the object of inner awareness, which exceeds the sphere of phenomena, and to which it is also difficult not to attribute more perfection than any phenomenon can present, a reality superior to that of sensations; if we consider, finally, how attached he is to the high morality that is hardly separable from spiritualism, one will rather be inclined to believe that the author of *Metaphysics and Science* will increasingly prefer, of the two paths between which he still seems to hesitate, the one leading to the lofty sites of science, to the summits on which revelled the thinkers, whose true philosophical genius he today sometimes even denies: the author of *Republic* and *Phaedo*, the author of the *Metaphysics*, and those of the *Meditations*, the *Theodicy*, the *Elevations*.

XV
Claude Bernard's Physiological Doctrine

A physiologist who has gained fame for major discoveries, Claude Bernard, after having been preoccupied, throughout his career, with questions of principle and method, has dealt with them expressly and at length in his 1865 *Introduction to the Study of Experimental Medicine*,[1] which is of eminent interest to general philosophy.

The aim of the book is to establish that medicine admits, like the physical and chemical sciences, not only observation, but experiments, and that it is only by experimentation that, in ascertaining with precision the phenomena with which it is concerned and their relations, it will pass from its still present state, from a science that is largely conjectural, to the state of a positive science, that is to say, to a science that can predict phenomena with certainty and, to a certain extent, modify them.

To demonstrate this thesis, Claude Bernard explains in detail the way in which he understands the objects considered by the science of life, and, consequently, its methods. Nothing is more instructive than the examples that such a master draws from his personal experience, than the picture he paints of the progress of his mind and work in discovering the truths he has arrived at. But here we have only to give an account of the general ideas and main results which he presents in their relation to philosophy proper.

Summing up Claude Bernard's work in this respect, we may say that, if he first relies on the general principles that form the basis of what may be called, with Auguste Comte, the positivist doctrine, such as the latter first conceived it and such as many physicians and physiologists still understand it, the illustrious scientist soon adds to it concepts which are his own, and which proceed from a quite different way of thinking.

Like those who call themselves positivists, and like all those who claim to derive all our knowledge from the data of the senses alone, Claude Bernard proclaims that nothing absolute is accessible to us, and that we can know only the relations expressed by phenomena. To find the laws of these relations, including the precise determinations of quantities, is in his eyes the goal of all science.

---

[1] Claude Bernard (1813–78), *Introduction à l'étude de la médecine expérimentale* (Paris: Garnier, 1865); *Introduction to the Study of Experimental Medicine*, trans. H. C. Greene (New York: Henry Schuman, 1949).

As Auguste Comte said, this is all that is needed to predict phenomena or to modify them for our purposes.

It is no less true that Claude Bernard has a completely different idea of science than positivism. According to the latter system, as expounded by Stuart Mill, science is formed by inductions which extend observed relationships beyond the limits of observation, inductions which are in no way deductions or instances of reasoning, for they are not based on any reason. Claude Bernard understood, like Leibniz, that to induct 'is always to draw consequences'; he was able to recognize that induction, at bottom, is a deduction; and, while Stuart Mill, after Bacon and Locke, reduces the syllogism to nothing, as merely the simplest expression of deduction, the physiologist who has enriched science with so many fruitful inductions is not afraid to say that all induction is nothing other than a syllogism.

Induction, according to Claude Bernard, is a conjecture by deduction. How, then, can the conjecture be proved? By verifying the consequences to which, in turn, it gives rise. For Claude Bernard, induction must therefore be a provisional and conditional deduction, which changes, through experiential verification, into an unconditional and definitive deduction.

Whereas, according to Stuart Mill, one passes, in induction, from an assertion about a fact to an assertion about an analogue fact, by a pure mechanism, for which no reason is to be found, according to Claude Bernard, on the contrary, in this passage we rely on a principle, on an a priori axiom, on a true innate idea, which, in truth, is fused with the very constitution of our intellect, namely that there is proportion and order in everything—that, in other words, there is nothing without reason. This is, incidentally, the predominant idea of the metaphysics concerning which the eminent physiologist is sometimes rather severe. He says somewhere, in terms which could be found in Descartes, in Leibniz, in Plato, and which form with Stuart Mill's doctrine of crude mechanism the most perfect contrast, that in the experimental method as everywhere else, the definitive criterion is the same as in all other methods: reason. Let us note here that Garreau, another philosopher-doctor who has often opposed materialistic physiology with just and elevated considerations, said in his 1842 *Essay on the Ontological Bases of Human Science, and on the Method Concerning the Study of Human Physiology*[2] that induction and hypothesis, in truth, are one and the same, and he added that it was the necessary idea of order that is always present to us which makes us move, when we induce, from the known order to the unknown order. From this he drew the consequence that the principle and the essence of induction was identical to reason, which is order itself.

---

[2] P. E. Garreau, *Essai sur les bases ontologiques de la science de l'homme, et sur la méthode qui convient à l'étude de la physiologie humaine* (Paris: Masson, 1846).

In a very similar sense, Adolphe Franck, in his *Report to the Academy of Moral and Political Sciences* on Javary's dissertation *Certainty*,[3] said: 'Unity and identity, or rather the notion of being which includes them both, is the principle of induction as well as of deductive reasoning.'

The physical form in which this general principle that everything has its reason is presented, so to speak, is that every physical phenomenon occurs under physical and defined conditions. Claude Bernard presented this principle with a new strength and precision under the name, which he gave it, of the principle of 'universal determinism'.

From the consequences he draws from it, from his application of it to organized beings, there results a theory which at first seems to reduce these beings to the condition of inorganic things and to support materialism, but which its author soon modifies by adding to it an element quite different from those of which it was first composed.

It is agreed that all the phenomena exhibited by inorganic bodies occur as a result of determined circumstances, which are what we call their physical causes. There is not the same agreement about physiological phenomena. It is often said, on the contrary, that they are the effect of a particular force called the vital force, and which acts with a certain independence in relation to external circumstances; the more complex and perfected the organism, the more it seems to be independent of its environments, and seems to determine itself with genuine spontaneity. This is because, says Claude Bernard, they possess an inner milieu home to physical conditions that escape superficial observation, but which are reached by deeper observation. The plant depends for its life, for its functions, on definite conditions of heat and humidity from the milieu in which it is located; the animal seems to be more independent of ambient circumstances and often even to free itself from them entirely by a spontaneous vital power. This is because it finds in the blood, contained within it but which is no less an ambient and external milieu for the organs immersed in it, the definite physical conditions of their functions; when these conditions are fulfilled, the functions of the animal are accomplished with the same necessity as those of the plant. In this way Claude Bernard brings under the law of determinism a number of facts that previously seemed irreducible to it, and behind which were entrenched, as if in a fort, the doctrines explaining at least part of the phenomena which occur in living beings by one or more forces superior to the inorganic order, doctrines that are more or less vitalist, including those that go no further than attributing to the organs or their elements what they call vital properties, and those explaining life by a vital principle really distinct from the organs, following Barthez, or even, following Stahl, by the thinking soul. Once the phenomena observed in organized bodies

---

[3] Adolphe Franck, *De la certitude: rapport à l'Académie des sciences morales et politiques* (Paris: Ladrange, 1847), p. 247.

have been brought closer to the ambient circumstances, including those of the inner milieux, we see that in the absence of these circumstances, these phenomena are never accomplished, but in their presence they are always realized; consequently, living beings do not possess the independence and spontaneity that is generally attributed to them, and the phenomena that they present take place within them in the same way and with the same necessity as physical and chemical phenomena.

Life and death, health and disease are therefore, says Claude Bernard, words to which nothing real corresponds. 'They are words which signify ignorance; for when we call a phenomenon vital, it is equivalent to saying that it is a phenomenon whose proximate cause or conditions we are ignorant of; they are purely literary expressions which we use because they represent to our minds the appearance of certain phenomena, but which express no objective reality.'

If this is so, organized beings, as Cabanis, Magendie, Broussais, Gall, and all the biologists who today belong to the positivist school, think, are only crude bodies more complicated than others; there is nothing in the world but crude bodies, only more or less complex machines, and universal determinism is a universal mechanism.

Granting that determinism, consisting in the connection of all phenomena with determinate physical circumstances, extends much further than vitalism supposes, we may still ask whether it is demonstrated, at least as Claude Bernard defines it, for all the phenomena offered by living beings. There is no proof yet that it extends to all the phenomena of movement, and that locomotion, for example, is always reducible to a purely physical and mechanical phenomenon. This is a question that we shall find again in connection with the discoveries and theories of modern physiology in relation to what it calls reflex movements.

But even supposing that the phenomena of organized beings are all similar in all respects to those of crude bodies and that our art can reproduce them, it does not follow, according to Claude Bernard, that organized beings themselves, the imitation of which is beyond our power, differ in no way from crude bodies. In addition to the phenomena, in fact, we have to consider the whole which they form, the order in which they are accomplished, and this is what physics and chemistry are insufficient to explain.

As long as we stick to the details, said Auguste Comte, the properties of organized beings can be more or less easily reduced to those of minerals. When we take the point of view of the whole, things are quite different.

A thinker like Claude Bernard understands better than anyone else that, in addition to the various phenomena which he explains by physico-chemical facts, there is in the organism the order and the concert which these phenomena form; he is struck above all by this order as it is manifest in the gradual evolution of organized beings, and, recognizing that such a regular and constant whole cannot be explained by the irregular and variable action of physical and external circumstances, he sees in it the effect of a definite, pre-existing type, to which the organism conforms just as a work of art is executed according to a predetermined thought; and he calls this type, in sequence, an 'organic idea'. This organic idea passes, he adds, by tradition from generation to generation—a conception reminiscent of Harvey's in his immortal *De generatione*.[4]

Claude Bernard expresses somewhere the idea that life can be defined as creation. That is why he calls the organic idea creative. Creative of what? Not, once again, of the particular phenomena, all of which must sooner or later be reduced by science to physical and chemical facts, but the machine to which they belong, which is the organism. 'In such a way that what characterizes the living machine is not the nature of its properties, however complex they may be, but the very creation of this machine.' When a chicken develops in an egg, it is not the chemical combinations of the elements that are to be attributed to the vital force, since these combinations are the result of the physical-chemical properties of matter; what belongs neither to chemistry, nor to physics, nor to anything else, but which is the characteristic of life, is the guiding idea of organic evolution. In every living germ there is a creative idea. The living being, as long as it lasts, remains under its influence, and death comes when it can no longer be realized. 'Everything is therefore derived from the idea which directs and creates alone; the physico-chemical means of manifestation are common to all the phenomena of nature, and remain jumbled together like the letters of the alphabet in a box where this force goes to find them in order to express the most diverse thoughts or mechanisms.'

As is clear, the creation of which Claude Bernard speaks, and which in his eyes is life itself, is the simultaneous and successive arrangement of the parts of the machine that make it an organism; it is, to use one of Auguste Comte's favourite formulae, both order and progress, and progress above all. To this order and progress there is a cause; this cause is an idea to which they respond and conform.

What is this theory, if not, as Paul Janet remarks in his review of Claude Bernard's work in the *Revue des deux mondes* (15 April 1866), a theory of what metaphysicians call final causation?

The final cause is that which answers the question 'why?' What then becomes in Claude Bernard's philosophy of the proposition that he repeats several times, following the example of the entire positivist school, that we can know the 'how' of natural phenomena, that is to say their physical conditions of existence, but never the 'why'? By his own admission, as soon as it is a question of life, consideration of the guiding and creative idea is indispensable; it is even what is most important; it is the proper object of science.

---

[4] Ravaisson is referring to Harvey's *Exercitationes de generatione animalium* (1651).

In the presence of this higher part of Claude Bernard's system, where his thinking changes entirely, the general theory of universal determinism becomes quite different.

In the interpretation he gave of it and the applications he made of it in order to bring the phenomena of life back to physics and chemistry, universal determinism meant that every phenomenon necessarily follows other phenomena of the same nature and order, which we call physical causes. From his reflections on the harmony and unity of life, there follows the conclusion that there is another kind of determinism, consisting in the fact that the organism, in its harmonic whole, has a cause quite different from the elements, from the parts of matter, a cause that Claude Bernard does not define, except by the fact that, under its influence, the parts, the material elements, come together and harmonize as if in the unity of one and the same thought. This is, however exactly we may understand it, a determinism quite different from the first, and which Claude Bernard himself calls a 'superior determinism'.

But how is the 'organic idea' actually a creative idea? In other words, how can we understand that it determines, in accordance with the order of which it is the type, the physico-chemical phenomena by which the organism is formed and maintained, and which are nevertheless always the necessary result of entirely physical circumstances? Perhaps it can be understood only if we assume an activity which the organic idea determines, and which arranges the parts according to its typical order, by means of suitable movements, in relation to the situations and distances that condition the physical-chemical phenomena; an elementary activity, comparable to Stahl's tonic activity, that would be something like an outline and a first state of that higher activity by means of which a being enters into full possession of the government of itself and makes its own destiny, that is to say, locomotive activity.

However one judges it, and whether or not it is possible to conceive of any other mode of action than movement for a power that tends towards a goal, an idea, a guiding and creative idea, cannot be understood without an intellect that conceives it, a will that pursues it. According to the theory with which Claude Bernard rises above materialism, which he describes as absurd and meaningless, it is difficult not to see the initial form of the only theory by which it can pass in some way from being figurative to being literal, from the abstract to the real. From the 'creative idea' the philosophical physiologist has to arrive, it seems, at mind, the only organizer and creator.

XVI

Philosophical Theology

Gratry

Several theologians belonging to the Catholic Church have opposed most of the doctrines discussed so far as incompatible with the dogmas of Christianity and even with natural religion and morality. It is not within the scope of the present work to give an account of the productions of those who work primarily from a theological point of view.

The same cannot be said of the works of Père Gratry, of the oratory. Père Gratry thought he had discovered in the idea of a modern German philosopher the principle of all that he found erroneous in modern doctrines, and with a directly opposed notion the principle that leads to all truth. He has established a whole philosophical theory.

A few years ago, it was thought that all the systems of modern philosophy, including eclecticism, contained the doctrine that identifies God with all things: pantheism. This idea was developed in particular by Abbé Maret, who has since become Bishop of Sura, in his *Essay on Pantheism* (1852);[1] by Abbé Bautain and, since then, by various other writers, most of whom belong to the Church. Adolphe Franck, from a very different point of view, has often expressed, with regard to various contemporary theories, comparable ideas. According to Père Gratry (and Buchez, in his *Logique*, had already said something similar), it is not pantheism which is the primary source of the errors of our time: pantheism is only a consequence of a philosophical proposition borrowed from Hegel, and which he himself had renewed from the sophists of antiquity, namely, the maxim that in the end everything is identical, and that consequently yes and no, being and non-being, are one. And to this principle, which destroys all reason, and to the method which is its development, Père Gratry opposes a principle and a method which, according to him, are suitable for strengthening everything threatened by what he calls modern sophistry. This is the main object of the various writings he published from 1851 to 1864, namely: a *Study of the Contemporary Sophists, or Letter to Vacherot*; a *Treatise on the Knowledge of God*; a *Treatise on*

---

[1] Ravaisson is perhaps referring to a later edition, but Henri Louis Charles Maret's *Essai sur le panthéisme dans les sociétés modernes* first appeared in 1840 (Paris: Débécourt). Maret (1805–84) was a liberal Catholic theologian much influenced by Lamennais, but this text contained a virulent critique of Cousinian orthodoxy as leading to pantheism.

Knowledge of the Soul; a *Logic*; and finally *The Sophists and Criticism*, a work composed on the occasion of Renan's *Life of Jesus*.[2]

The authors whom Père Gratry has especially in view—Vacherot, Renan, Scherer—have expressed themselves concerning Hegelianism, in many respects, with favour; one finds in their theories certain tendencies or certain results analogous to the main tendencies and results of Hegel's philosophy. But it is not obvious that they have adopted his principles or followed his method; above all, it is not evident that they have, following his example, set up as a rule the identity of contradictories, the negation of the principle of contradiction.

Vacherot, as we have seen, separates, and even opposes as completely incompatible, the real and the ideal or rational, and consequently denies God any reality. Hegel, on the contrary, said: 'What is rational is also real, and what is real is also rational'; he treated as superficial and false the theory according to which the very perfection of the ideal is an obstacle to its reality. According to his expressions, which here return to those of Leibniz, 'God is the highest reality and, indeed, the only reality.' It is therefore far from possible to consider Vacherot's philosophy and that of Hegel as identical. Moreover, it is not clear that Vacherot anywhere invokes or puts to use the Hegelian maxim, whatever its true meaning, of the identity of opposites, nor that, consequently, he ranks himself, or can be ranked, among the supporters of the system of absolute identity.

The same is true of Scherer. In an article in the *Revue des deux mondes* (15 February 1862), entitled 'Hegel and Hegelianism', although he expresses great admiration for the greatness of the system and for the strength of mind of its author, he nevertheless declares that, in his opinion, Hegelianism is a 'system that is contradictory in its essence and terms, and, all in all, sterile'. If he seems to endorse the view, attributed to the German philosopher, that one assertion is not truer than the opposite assertion, it is in the sense that the contradiction of the opposite terms would always lead to a higher conciliation; and any such conciliation would, according to him, amount to the principle that 'absolute judgements are false', because 'everything is relative'. This is a maxim common to Scherer and Renan, and, as we have seen above, it is the fundamental maxim of the positivist school. But what could be further from Hegel's intention?

---

[2] Ravaisson is referring (loosely) to Auguste Joseph Alphonese Gratry's *Etude sur la sophistique contemporaine où lettre à M. Vacherot* (Paris: Douniol, 1851), which was first published earlier in the year as *Lettre à Vacherot, directeur des études de l'Ecole normale, par l'abbé Gratry, aumônier de l'Ecole normale*. Gratry (1805–72), a product of the Ecole Polytechnique who became a priest attached to the Ecole Normale, and one of the most important Catholic intellectuals of the century, attacked the historical theses concerning Christianity advanced by the Ecole's director, Vacherot, in the third volume of his 1851 *Ecole d'Alexandrie*. Ravaisson refers also to Gratry, *De la connaissance de Dieu* (Paris: Douniol, 1853), *De la connaissance de l'âme* (Paris: Douniol, 1857), *Logique* (Paris: Douniol, 1856), and *Les sophistes et la critique* (Paris: Douniol, 1864), written in response to Ernest Renan's best-selling *La vie de Jésus* (Paris: Lévy, 1863).

It is therefore doubtful whether Père Gratry is justified in signalling in Hegelianism the common source of the theories of Vacherot, Renan, and Scherer, and in saying that the Hegelian principle of the identity of contradictories is the key to what he calls modern sophistry.

As for the general maxim in which Père Gratry finds the essence of all Hegelianism, perhaps it is not enough, in order to appreciate it, to compare it, as he does, with what the sophists of antiquity said that was similar. In his *History of Philosophy*, Hegel himself pointed out this similarity. But, as he also pointed out, it is not enough to identify two systems, to note two propositions, even important ones, very similar to each other; it is necessary to examine the direction in which they are going and where they come from. 'Videndum est', says Cicero, 'non modo quid quisque loquatur, sed etiam quid quisque sentiat, atque etiam qua de causa quisque sentiat.'[3] Even if there is, in appearance or in reality, something sophistical in Hegel's method, it is difficult to confuse the modern doctrine where everything is reduced to thought with the ancient sensualism of Protagoras and Gorgias. Hegel's view is, basically, that the oppositions, the contrarieties even, presented by the lower degrees of either existence or knowledge find their harmony, their unity, in a higher degree; and, moreover, that it is the function *par excellence* of thought, in its highest perfection, to bring about this marriage, this intimate union of opposites. Is such a conception, whose proximate origin can be traced back to Schelling and Fichte, back to Kant, but to which in antiquity the very doctrine of the greatest opponents of the sophists was not foreign, only contemptible? It perhaps remains to determine, beneath the formulae by which Hegel expressed this alternate succession of contrarieties and harmonies, what its principle is; and perhaps he made the error here of taking the form for the content, and, in general, of reducing everything to logic, to the rational alone. He will nevertheless have the merit of having shown with a completely new precision, as well as with a rare breadth of vision, the rational chain of logical conditions which form, as it were, the mechanism of the intellectual world.

Père Gratry believes he has found an intimate relationship between the Hegelian system of universal identity and the method of deduction. This method consists, he claims, in a series of transformations by which, developing a notion without adding anything to it, one goes from the same to the same. In this way we learn nothing; on the contrary, learning is adding to a notion a notion which is not contained within it; and this is what is achieved by the method of 'transcendence'.

This method, opposed to deduction, is, for Père Gratry, induction. Induction, which he takes to be identical with Platonic dialectics, would have found,

---

[3] Cicero, *De officiis* I, xli, 7: 'in deriving counsel from one of these, we have to see not only what our adviser says, but also what he thinks, and what his reasons are for thinking as he does' (trans. W. Miller, *On Duties*, Loeb Classical Library, Harvard University Press, 1913).

moreover, its most perfect form in the kind of calculation constituting the highest part of mathematics, that is to say differential and integral calculation, and which is called infinitesimal analysis. The true philosophical method, diametrically opposed to the method of deduction and identity, would therefore be the method of the calculation of the infinite applied to metaphysics, to natural theology.

The great problem of philosophy is, says Père Gratry, that of reaching the infinite, which is God. The deductive method, proceeding from the same to the same, can, in his opinion, in departing from the finite to arrive at the finite, only identify the infinite and the finite, which is pantheism. The infinitesimal method, which, by way of induction, according to Père Gratry, proceeds from the finite to the infinite, is therefore the very method by which the main problem of philosophy must be resolved. 'What do we do when from the finite perfections found in us, from will, from intelligence, we conclude, following the path traced by Descartes, with infinite perfections in God? We proceed, as in the infinitesimal calculus, from the finite to the infinite. Thus the method of the infinitesimal calculus is the same method by which the existence and nature of God is demonstrated. Natural theology proceeds exactly like higher mathematics; on both sides, the same procedure and the same certainty.'

As for the connection which the learned and eloquent author establishes between the system of universal identity and the deductive method, it may be worth noting that if deduction consists, indeed, in drawing consequences from a notion, in developing what it contains, and, consequently, in showing that each consequence is only the principle itself, presented in a different condition and form; and if we may even add, with Aristotle and Leibniz, that all regular deduction, all demonstration comes back to a definition that is a reciprocal or identical proposition, where the subject and object are the same thing; and if, moreover, the axioms to which all deductions are subject as to universal rules are reducible to identical truths, it does not follow from this that all the notions serving as special principles for different series of deductions are the same, and that, consequently, everything is identical.

Concerning the fact that, in order to escape this universal identity to which he believes the use of deduction leads, Père Gratry would like to see employed in philosophy only induction, which, instead of deriving one notion from another, would add to a notion a different notion, as experience does—and this is a thought in which he agrees with all those who take their starting point in the mere observation of phenomena, and particularly with Stuart Mill—there is reason to notice, perhaps, that induction, according to Claude Bernard's observation, in agreement with Leibniz, is itself ultimately reducible to deduction—but to a hypothetical and provident deduction that is combined with experience.

Due to the provisional, hypothetical, and, consequently, merely probable consequences of induction, it is doubtful whether it is possible, as Père Gratry suggests, to confuse it with analysis, and particularly with infinitesimal analysis. The learned author believes he can rely on the considerable authority of Wallis, Newton, and Laplace on this point. If, however, we look closely at the passages of these great authors to which he refers, it is difficult to accept the interpretation he gives of them. Wallis, in his *Arithmetica infinitorum*—in which, as Leibniz said, he paved the way for differential calculus by considering numbers, just as, on the basis of openings provided by Galileo, Cavalieri had done so by considering figures—had made great use of induction in the formation of convergent series. He saw it as an excellent mode of investigation and, in certain cases, a sufficient method (*satisfactoria*) of demonstration. Nowhere did he confuse it with analysis, which can be rigorously demonstrative.—Laplace defended Wallis against Fermat, who would have wanted everywhere, instead of inductions, rigorous demonstrations by the geometrical method of the ancients; he approved the use of induction as a means of research and often even of proof; he did not therefore say that analysis and induction were the same thing.—Newton, in the concluding pages of his *Mathematical Principles of Natural Philosophy*, said that the method of discovering the laws of nature is induction, which, by collecting analogies, reduces complex facts to simpler and therefore more general ones. But he saw as well, and stated as strongly as anyone else, in these same passages, that induction can only give a greater or lesser probability, depending on the number of experiments. He seems not to have identified anywhere induction and analysis. What he did say, or imply, is that analysis is the genus of which induction is a species.

Père Gratry has reproduced and developed the idea that the method of infinitesimal calculus is the one by which we rise from the finite creature to the infinity of God. Until now, on this point, he has found fewer supporters than opponents. And, indeed, the infinitesimal method is based on the principle, formulated by the one to whom it is most indebted, that 'the reasons or relations of the finite succeed in the finite'. It consists in concluding, from the relations of two quantities of which one varies with the other according to a law, to what they become if we suppose the two quantities reduced to a value smaller than any assignable value; and, consequently, in determining, by means of the relations of finite quantities, those of their infinitesimal elements. From this results, with the law of generation of these quantities, the discovery of a great number of their properties, inaccessible to ordinary geometry and analysis. But the infinitesimal that the geometer thus calculates is only a logical entity, comparable, says the principal inventor of differential calculus, to the imaginary roots of algebra. Is the method that leads us to this ideal limit of the gradual and continuous decrease of real magnitudes the same method by which we rise to this absolute of reality, which is the infinite considered by metaphysics and theology?

Just as, in a general way, inferior things can serve to make us perceive superior things—sensory things, for example, allowing us to grasp intelligible things—without helping us genuinely to understand and prove them, and just as it is through the superior, on the contrary, that the inferior is understood and demonstrated, so too it is not what is called infinity in mathematics, which is only its shadow, that can serve as a scientific demonstration of the true infinite, the object of metaphysics. It is rather through the true infinite that the infinitesimal of the geometers is intelligible.

Descartes was able to represent our mind rising from the consideration of its limited perfections to the unlimited perfections of God. He knew no less well and expressed no less strongly that we have first of all intimate knowledge of the true infinite. Otherwise, how would we recognize it in particular forms, in particular limits? The infinite is the inner light by which we originally see both itself and everything else. It is not through the infinitesimal of mathematics that we can acquire a more perfect knowledge and a more exact demonstration of divine infinity.

In the differential calculus we are not dealing genuinely with the infinite, but with something which is an incomplete imitation of it, with a quantity considered in a degree of smallness inferior to any given value, which we express by the fiction or symbol of something infinitely small. This is a fiction, because for something infinitely small, rigorously speaking, to be possible, it would be necessary that the number of divisions or subtractions by which it could be arrived at be infinite, and an infinite number is a contradiction. But if we can continue indefinitely between two quantities the same ratio below any given value, or beyond any limitation of these quantities, this is because, the same reason always existing, we are always entitled to continue as we have begun. It is in the same way that we conceive that there are no assignable limits to either time or space. The source of this idea of a thing, independently of limits and quantities, is therefore the idea that we carry within us of the absolute and of perfection independent of all limitations. 'The true infinite is not to be found', says Leibniz, 'in wholes, composed of parts, formed by successive addition. It is, however, to be found elsewhere, namely in the absolute, which is without parts, and which has an influence on composite things, because they result from the limitation of the absolute.'[4] And elsewhere, after explaining that we extend our ideas of space and time indefinitely because we always conceive the same reason for doing so, he adds: 'This shows how our ability to carry through the conception of this idea comes from something within us and could not come from sense experience. The idea of the absolute is in us internally like that of being.'[5] And elsewhere: 'We have the idea of an absolute in perfection, because for this we need only conceive of an absolute, putting limitations aside. And we have the perception of this absolute because we participate in

---

[4] Leibniz, 'Quelques remarques sur le livre de Mons. Lock intitulé Essay of Understanding' (in the Akademie-Verlag of Berlin edition of the *Nouveaux essais sur l'entendement humain*), p. 7.

[5] Leibniz, *New Essays* II, xvii, §3, p. 158. Ravaisson contracts this passage slightly.

it as we have some participation in perfection.' Far from consideration of the differential calculus being able to contribute anything to the demonstration of the infinite, it is from the notion of the true infinite, which is the absolute, the innate treasure of our reason, that the notion of this apparent and imaginary infinite of quantity is formed, whose true name, as Descartes said, a name which expresses only the possibility of always going beyond anything finite, is the indefinite.

But is it true that infinitesimal analysis possesses the characteristic, which Père Gratry attributes to it, of passing 'as if by a leap' from one notion to a notion of a different order? According to Leibniz, on the contrary, continuity is the essence of the infinitesimal method. 'One postulate', he says, 'is its foundation: whenever it is a question of a continuous passage ending at some limit, one can institute a reasoning whereby this limit itself is understood.' Finally, can we admit that, in a general way, the characteristic of a true method is to proceed by 'jumps', by 'leaps', by 'impulses', as Père Gratry usually puts it? Is this characteristic not rather that of attaching a notion to a notion by a continuous and imperceptible sequence? 'Nature does nothing by leaps and bounds,' said the man to whom we owe both the sublime calculus, which is an application of the law of continuity, and this very law. The same could be said of science: 'everything is connected within it', said Descartes.

Gratry's theories on methods, theories to which he gave a stamp that is eminently his own, can nevertheless be explained by the maxim generally accepted since the last century, as we saw above, that we know positively and directly only those phenomena that are the object of experience. Hence it follows that we can reach principles of another order only by leaping, as it were, from this sensory world, which is like the ground under our feet, into the higher world of pure intelligibles. Emile Saisset, a severe critic of Père Gratry, is in complete agreement with him in this respect. He disapproves of his attempt to apply the method of differential calculation to metaphysical matters, but he agrees that one can pass from the finite to the infinite, from the sensible to the intelligible, only by a sort of 'jump'.

But just as eclecticism, losing the hopes it had long founded on a method of 'transcendence', according to Père Gratry's expression, has inclined, in the end, as is evident above all in Emile Saisset's *Religious Philosophy*,[6] towards replacing it by an immediate experience and a direct view of the intelligibles, so too, while still maintaining his ordinary theories, but nevertheless drawing inspiration from a significant author from the old Oratory, Père Thomassin, who himself drew inspiration from both St Augustine and the Neoplatonists, Père Gratry has attempted to establish that we do not only

---

[6] Emile Saisset (1814–63), *Essai de philosophie religieuse* (Charpentier: Paris, 1859).

conceive of God, but that we have, strictly speaking, a feeling of him, an experience of him. There exists in the soul, he says with Thomassin, a secret sense by which it touches, rather than sees or hears, God. It is possible, he says, to re-establish the famous axiom: nothing is in the understanding which was not first in the senses. It can be argued that all knowledge comes from the senses. Experience has driven out of natural science the scholastic rationalism which claimed, by means of abstract maxims, to construct nature a priori, and which reappears in Hegel 'dealing with the visible world', in the name of pure reason, 'from creator to creature'. Experience will one day also banish rationalism from the science of the soul and the science of God. This will be when, instead of limiting ourselves to the combination or analysis of abstract ideas and general maxims, we are able to find in our consciousness the higher principle which it reflects, to feel, to touch in our own depths, beyond our own personality, immolated and sacrificed, that which is better than ourselves.

Père Gratry says: 'God himself is the primary root of our freedom. We draw from God the strength to will, to will well; we draw this strength from God through love.—But what is love? It is to unite, to conform. Sacrifice is morality itself. Sacrifice is the only way to God; it is the necessary relation of the finite life to the infinite life. The act of freedom which sacrifices, that wants God before itself, brings us closer to God, brings us closer to ourselves, increases our freedom, while the opposite act, which does not sacrifice, which wants itself before God, takes us away from ourselves and decreases our freedom.' This is the word of the Gospel: 'he who wants to save his life loses it; he who consents to losing it, saves it'.

By the developments which he has given to these high maxims, full of the purest spirit of Christianity, even more so perhaps than by his ingenious but questionable theories on methods, the eloquent Oratorian has brought great merit to philosophy and natural theology.

XVII
Philosophical Theology
Saisset, Simon, and Caro

Like Père Gratry, in the name of the common interests of religion and philosophy as well as in the name of philosophy proper, the late Emile Saisset, who was prematurely taken from her, Jules Simon and Caro have attempted within remarkable works—the first in his *Religious Philosophy*, the second in part of his *Natural Religion*, the third in his *The Idea of God and its New Critics*[1]—to maintain the absolute of divine nature against theories which tend to enclose all reality within the limits of relative existence.

Jules Simon and Emile Saisset did not set out to demonstrate once again, by the arguments that metaphysics has so often reproduced, the existence of God. Both showed themselves willing, as was the head of the school which counts both among its most renowned masters, to abandon in the face of Kant's criticism the traditional proofs of this great existence, and especially the one that, according to Kant himself, is the nerve of the others, the one that Descartes had recognized and honoured, and which derives from the very idea of the divine nature. Both showed themselves willing to think that the existence of God should rather be considered as beyond demonstration, and as possessing self-evidence that argumentation could only obscure. Both also proposed above all to prove that God is a person. Emile Saisset, in particular, sought to draw out from the main philosophical systems of our time and even of the past what he calls the mother idea of pantheism, to show its defects, and to bring to light the arguments which seem to him to establish, against pantheistic systems, which confuse God with nature and humanity, the necessity of a superior Being in whom is found the perfection of intellect and will. Both of them have been able to bring out the weakness of the usual argument advanced by the opponents of divine personality, that personality is a determination, and that, since all determination is, as Spinoza said, a negation incompatible with infinity, infinite being can have nothing personal about it; or again, and this is the same idea presented from the psychological point of view taken by Hamilton and Stuart Mill, that consciousness as an attribute of personality cannot be found in God, because consciousness implies a duality, and consequently a reciprocal limitation of the object thought and the

---

[1] Jules Simon, *La religion naturelle* (Paris: Hachette, 1856) and Elme-Marie Caro, *L'idée de Dieu et ses nouveaux critiques* (Paris: Hachette, 1864).

thinking subject, which the unity and infinity of God do not admit; and likewise for will or love. The defect of this argument is that it takes as an absolute condition of existence what is merely a condition relative to a particular definite state of our finite nature, and which in the infinite vanishes. This is what the author of the *Ultimum organum*, which will be discussed below, has made clear, and what one of the most distinguished philosophers of contemporary Germany, Lotze, in his *Microcosm*, has explained with remarkable clarity.[2]

Jules Simon and Emile Saisset have above all defended the belief in the personality of God against what they believed to be more or less contrary to this belief in the systems of Spinoza, Kant, Hegel, and even Descartes, Malebranche, and Leibniz. Caro defends it, as the very title of his book indicates, against more recent theories. In addition, Caro added the question of the immortality of the human soul to the question of divine personality.

In *The Idea of God*, Caro applied himself above all to demonstrating what is superficial, erroneous, and even contradictory in the doctrines, stemming from positivism or more or less inspired by its principles, which we have already addressed, and which try to replace the God of spiritualism by natural forces more or less proximate to mere matter. In this book, he did not seek to renew or substantiate by his own research the doctrines he defends. Nevertheless, in the developments which led him to the critique that is his principal object, it is possible to make out views which go beyond the ordinary horizon of these doctrines. This is an idea that we have encountered in what we have had occasion to quote from the learned mathematician Sophie Germain, but which Caro has several times reproduced with features peculiar to him, in *The Idea of God* and a still more recent book on Goethe's philosophy: that the principles of the order manifest in things belong, before any experience, to reason. Therein lies, he remarks, the foundation of induction: 'We presume, we affirm a priori, that the cosmos is intelligible, that is to say that its phenomena are of a nature reducible to a rational unity. Is this kind of pre-existing agreement between our intellectual constitution and the rational constitution of the world, between the mind and nature, not a singular fact? And this sense of order, what else is it, in vague and obstinate forms, but the belief in an intelligent cause?'[3]

If we have a natural conception of order, a conception which proves a natural belief in an intelligent cause which understands and wills it, this is because order is not only an object and a goal for intellect, but intellect itself. In recent lectures on human personality, indeed, Caro has shown himself ready to embrace, instead of the half-spiritualism of the eclectic school, a true spiritualism that finds something immaterial in matter and that explains nature itself by spirit.

---

[2] *Ultimum organum* is the work of De Strada that Ravaisson discusses in the following section. Ravaisson also refers here to Hermann Lotze's *Mikrokosmos: Ideen zur Naturgeschichte und Geschichte der Menschheit. Versuch einer Anthropologie* (Leipzig: Hirzel, 1856–64).

[3] Elme-Marie Caro, *La philosophie de Goethe* (Paris: Hachette, 1866).

XVIII
Philosophical Theology
Ontologism

A remarkable movement has arisen in recent times among philosophical theologians, under the name ontologism, in opposition to both traditionalism and psychologism.

To what it called psychologism, born of the use of reflection, as understood not by Descartes, who made it the starting point of philosophy, but rather by Locke and his successors, and which seemed to make truth and certainty depend too much on the opinions of each individual, the traditionalist doctrine had believed it could oppose unanimous consent, the universal tradition. But in order to judge traditions, to distinguish those that are only particular and temporary from those that are truly universal and constant, and, moreover, in order to establish the very principle that the universal and constant tradition must contain the truth, we have to return to reason. After traditionalism was thus destroyed by the contradiction contained in its principle, another doctrine arose, which no longer claimed to show truth independent of reason, but rather, by showing reason to be independent of personality, re-established its authority. This doctrine consisted in placing reason in immediate relation with being, as with an object external and superior to us: hence the name it took of ontologism. It was first expounded by theologians at the University of Louvain, and constituted the basis of the teaching of Abbé Baudry, professor of philosophy at the major seminary of Saint-Sulpice, who has recently died as Bishop of Périgueux, and we find it developed in a work published in 1856, under the title *Ontology, or Study of the Laws of Thought*, by Abbé Hugonin, then director of the ecclesiastical division at the Carmelite school. In this book, Abbé Hugonin, in accord with the ideas of Abbé Baudry, explained how our intellect has for its highest immediate object ideas which are not its own operations or products of its operations, but which are independent of them, which are, at bottom, being itself, the universal being, the absolute being, God.

Abbé Rosmini believed that the intellect had as its universal and necessary object in all particular and contingent objects what he called indeterminate being, which exists, since the mind apprehends [*aperçoit*] it, but with an existence that could be called 'projected' or virtual, quite similar to that of the ideal in many of the contemporary theories we have previously reported on. The universal being innate to our intellect was thus not, in this conception, something real and subsistent, but merely a logical principle, a rule for directing our mind. If one were to disregard the mind that considers it and that it directs, it would no longer be anything.

Whatever the differences between Rosmini's ideas and those of Vacherot and de Rémusat, we see here how similar their principles are. This is because they have more or less the same way of understanding the objects of intellect as entities separate from all reality.

The ontologists try to show that the ideas by which the intellect regulates itself and which serve to understand and measure everything else are not only objects of conception, but that they are modes of a real, actual existence, which is none other than God. This is—say these authors, as well as Abbé Blampignon, author of a theological thesis on Malebranche—the doctrine of Malebranche and of St Augustine; it is also, according to them, the doctrine of Plato. Aristotle, as Abbé Hugonin says somewhere, was a psychologist; Plato, an ontologist.

Plato, indeed, seemed to make of the notions by which we understand things distinct realities contained in a total reality that would be God. It is doubtful, however, whether he put these limits and diversities into God; it is doubtful whether he should be counted among the ontologists, in the sense of the doctors of Louvain and Abbé Hugonin, the one who sought God, even beyond anything that is called being, in an absolute unity.

Aristotle wanted to place only within us the diversity and distinction of ideas. It is doubtful, however, whether it should be necessary to reduce to psychologism the one who saw, and saw the first, in God, not only, as ontologism says of being, the highest object of intellect, but supreme thought, the source of all thought.

Finally, it is doubtful whether we could perfect Rosmini's conception sufficiently by taking 'being', as he does, as principle, while adding that it does not exist only potentially, as the Italian philosopher said, but that it really subsists, that it really is. Hegel did not say without reason, it seems, that the idea of being is the most impoverished of ideas, and that to be without anything more would be equivalent to not being.

Perhaps ontologism is only a first form of a more definite doctrine, where being will be defined by life and thought. However, among the philosophical theologians who profess it, as well as among Père Gratry and the Bishop of Sura, to the various causes which always make it difficult to pass from these logical generalities, which stand between the mind and realities, to these realities themselves, there is added a special reason to remain often with ideas and expressions incompletely defined: the constant concern about working with reason in the domain of faith, and, in the things which seem to belong to the province of reason alone, of not being in sufficient agreement with decisions taken or to be taken by the canonical authority. Père Gratry, Abbé Maret, and Abbé Hugonin call the philosophy that refuses the enlightenment provided by Christianity 'separate philosophy'. That of theologians in general could be called, even more so today than in the Middle Ages, a dependent philosophy. But philosophy wants, it seems, perfect freedom.

A time will come, perhaps soon, when the idea of development will prevail in religion, no less than in any science, as, for example, it is expounded by the eminent Catholic scholar Newman—an idea which is gaining more and more minds every day. In this time a broader doctrine of interpretation will be established. Freer, theology will find more utility in philosophy, and will also be more useful for it. And it is then that we will be able to see proved at last that great statement of St Augustine, that true religion and true philosophy do not differ.

XIX
De Strada's Metaphysics

An author who had already published various works in prose or verse under the pseudonym de Strada published in 1805 an *Essay on an Ultimum Organum or Scientific Constitution of Method*, first series, *Grounds of Metaphysics*,[1] in which he expresses ideas which are not at bottom without analogy with those of the ontologists, but from a quite different point of view and with a greater freedom of thought.

If we look for the thought he wanted to express under the often unusual forms of his language, we find that, in the face of tendencies which seem, at least at first sight, to dominate the time in which we live, he has set out to restore metaphysics, the science of the supernatural, to its former glory.

'The ill of our time', he says, 'is that thought, weary from its efforts and not knowing where to settle, clings to material reality and rests on it. Truth is no more, and with it die the highest ideas. The mind, deprived of a criterion for estimating truth, of a method for attaining it, stumbles as if suffering from vertigo and finally falls into atheistic materialism.'

De Strada wastes little time criticizing the theories, all too obviously incomplete and superficial, that reduce everything to matter and the senses, and which he calls, with a name that we should maintain, 'pseudo-positivism'; but he shows how, in metaphysics itself, a physical element has crept in which alters it.

'The object of knowledge is', he says, 'being; but being, in whatever form it presents itself, has certain constitutive qualities, which are, consequently, for every existence in which being is realized, conditions, laws. And this is why everything can be deduced, everything can be proved.' Unlike most of those in recent times to have defended metaphysics against its opponents, and who, for the reasons we have indicated, generally show little confidence in the regularity of reasoning, and prefer either an induction that proceeds, as they put it, by leaps and bounds, or inexplicable revelations of a mysterious reason, de Strada maintains that there is nothing to which reasoning does not extend. The necessary qualities of being can,

---

[1] Jules de Strada is the pen name of Jules-Gabriel Delarue (1821–1902), a metaphysician, poet, and painter from the Poitou region of France whose first major metaphysical work was the 1865 *Essai d'un ultimum organum ou constitution de la méthode* (Paris: Hachette). It is remarkable that Ravaisson dedicates an entire section of his report to this work, given that otherwise, as Lucien Arréat wrote thirty years later, 'Strada had the singular fortune of passing his life almost entirely neglected by the official philosophical public, although he has published more than twenty books on philosophy, social science, and history, not to mention an enormous poetical work, *L'Epopée humaine*, which already embraces nineteen volumes' ('Literary Correspondence. France', *The Monist* 7/2 (1897), pp. 287–94, p. 292).

in his opinion, be reduced to the following three: determination by the expansion of force, identity in duration or permanence, and essence, in which the first two are combined. The necessary constitutive qualities are, he says, the object of thought; the contingent realizations are the object of experience; every contingent realization necessarily contains the constitutive qualities. At the same time, therefore, that we perceive an object as sensory, we think it as intelligible.

Perhaps it would be appropriate to add, with Bossuet and Kant, that we also imagine it. We know Kant's theory according to which the sensory elements are first brought together into a whole by the imagination, and it is a result of the synthesis of the imagination that the higher synthesis of the understanding takes place. Bossuet had already said that we do not perceive anything through the senses without immediately imagining it. With this insertion of the middle term of the imagination between sensation and thought, de Strada would perhaps justify more fully his theory that the properties of objects correspond to three means of knowledge: for the real, experience; for the numerical, calculation; for the ideal, syllogism—a theory which recalls the threefold division of science by Plato and Aristotle into physics, mathematics, or the science of the 'things of the middle region', and philosophy. Perhaps we could say, in combining the ideas of these ancient thinkers with those of Leibniz and Kant, that quantity, which is the special object of mathematics, is properly the world of the imagination, an intermediary between the domain of the senses and that of pure intellect.

In any case, according to de Strada, such is our condition that we take cognizance at the same time, by independent faculties, of different parts of things, without it being possible for us to draw them from each other, or, with one way of knowing, to do without another. The materialist will vainly try to explain the intelligible by the sensible; but the spiritualists will also vainly try to predict, to construct nature a priori by means of pure ideas. If they seem to succeed in doing so sometimes, as Hegel does, it is because they have in advance transported into the intelligible the sensible properties that they imagine they derive from it, and which they then appear to derive from it. Yet Hegel will find in nature a host of details for which all his logic cannot provide the slightest explanation, and which he will be content to ignore. Vacherot had already made a similar observation.

In contingent realizations, we all perceive, de Strada says, the necessary qualities that they imply; we do not all perceive them to the same degree. To see clearly in contingent realizations the necessary qualities is the characteristic of genius. Rising above external circumstances, or, as we say, the realms on which vulgar intelligences depend, and which are more or less sufficient to explain them, genius 'plunges straight and without bias into the absolute, and thus its work is true for all places and all times'. It is therefore—everywhere, always—genius that discovers, because it is in immediate communication with the absolute, with the divine; the crowd only follows behind.

Now, it is not enough to show in everything experienced the ideal that it implies; it is necessary, in order to constitute metaphysics, to show that the ideal, that the absolute is independent of the physical, the sensible, the contingent. Most of the time, on the contrary, the inferior element is made to penetrate the superior, and thus physics into metaphysics. Kant knew very well that everything in nature is presented in the form of oppositions, antinomies, everything being formed of opposites. Hegel did more: he brought antinomies to the heart of the absolute; he made them the elements of its constitution. These two great thinkers, especially the latter, have been accused of audacity. Far from it, says de Strada; it is their metaphysical timidity for which we must reproach them; 'this great spectacle imposed on them too much'. They accept the antinomies from experience, and set them up as universal and necessary principles; their philosophy therefore consists in taking metaphysics physically. The same must be said of those spiritualists who place in God separate and consequently finite notions; by carrying multiplicity into him, they make him finite himself.

Philosophy, says again the author of the *Ultimum organum*, has the antinomies for its object; but it must understand that they come only in second place, below the absolute, which is free of them. Without doubt, in the presence of the negative, and limited by it, the positive itself becomes negative, and it seems that the one, like the other, exists only on condition of the other, and as relative to the other. This is what, as we have seen, not only Hegel says—who, at least, according to de Strada, senses the inadequacy of this point of view, and who aspires to the resolution of his antinomies—but also Kant, and Hamilton, and all those who pretend to set up opposition and relativity as a universal law. Yet the negative and the positive to be found in all things are equal or equivalent only mathematically, says de Strada, that is to say, as the abstracts 1 and 1 are equal in a number, whatever realities they correspond to. The negative borrows from the positive everything real in it; negation is a derivative of affirmation; affirmation in itself has no need of negation. 'An affirmation is posited; I negate it. My negation instantly gives the affirmation the quality of negation of my negation (this is Hegel's argument). But is it by itself that the affirmation is negation? No; it is by a negation.' It is therefore futile to exalt negation and non-being to the point of equality with being and affirmation. Since all negation has the right to be only in and by reality, the negative is secondary, the positive is primordial. The positive is to the negative what 1 is to 0, what reality is to nothing. 'The day will come', says de Strada, 'when to explain, in metaphysics, by the union of non-being with being, will seem as puerile as it would be today in physics to explain by the vacuum united with matter. It is time that we understand that, if in nature reality shows itself to be everywhere limited, limitation is not for that reason of its essence.' The metaphysical spirit consists, therefore, according to him, in understanding that there is, above the state of antinomy and contradiction, which is that of nature and up to a certain point ours, an absolute state in which negation, which seems to us here below the very condition of existence, has no place, and where there is only reality; this is the proper state of being.

Being is the object of mind; solicited by being, mind appropriates it, in a way that is both necessary and free, 'by abstraction and extraction'. Being serves mind as food serves the stomach, as air serves the lungs. Since mind thus responds to being, the various properties of being correspond to the various functions of mind. In each reality are to be found, though in different ratios, all the qualities of being. 'Man hears God in everything and in every fact; he is as if deafened by the eternal and incessant rustling and clamouring of the absolute.' In the same way, in each act of the mind, even in the first, the simplest, all its faculties, all its operations are found in different degrees of development. There is no perception, however elementary, which does not contain all reasoning and all method. It remains to be seen how, in what way; to see, in other words, what method derives from these principles.

The method, for de Strada, is the movement, the advance of the mind. Each individual, each people has its method, which comes from some inventive initiator genius, and which, more than the external circumstances of time and place, explains its history. Humanity develops in spheres as different as our faculties, and that are to a certain extent independent of each other: religions, arts, sciences, social and political institutions; in this way, independently to a certain extent of each other, live the lungs, the heart, the brain. These free, yet harmonious, developments have one and the same principle, from which they derive cohesion and unity: this principle is method, thought. 'An idea recognized as true is, indeed, the basis and the core of any gathering of men. It has often been asked where the nation [*la patrie*] is to be found: it is here.' Method itself is the development in the human mind of the necessary laws which, at the same time, develop in things. 'God and man make history: God, by necessary laws; man, by his method. This in such a way that intelligence, by its constitution, which is method, by its knowledge, which is derived from necessary laws, generates all the materiality of events which is only a garment... It is mind that is history. The cause of changes in religions, institutions, philosophies, is the mind in search of method.'

In turn, method is reduced to a *criterion*. The criterion is the principle according to which we estimate the true, the absolute principle of certainty. If methods are the basis of history, this is because at the basis of methods lie criteria, sources of convictions and passions. Nations seek a criterion; it is in pursuit of it that they are constantly changing. 'Who makes man mobile? It is his search for the absolute. His passions drive him to it as much as his reason. In such a way that man is variable only with the aim of no longer being so: great attraction of the stable and the unchanging, sublime anxiety and mobility, which will only be more sublime if resting in necessary laws discovered and certified.'

Several criteria, several alleged principles of certitude, have dominated in turn: among primitive peoples, force; observation and logic among the Greeks; in the Middle Ages, faith; since Descartes, evidence—all incomplete, insufficient. Force is foreign to the mind; observation and logic need principles; faith needs proofs; supposed evidence sets everyone up as the supreme judge. Today, that is combat and reciprocal destruction of enemy criteria. 'In this way are to be explained the contradictory phenomena, which have remained problems, horrific problems: increasing materialism in a society which aspires to the absolute; freedom unable to establish itself in an age of ardent independence; the metaphysical sciences dying, and the highest science and thought in ruins. Already one trembles to see the efforts of our age ending in the abyss of the immorality and slavery of the ancient world. Are we perched on the ruins of spirit and of freedom? Is it but a vain dust that the centuries bring to us? Must the wind of despair dissipate all human affairs, all the thoughts of genius striving towards absolute truth?'

No, adds de Strada. A criterion remains to be found, and is close to being found, which must resolve the contradictions, ground the uncertainty. This criterion, which must, by definitively founding method, constitute science and civilization on a new and solid basis; this infallible, absolute criterion, is the fact.

In relation to things, it is an error to remain with the inferior point of view of antinomies; it is a similar error, as regards the relation of the mind to things through knowledge, to hold to the particular criteria dominant up to now and by which the limited individual makes himself a principle and a rule. These are particularly those which have been present since the time of Descartes, faith and evidence, and for which reasoning has been abandoned.

To appeal to faith is to hold on to a feeling for which no reason is given; the same goes for evidence, a term derived from sight; to rely on evidence for everything is to hold on to simple states of mind, with no other guarantor than themselves. Faith also seeks external support: 'There is faith only when there is evidence, if not of all the statements, then at least of the general truth of the doctrine. And as for the evidence, which is disputed, it refers to a reason.' So faith and evidence operate only through reasoning, even when we believe without reasoning, even when we see without reasoning. St Augustine had a sense of this truth when he said: 'We could not even believe if we did not have reasonable souls, capable of reasoning.' It is therefore reason and the operations of reasoning, that is to say experience, calculation, and syllogism, which make us capable of faith as well as of science.

De Strada adds: 'I was therefore right to maintain that Descartes leaves thought in an anti-methodical state, analogous to faith. But whereas faith attached man to God, evidence only attaches him to himself. Descartes leaves man in the pettiest, the most childish, and the most impossible of faiths, faith in himself. The consequences are palpable in societies: the Middle Ages had the elevation of its instinctive and emotional link to its God; the modern age has the bastardization of individualism and personal autocracy. It says with the crude Protagoras: man is the measure of things. Ignobility without solidity.'—'What, moreover, does it mean to say of the mind that it can see by evidence? It is to say that it sees because it sees. It is rather convenient to pass over all this beautiful and secret mechanism of thought, all its beautiful harmony with being, all its wonderful intertwining with each modality of being, and to exclaim in the end, as if one had discovered the secret: I see because I have the virtue of seeing.'

Descartes had confidently opposed to the syllogistic method of the Middle Ages, which drew endless series of useless consequences from principles that were more or less accepted, the simple light of evidence, to which Scottish and eclectic 'common sense' also returned later on, but Leibniz judiciously remarked that this was a very summary method, and that it substituted arbitrariness for science. Even if true evidence were the ultimate reason, it would still be necessary to realize whether one had reached it. Nothing was genuinely obvious except identical propositions, which are reason itself; any apparent truth had to be reduced, by means of analysis, to these identities in order to be judged and appreciated at its true value.

'Everything can be demonstrated,' says de Strada in a similar vein, 'although not by just any science. The secondary sciences accept from the primary sciences the notions on which they are based without defining them. Thus metaphysics defines the notions of time, space, etc., and passes them on to geometry, which, with its eyes closed, accepts and then establishes its own axioms, definitions, and hypotheses, and operates by the methodological instrument appropriate to it until it is demonstrated; in such a way that, in the entire circle of knowledge, everything is defined and everything is proven.' Moreover, there is nothing so reasoned as axioms; they are the results of reasonings so necessary and so frequent that we no longer notice them. In the same way, without paying attention to it, without being aware of it, we inhale and breathe in air incessantly.

It is therefore through all our faculties, it is through reasoning combined with calculation, together with perception, that, necessarily and freely, we form our knowledge and, above all, the simplest elements of our knowledge.

In the name of what principle? In the name of, by virtue of, the fact.

For de Strada, the fact is not only what strikes the senses; it is reality, whether it is addressed to the senses or to the mind. His constant preoccupation is to give certainty a principle superior either to materiality, which alone is nothing, or to individuality, which alone is also nothing; he finds this principle in the fact conceived in its totality filled with what he calls the necessary qualities, filled with the absolute, containing in its depth the substance of universal being. 'The fact', he says, 'is the link between the natural and the supernatural. One wants to deny any marvels: the life of thought is a perpetual marvel; God becomes nature in every fact; the infinite spirit in every notion becomes human spirit; in every fact spirit possesses God.'

The criterion is the fact, therefore the criterion is God. 'God the criterion, tangible by the fact, is all in one: this is the basis of the whole doctrine and of the whole methodological revolution. The day man feels this truth, he will feel that he is ignorant of nothing that is necessary for him.'—'Since I have understood it,' says the author we are analysing, 'I am at rest in clarity, for every fact manifests God, for I see man feeding on the substance of God through the fact. And therefore I listen to him now with my heart as well as with my mind. We must love him as well as study him. The basis of science is not beautiful syllogisms, beautiful experiments, but rather communion with being and with God through that blow to the inner sanctum of the heart that the thing, the idea, the great work of art, of science, or of virtue give you; it is life for two, which takes place only through knowledge and love. This is the soul of the method: experience, faith, syllogism, are its exterior and outer layer.'

The mind, in the presence of the fact, begins, in its eagerness to possess it, and to explain it to itself, with the a priori, the hypothetical: this is the first step of science. Then comes the a posteriori, the verification, the demonstration; through that, possession. Such is the necessary advance of the method: hypothesis, immense desire, certainty, appeasement, and endless joy. Method is life itself; life is assimilation, transubstantiation, the transformation of being into thought.

In order to express this union, this marriage of being and thought, de Strada finds fiery words; his work ends, as he says, with a sort of hymn of hymns to Science and Metaphysics, and with the ardent invocation: 'O God heat, O God thought, O God blood, O God voice, truth and life, O God fixed and ever present control, come. Man calls for you; his weakness thirsts for your power; his ignorance, for your knowledge; his smallness, for your infinity; his error, for your certainty; his negation, for your affirmation. Come, man cannot ascend to you without you, ever present by the fact. Come, and let us be one with you, by the thought you solicit, by the love you raise, in that communion of the absolute, which is life through science, art, and virtue.'

And finally, in a short postface, addressing contemporary philosophers: 'I have attacked you all. I am the living reaction to your methods. I have said to you: You are all in the wrong...I have attacked you all. None of you will support me. Will you speak, theocrats? I fight you. Is it you, physicists? I fight you. Is it you, evidentialists? I fight you. I fight you, but to unite you. I fight you, because I fight man and I defend God. I am the most realistic of philosophers, because I say what no one has dared to say: that the fact is the criterion. I am the most spiritualist of them all, for it remains demonstrated that man judging by the criterion-fact judges only by God. The old antagonisms will fall away when we have understood the fact and its link with being, that is to say with the absolute truth of which it is the incessant, always present, and everywhere vivacious manifestation. If I have been obscure, I will explain. If there are gaps, I will fill them to the best of my ability.' And he calls to him those who want to found with him 'the school of being and of the basic fact, mediator and criterion of knowledge, the school of the universal reality of being, the school of the God method with the permanent criterion-fact'.

However obscure de Strada may be, as perhaps more concerned with rendering his thoughts in all their force than with clarifying them, and with presenting them in their thousand dazzling faces than with ordering the elements they imply, we can at least see clearly the goal towards which he tends, which is to draw science out of the narrow circle in which it is enclosed by the exclusive or almost exclusive consideration of what belongs either to nature or to man, and to turn it towards the supernatural which pierces and radiates through all these clouds, towards that absolute and infinite of which finite and relative things are, according to Leibniz's expression, only fulgurations.

But in this enterprise, which he has embraced with such ardour, perhaps he is not as alone as he thinks. If we consider the past, we will find that, among physicists, the greatest have known that, whatever the usefulness and necessity of experience, it is reason that makes the final judgement: witness, from the Renaissance, before Galileo, Leonardo da Vinci saying: 'We have to go from experience to reason, but nature goes from reason to experience'; and that the greatest of theologians have recognized that faith has knowledge as its principle, and knowledge as its end (witness St Anselm entitling his first work 'Faith seeking to understand'). As for philosophers, Descartes himself, although in the presence of the abuses of empty reasoning he may have seemed to give too much to simple evidence, and thus to subject science to the discretion of a so-called common sense, said that the true criterion for estimating all truth, for giving all certainty, is the idea of God, and that all truths, starting from this supreme truth, follow each other and are linked together.

As for our time, from all of the works relating to metaphysics and general philosophy which we have accounted for, it emerges that, if minds have seemed heretofore divided between pseudo-positivist theories, inclining to materialism, and semi-spiritualist theories, according to which we have of the higher principles only a mere general conception from which reasoning cannot deduce any of their effects, or an almost equally inadequate feeling, it is no less true that a doctrine shows itself to the attentive eye, which only a few have sketched out in its entirety, but whose secret influence these different systems nevertheless undergo, and around which they tend more or less, but more and more, to gather. And this doctrine is the one that gives to things a principle that is intelligible and real at one and the same time, a principle superior to the external and sensory appearances with which pseudo-positivism is satisfied, and to the abstractions that the understanding forms to explain them to itself. This is the principle that the author of the *Ultimum organum* and the ontological school have in view under the name, still incomplete and obscure, of 'being'. This will be confirmed, if we are not mistaken, by the account we have yet to give of the principal works that, in the period we are dealing with, have addressed the various parts of philosophy and the various questions which are related to them.

XX
Magy on Physics and Metaphysics

Before proceeding to these more specialist works, we must mention a recent work that, though undertaken mainly in order to determine the most general principles of physics, could perhaps contribute to a more precise definition of the object of metaphysics. We are referring to Magy's *Science and Nature* (1868).[1]

Descartes had admitted two substances: body, consisting of extension; mind, consisting of thought. Spinoza had seen in extension and thought two attributes of a unique substance. Leibniz, reducing extension and time to a mode of our way of knowing, considered as substance only that which acts, only force. There was in bodies, according to him, something substantial: in addition to extension, there was something active that was the source of movement. The ground of force is, he added, perception and appetite, which Descartes had named in the single word 'thought'.

Malebranche, who abhorred Spinoza's system, distanced himself less from it than Leibniz. There were, he said, two kinds of ideas: ideas of magnitude, the object of mathematics, and ideas of perfection, the object of metaphysics. This comes back to the common division into matter, identified by Descartes with extension, and spirit, whose own nature is to be determined by the good, or perfection, and which is perfection itself. These two heterogeneous elements were united in God. It was necessary to conceive in God not only thought, the supreme perfection, but also extension; not, it is true, the material and sensible extension that body offers us, but an intelligible extension, in which material extension had its source.

Bordas-Dumoulin, in his *Cartesianism*,[2] adopted Malebranche's ideas and generalized them. What Malebranche had said about God, he said, had to be said about any substance. For him, all substance is composed of two elements: the one capable of precise evaluation and calculation is magnitude; the other, which escapes any exact measure, was perfection, or, since perfection is synonymous with completion, life or force, which is its cause. In the inorganic

---

[1] François Magy (1822–87), *De la science et de la nature: essai de philosophie première* (Paris: Ladrange, 1865).
[2] Jean-Baptiste Bordas-Dumoulin, *Le Cartésianisme ou la véritable renovation des sciences* (Paris: Hetzel, 1843).

world, quantity or extension predominates; in the organic world, force. Among the sciences, there are some in which quantity alone is the object: these are arithmetic and geometry; there are others in which it serves only as a support and symbol for the ideas of force and perfection. These are the sciences which consider living beings, such as natural history and medicine, and even more so those which relate to things of the intellectual and moral order, namely metaphysics, theology, morals, and politics. Of these two kinds of ideas, the first are both the easiest to grasp and the easiest to deal with; they can be represented exactly by symbols, numbers, or letters; so that by operating on these symbols according to certain very simple rules, one arrives at infallibly true results, a property which is due to the fact that quantity is by essence divisible into equal parts. Whence the constant disposition of the human mind to relate everything to ideas of magnitude, to see everywhere only extension and mechanism. In contrast, the ideas of perfection escape any rigorous definition, any exact representation by any kind of symbol. This is why, according to Bordas-Dumoulin, the enterprise, dreamed of by Descartes and Leibniz, of a universal philosophical language that could demonstrate and calculate everything, is futile.—Several of these ideas had been mentioned by Destutt de Tracy; Bordas-Dumoulin followed him in the war he declared on logic as a vain and sterile imitation of calculus.

Magy, in his pamphlet, has supported and ingeniously developed ideas similar to those of Bordas-Dumoulin by applying them to nature. Only, instead of calling his two principles magnitude and perfection, according to the terms the latter borrows from Malebranche, he calls them extension and force. Moreover, Magy tries to explain how we can understand that, through movement, the second of the two principles is a product of the first: this is what he calls the dynamic explanation of space. In the end, instead of considering the two principles as essential to any substance, he tried to show, as Leibniz had already done, that of these two principles, the first, which responds to sensory phenomena, is but subjective, or, as Leibniz put it, imaginary, while the properly intelligible principle, force, is the very foundation of all reality.

It may be said that Bordas-Dumoulin, who believed his two principles to be everywhere inseparable, showed himself to be a physicist in metaphysics, like the Stoics in the past and like Spinoza and even, to a certain extent, Malebranche, and that Magy, in his essay on general physics, showing the superior principle to be independent of the lower, has proved himself to be above all a metaphysician. When he takes metaphysics as the special object of his meditations, he will undoubtedly follow in the footsteps of Leibniz and, after having completed the task of bringing to light the full independence of the higher principle, reveal and demonstrate its essentially spiritual nature.

Finally, we should mention, among the works of which the metaphysics of our time can be proud, the *Lectures* given in Lyon for many years by Abbé Noirot, of which it is regrettable that we still have all too brief summaries; also the extensive work, in which we can see a number of strong and ingenious ideas, which one of his pupils, Blanc Saint-Bonnet, published a long time ago under the title *Of Spiritual Unity*; and other publications by Lefranc, Charma, etc.[3]

---

[3] Antoine Blanc de Saint-Bonnet (1815–80), *De l'unité spirituelle*, 3 vols (Paris: Pitois, 1845 [1841]).

XXI
Physics and Philosophy
De Rémusat and Martin

In the period we are dealing with, given that the dominant philosophy kept itself quite separate from the sciences, there have been few important publications concerning what has been called the metaphysics of physics. We should mention as worthy of note, however, Charles de Rémusat's inquiries concerning matter, part of his *Essays*,[1] wherein, as we have already had occasion to say, he is attached to the ideas expressed by Kant in his *Metaphysical Principles of the Science of Nature*,[2] as well as *Spiritualist Philosophy of Nature* by Henri Martin, author of numerous and learned publications relating to the history of the mathematical and physical sciences in antiquity.[3]

---

[1] Charles François Marie de Rémusat, *Essais de philosophie* (Paris: Ladrange, 1842).
[2] Immanuel Kant, *Metaphysical Foundations of Natural Science*, ed. M. Friedman (Cambridge: Cambridge University Press, 2004).
[3] Thomas Henri Martin, *Philosophie spiritualiste de la nature* (Paris: Dezobry, 1849). As noted in the introduction to this volume, Louis Léger imagines Ravaisson working with Martin (1813–84) at the Rennes Faculty of Humanities, where he became the rector, but Bergson convincingly rejects this.

XXII
Psychology
Habit, Memory, and the Association of Ideas

Among the numerous productions relating to psychology, among which we must mention, in addition to those we have already cited in speaking of eclecticism, the special works of Abbé Bautain and Waddington-Kastus,[1] Paffe's *Essay on Sensibility*,[2] etc., and many articles in Adolphe Franck's *Dictionary of the Philosophical Sciences*, several of which are due to that author, in recent times two remarkable theses have been defended at the Paris Faculty of Humanities, one by Mervoyer, the other by Gratacap, examining the question of the association of ideas and memory, to which is closely connected the general question of the constitution and mode of development of the intellect.

Hume, as we have recalled, had reduced all that exists to impressions and to the ideas that were, according to him, only their copies; this is, as we have also stated, the principle of the philosophy which takes the name of positivism. Noting, moreover, that after certain ideas certain others are ordinarily presented—and instead of confining himself to this phenomenon, as he should have done if he wished to be in perfect accord with his general theory, which reduces all causality to a pure illusion, as Stuart Mill wishes to do—he imagined that just as Newton explained chemical phenomena by a kind of reciprocal attraction of bodies, this fact, that particular ideas are ordinarily succeeded by such others, can be explained by supposing between them a comparable attraction. Perhaps, since it was a question of a phenomenon relating to particular circumstances, different according to the different characteristics of the ideas between which it takes place, a more apt comparison would have been to the elective affinities of the chemists rather than universal gravitation. What are these circumstances, what are these characteristics to which the mutual attraction, or, as we say using a term which implies no theory of the cause of the fact, the association of ideas, is subordinate? These are, according to Hume, resemblance, contiguity of place and time, and causality; an enumeration which the Scots sought to complete by adding to the relations of things to each other their relations to us, and which, moreover, could

---

[1] Ravaisson is referring to Louis Eugène Marie Bautain (1796–1867), *Psychologie experimentale* (Paris: Dérivaux, 1839), published in a second edition as *L'esprit humain et ses facultés* (Paris: Didier, 1859), and C. Waddington-Kastus, *De la psychologie d'Aristote* (Paris: Joubert, 1848).

[2] Ravaisson seems to be referring to Markus Paffe, *Considérations sur la sensibilité mise à sa place, et présentée comme essentiellement distincte du principe intellectuel* (Paris: Le Normant, 1832).

easily be reduced to a simpler classification if we observe the close relationship that exists between resemblance and contiguity, as well as, following Hamilton, that between resemblance and causality.

Herbart, in Germany, expounded a system of psychology whose principle was a conception quite similar to that of Hume, but it was a more distinct conception, including as one of its elements quantity, and by that very fact susceptible of quite different developments, of a quite different variety of applications. According to Herbart, everything can be reduced to ideas or representations that come together, obstruct each other, hold each other in equilibrium, or drive each other apart according to exact laws of statics and dynamics, the effects of which are therefore calculable. All representations, at bottom, exist simultaneously; only some of them obstruct or cooperate with others; they prevent each other, or add to each other, or intermingle with each other; whence all our ideas and our desires. By the combination of representations is formed what we call reason and what we call sensibility and will. We find the same conception in England, elaborated in a more or less different way by the philosophers who belong to or can be related to the positivist school: Stuart Mill, Samuel Bailey, Alexander Bain, Herbert Spencer. The latter in particular has expounded, with remarkable lucidity, the theory that the whole vast body of our knowledge is the result of accumulated experiential perceptions, just as islands, whole continents, have been formed by the successive accumulation of almost imperceptible zoonites.

Nature, says Spencer, offers us facts forming regular series. Facts are answered in us by representations; series of facts are answered by series of representations; the more the latter are repeated, the more the former also, in being repeated, become unchangeable. In this way general propositions are formed by the repetition of particular propositions. If we now consider that acquired ideas, having become part of the intellectual constitution, are inherited, and in subsequent generations become innate ideas, we shall understand how instincts, and particularly those intellectual instincts which are sometimes called a priori judgements, can be explained in a general way. What are these judgements? They are naturally those relating to the most elementary phenomena. The simplest phenomena are also, as Auguste Comte remarked, and as had been remarked long before him, the most general, those which occur everywhere and in everything; they are therefore those whose representation is impressed upon us the earliest and the most strongly. We find in ourselves judgements representing the most elementary sequences or connections, rooted by heredity for many generations, but without seeing their origin, without being able to get rid of them. The opposite seems inconceivable to us; they are what we call, therefore, irresistible beliefs, absolute judgements, necessary truths. Such is the theory of the formation of ideas, or, in Spencer's phrase, of the 'growth of intelligence', a theory which is common, with only slight differences, to Spencer, Bailey, Bain, and Stuart Mill, and which, indeed, is the basis of what may be called positivist or empirical psychology.

This is still Hume's system, for it invokes, in order to explain the necessary relations to which things seem to be subject, not the relations of their ideas reduced until we come, as Leibniz said, to identical truths and the very attributes of God, but the merely external and accidental relations of our perceptions in space or time.

Mervoyer has reproduced, in a thesis entitled *The Association of Ideas* (1865),[3] some of the main features of this doctrine, which he approves, especially as expounded by Bain.

Gratacap, in his 1865 thesis *Memory*, took a completely opposite view.[4]

Reid had said, without attempting to prove it, that the association of ideas must be grounded in habit. In contrast, Dugald Stewart, much more inclined than his teacher to explanation by means of phenomena alone, to which his successor Brown soon gave himself up almost entirely, was of the opinion that it was rather habit that should be explained by the succession and association of ideas. The author of a thesis on habit, submitted in 1838 to the Paris Faculty of Humanities, in drawing the association of ideas back to this phenomenon, explained habit by the inclination one has to repeat and to imitate oneself, an inclination that itself can be reduced to the tendency, to the effort of all things to persevere in the action that constitutes their very being.

Gratacap has sought to show that both memory and the association of ideas, which hardly differs from it, find their explanation in habit. 'Most often', he says, 'we want to explain memory by the traces that remain in the brain of the impressions made on us by things outside, by movements that continue, vibrations that are prolonged: instead, it is the soul that we must ask for its secret.' We attempt to explain the fact that we call association, namely that one idea presenting itself to us immediately brings another with it, by the properties of the objects to which these ideas correspond, properties which are translated in our organism by movements and impressions. On the contrary, according to Gratacap, association can be explained only by the operations of the subject who knows. As Reid and Royer-Collard pointed out, we do not remember the things themselves, strictly speaking, but the perceptions we have had of them; in the same way, if on the basis of one thing we remember another, this is because we had already united them in the same perception, in the same consciousness. And, indeed, the more the perception was unitary, the more indissoluble the association, the more indestructible the memory. What we have done, we naturally tend to do again. What comes to us from outside soon fades and disappears; what comes to us from within grows and is strengthened: this is like a spring which, as it acts, becomes tighter and tighter instead of slackening. Thus is formed what is called habit; thus are formed memories. 'Everything that imposes itself on the thinking principle, coming from outside and finding an obstacle in its inertia,' says Gratacap, 'worries and

---

[3] Pierre Maurice Mervoyer, *Etude sur l'association des idées* (Paris: Durand, 1864).
[4] Antoine Gratacap (1788–1877), *Théorie de la mémoire* (Montpellier: Boehm, 1866).

troubles it for a moment, but soon disappears along with its cause without leaving any trace of its passage. But when the thinking principle exercises itself spontaneously, it contracts, while acting, a secret aptitude to act again: this is active habit, and this habit is memory itself.' Hence, as Gratacap remarks, 'memories are all the more rapid, and more sure, and more in our power, when they are those of more intellectual operations'.

Perhaps he will feel the necessity to add to this theory that two perceptions do not recall each other only in the case where they have in fact been together, which is the case to which positivism reduces all their relations, but also, and especially when they rightfully, so to speak, enter into the same consciousness, when they seem to be parts of the same idea, and that by the one the mind completes the other. Just as the eye, on perceiving a colour, immediately sees all around it the colour which is its complement; just as the ear, on perceiving a sound, immediately hears different sounds with which it forms chords; in the same way, and even more so, the intellect, when a notion is present to it, immediately conceives what, in one way or another, completes it: not only, therefore, the external and accidental circumstances among which it once conceived it, but still more what is either similar or contrary to it, what depends on it or on which it depends. In other words, the principle of association and memory is none other than reason.

It may be added that, by these relations in knowledge as well as in reality, everything standing more or less at a distance, from one object the mind passes not only to a second object, but from this one to a third, and so on indefinitely, so that, with each impression that shakes it, it evokes, all together perhaps, though without bringing it entirely to the light of full consciousness, the almost infinite multitude of its ideas.

It is materiality, on which our senses are partly dependent, which begets oblivion;[5] pure mind, on the contrary, is all action, and thus all unity, all duration, all memory. It is always present to everything and to itself, unfailingly holding under its gaze all that it is, all that it was, perhaps even, if one dares to go as far as Leibniz, all that it will be, and thus sees all things, according to a dictum we have already quoted, in the form of eternity.

The positive doctrines or doctrines of exclusive empiricism believe that they explain the formation of our knowledge and our memories by accumulated sensations alone; they forget the intellectual action that, after having composed from sensory elements a particular perception, makes of several perceptions groups, wholes, whose different parts then recall each other. 'Materialism', says Gratacap, 'is a strange error: it takes from the soul its ways of being, projects them and spreads them outside of it, constitutes matter with them; and the soul thus stripped out in favour of bodies it then denies.'

---

[5] I have borrowed N. M. Paul and W. Scott Palmer's magnificent translation of '*qui met en nous l'oubli*' as 'begets oblivion'; see Henri Bergson, *Matter and Memory* (London: George Allen and Unwin, 1911), p. 232.

As we have seen, the theories that claim to explain vital actions by the organs seem to be shaken at their base; we are beginning, it seems, to agree more than in the past that it is precisely vital action that constitutes the organ, that to live, according to Claude Bernard's expression, is to create—but to create what? The organism. In the same way, although the theory claiming to explain intellect by the senses, which we can call its organs, has made considerable progress in the hands of Herbart, or of other German or English psychologists, and although it accounts, with a completely new precision, for the empirical conditions of the development of the intellect, it seems that thereby we see better, or will see better, that a share of this development belongs to the intellect itself, and that this part is almost everything; that the action of the mind consists, at bottom, in finding everywhere, in expressing the whole of mind, and, consequently, even as it takes nature as its object, in acquiring, on the occasion of and by means of nature, a more extensive knowledge of what it can do and of what it is, and in entering, with the help of what it encounters that seems opposed to it, into a more profound and intimate possession of self. We see better that sensations are only material for intellectual activity, and that it is intellectual activity that has prepared these materials for itself in an earlier phase; and that if the soul needs the fabric offered to it by the external world in order to present itself to itself, it has woven this fabric from its own substance.

'If we want', said the author of the *New Essays on Human Understanding*, 'the principles of things to be deposited on our intelligence as on a kind of cloth, it must be an elastic and active cloth, one that modifies what it receives.'[6]

---

[6] Ravaisson is here paraphrasing Leibniz, *New Essays* II, xii, §2, pp. 144–5.

XXIII
Animism, Vitalism, and Organicism

In the first half of the present century, philosophy had little to do with physiology. Neither Maine de Biran, who defined the human being by the will in order to establish its independence with regard to sensation, nor eclecticism, which confined itself to the observation of what it called the facts of consciousness, concerned itself greatly with physiological facts except to signal what distinguishes them from those of psychological facts.

In a work *Of Habit* mentioned above, habit was presented as a sort of middle term between instinctive and natural operations, which seemed to suggest, as Stahl said, beneath the diversity of effects, an identical principle.

The question of the relationship between the physical and the moral became, at about the same time, the subject of completely new studies.

1843 saw the birth of the *Annales médico-psychologiques*, a journal concerned with anatomy, physiology, and the pathology of the nervous system, which was intended to collect all the documents relating to insanity, neurosis, and the legal treatment of the insane,[1] and which was edited from 1845 to 1848 by Baillarger and Cerise; from 1849 to 1854 by Baillarger, Brierre de Boismont, and Cerise; and since 1855 has been edited by Baillarger, Moreau (of Tours), and Cerise. The philosophy of mind will find useful material and observations within it. The same is true of Brierre de Boismont's work *Hallucinations*, which reached its third edition in 1862, and of his treatise *On Suicide and the Madness of Suicide*,[2] the second edition of which appeared in 1865; of various publications by Falret, Durand (de Gros), etc., and of pamphlets, some favourable to, others opposed to materialism. Among the latter, particularly noteworthy are Jules Fournet's *Law of the Two Substances and their Hierarchical Concurrence*,[3] and Chauffard's lecture on

---

[1] The full title of the journal is *Annales médico-physiologiques, journal de l'anatomie, de la physiologie et de la pathologie du système nerveux, destiné à receuillir tous les documents relatifs à l'aliénation mentale, aux névroses et à la médecine légale des aliénés*. In the body of the text, and in order not to break the editorial rule of producing the titles of journals in the original language, I have translated the long subtitle but not presented it in italics as an actual subtitle.

[2] Alexandre Brierre de Boismont (1797–1881), *Des hallucinations, ou Histoire raisonnée des apparitions, des visions, des songes, de l'extase, du magnétisme et du somnambulisme* (Paris: Germer Baillière, 1852) and *Du suicide et de la folie du suicide* (Paris: Germer Baillière, 1856).

[3] Jules Fournet (1811–85), *La loi des deux substances et de leur concours hiérachique, ou Du principe de la vie* (Paris: Masson, 1863).

positivism, as well as his *Fragments of a Medical Critique*.[4] In the end, the old quarrels of organicism, vitalism, and animism arose once again.

Aristotle, this time in agreement with Plato, had thought that the concert, the order which appears in the operations of living beings, however each particular phenomenon may be explained, marks a tendency towards a goal and, consequently, an action dependent on some intellect. Moreover, between the phenomena of life and those belonging to the thinking soul he noticed a connection, a continuity which precludes their being attributed to two different principles. According to him, therefore, life came from the soul, from what feels and thinks.

The soul, as Descartes held, is that which thinks. It is therefore impossible to attribute to the soul vital phenomena of which we are not aware.

However, Leibniz observed that there exist confused, indistinct perceptions, of which we are unaware. Stahl did so also, and he did more: he showed that there are operations which, though they proceed from intellect, cannot be the subject of either memory or reflection; these are the operations that, without relation to anything extensive and figurative, cannot be objects of the imagination. Only imaginable things, involving figure and extension, can be the matter of what is called reasoning. Vital, internal operations, although they escape reasoning, because they do not involve any perception of appreciable distance, are nevertheless operations of reason. Without consciousness? No; but without that express and distinct consciousness to which only reflection and memory apply.

Leibniz differs from Stahl on one point: according to Stahl, the soul is really and in every sense the cause of movement in the body it animates; according to Leibniz, the soul has no direct action on the body, and only accompanies with its will and its consciousness movements that are consequences of previous movements. But for Leibniz, as for Stahl, nothing happens in the body without something in the soul corresponding to it; in the soul, that is, in thought, and, however weakly and obscurely, in consciousness.

Since Bichat's time, organicism, in appealing to that great physiologist, reigned almost unchallenged in the Paris medical school, whereas vitalism, systematized by Barthez, governed that of Montpellier. Organicism explains life by properties of the organs; vitalism explains it by a special principle different from matter, which is no less different from spirit. Animism, which relates life to the soul, had almost no supporters. An Italian theologian, a Theatine named Ventura already known from various philosophical publications, attacked in 1853—in the name of the Catholic faith, which demanded, he said, the unity of the principle of thought and that of life—the Montpellier vitalist doctrine. Barthez's pupil and successor, Lordat, in his *Responses to Objections Made against the Principle of the*

---

[4] Paul-Emile Chauffard (1823–79), *De la philosophie dite positive dans ses rapports avec la médecine* (Paris: Chamerot, 1863) and *Fragments de critique médicale: Broussais—Magendie—Chomel* (Paris: Germer Baillière, 1864).

Duality of Human Dynamism, defended the doctrine of his master and most of his colleagues, and it should be added that the Bishop of Montpellier publicly congratulated him.[5] Abbé Flottes, professor of philosophy at Montpellier, at least tried to prove in a short pamphlet that vitalism and animism were equally compatible with religion and morality. Nevertheless, after Abbé Gunther, in Vienna, and then Canon Baltzer, in Breslau, advanced opinions which can be related to vitalism, a papal brief dated 30 April 1860 declared that the doctrine of the substantial unity of the principle of life and that of thought was the faith, and condemned all contrary opinions as inconsistent with Catholic dogma.

Whatever we are to make of this intervention of theological authority in a question which seems to be a matter of science rather than belief, the controversy continued and expanded. Several of the most prominent members of the eclectic school started to take part in it.

In 1857 the Academy of Moral and Political Sciences put the philosophy of St Thomas up for examination: it was an opportunity for scholars to study, among other questions, the relation of soul and body, which the Angel of the Schools had explored in depth following Aristotle, and resolved in the same sense as he had. The author of the winning entry, Charles Jourdain, took sides with Aristotle, with St Thomas, and with animism. In his report on the competition, de Rémusat, without formally pronouncing himself in favour of animism, declared that he saw it as a plausible doctrine.

In the same year, Francisque Bouillier—the author of a scholarly *History of Cartesianism* that was jointly honoured with Bordas-Dumoulin's *Cartesianism*, and of a *Theory of Impersonal Reason*,[6] focused on presenting and defending Victor Cousin's ideas about reason—taught at the Lyon Faculty of Humanities the identity of the thinking soul and of the vital principle; he published a summary of his lectures the following year. That year, Jaumes defended the Montpellier doctrines against him in his dissertation *On the Soul and the Vital Principle*[7] and in an *Introduction to Medical Philosophy*, published in 1861. Richard de Laprade, in a dissertation entitled *Animism and Vitalism* that the Academy of Lyon included after the author's death in its 1860 anthology, also took up the argument against Bouillier in defence of the Montpellier doctrines.[8]

---

[5] Jacques Lordat (1773–1880), *Réponses à des objections faites contre le principe de la dualité du dynamisme humain* (Montpellier: Sevalle, 1854).

[6] Francisque Bouillier, *Histoire et critique de la revolution cartèsienne* (Lyon: Boitel, 1842), which was developed as *Histoire de la philosophie cartèsienne* (Paris: Durand, 1854), and *Théorie de la raison impersonnelle* (Paris: Joubert, 1844).

[7] François Anselme Jaumes (1804–68), *De l'âme et du principe vital, étude psychologique et médicale faite à l'occasion d'un travail de M. Bouillier contre le double dynamisme* (Montpellier: Boehm, 1858). Ravaisson seems to miscite the title of Jaumes's 1861 *Introduction à l'étiologie morbide* (Montpellier: Boehm, 1861). Jaumes, professor at the Montepellier Faculty of Medicine, seems not to have written an *Introduction à la philosophie médicale*.

[8] Jacques Julien Richard de Laprade (1781–1860), *L'animisme et le vitalisme* (Mémoires de l'académie de Lyon, classe des lettres, 1861).

Albert Lemoine, in a 1858 dissertation read to the Academy of Moral and Political Sciences entitled *Stahl and Animism*, set out in great detail and with great accuracy Stahl's ideas, and drew attention to a considerable part of the truth which they seemed to contain. Nevertheless, he did not agree that vital operations could be attributed to a reasoning cause. From Stahl's doctrine, he said, he accepted the vitalism but not the animism.

Emile Saisset, in an article in the *Revue des deux mondes* of 15 August 1862, entitled 'Soul and Body', similarly declared himself in favour of vitalism.

Adolphe Garnier made similar declarations in a report to the Academy of Moral and Political Sciences on Bouillier's book,[9] as did in the same year two distinguished physicians: Bouchut, in his *Life in its Attributes in their Relation to Philosophy: Natural History and Medicine*, and Jules Fournet, in *The Law of Two Substances*, which we have already mentioned.

In 1863, Charles Lévêque, within the *Journal de l'instruction publique*, also sought to demonstrate that animism misappropriated the authority of Aristotle; Philibert also argued this in a thesis presented to the Paris Faculty of Humanities in 1864 on the principle of life in Aristotle.[10]

Tissot, the translator of Kant and Henri Ritter, defended animism in various articles in the *Revue médicale*[11] and in an extensive work entitled *Life in Man*, published in 1861.[12] In the same year, Charles presented a thesis, *De vita naturae*, at the Paris Faculty of Letters, in which he showed himself to be quite favourable to vitalist opinions.[13] A physician-philosopher whom we have already mentioned, Carreau, in a treatise *Of the Difference between Organism and Mechanism*, also published in 1861, sought to counter Stahl's animism with the occasionalism of Descartes and Malebranche, the system according to which, in the very phenomena that are called voluntary movements, the will alone is ours, and the movement is God's.

In 1862, Bouillier developed his opinions and answered the criticisms addressed to them in a work entitled *Of the Vital Principal and the Thinking Soul*,

---

[9] This report was published separately as Adolphe Garnier, *Rapport sur trois ouvrages: 1) Du principe vital, par M. Bouillier; 2) La vie, par M. Bouchut; 3) Du principe vital, par l'abbé Thibaudier* (Orléans: Colas, 1862). Ravaisson also refers to the second of the works that Garnier reviews: E. Bouchut, *La vie et ses attributs dans leurs rapports avec la philosophie, l'histoire naturelle et la médécine* (Paris: J.-B. Baillière, 1862).

[10] Henri Philibert (1822–1901), *Du principe de la vie suivant Aristote* (Paris: Durand, 1865).

[11] Albert Lemoine, *Stahl et l'animisme* (Paris: J.-B. Baillière, 1858). Lemoine (1824–74) taught philosophy at the universities of Nancy and Bordeaux, and then at the Ecole Normale Superieure. Ravaisson cites Lemoine's work—on sleep and madness, as well as on the questions of vitalism and animism—several times in the report, but in his 1875 posthumous *L'habitude et l'instinct: études de pscyhologie comparée* (Paris: G. Baillière) Lemoine did not repay the compliment. Without ever referring to it directly, Lemoine attempts to gain critical distance from Ravaisson's approach in the 1838 *Of Habit*. On this point, see chapters 2 and 3 of my *Being Inclined: Félix Ravaisson's Philosophy of Habit* (Oxford: Oxford University Press, 2019).

[12] Joseph Tissot, *La vie dans l'homme* (Paris: Masson, 1861).

[13] This is the secondary, Latin doctoral thesis of Emile August Charles (1825–97): *De vitae natura, dissertatio* (Bordeaux: Delmas, 1861).

or Examination of Medical and Psychological Doctrines on the Relations of the Soul and Life.[14]

Bouillier declared himself almost entirely Stahlian. He has forcefully brought out the reasons which oppose the explanation of life either by matter or by an immaterial principle different from the thinking soul. He stops on one point, and this point is essential: like Lemoine and Lévêque, like all the partisans of vitalism, he cannot admit with Stahl that the vital functions are the work of thought; but, for him, they are no less, like the most perfectly intellectual operations, the work of the soul.

The point is that it is an error, in his eyes, to define the soul, as Descartes did, by thought; he refuses all the more to subscribe to the Leibnizian theory according to which thought is the essence not only of human souls as Descartes wanted, but of an infinity of simple principles or monads spread throughout the universe, and which represent by more or less confused or distinct, obscure or clear perceptions, the infinity of phenomena of which the universe is composed. According to Bouillier, the essence of the soul, of all souls, of all monads, is not thought, not will, but action, of which thinking and willing are only the most perfect forms, belonging only to a higher state, which is the state of reason. Vital functions are not for him operations of reason, even defined as Stahl defines it, 'but', he says with Lemoine, 'of an instinct without intelligence, without consciousness of itself, of a blind instinct'.

However, once it has reached the state of reason, the soul, according to Bouillier, becomes, to a certain extent, conscious of its instinctive operations; from the lower order in which they are carried out, they resound, as it were, in the higher order; and, in turn, the higher reacts on the lower, the spiritual on the vital and the physical. The unity of the living and thinking being is thereby perfected.

In these terms, Bouillier invites the philosophers of the school to which he belongs, and in general the partisans of spiritualist doctrines, to abandon an all too narrow and abstract psychology and to join him in the animism which he considers to be the true spiritualism.

One might ask, however, whether explaining life by actions of the soul that are in no way intellectual is not still to profess, under the name of animism, a simple vitalist doctrine. Where does Stahl's reasoning begin? From order and concert, the characteristics of life, which mark a tendency towards a goal: hence reason, intellect. It is therefore not enough to say that vital functions are the product of a force, the work of an instinct; we must necessarily add: of a force that tends towards a goal, of an instinct that accommodates itself to an end, and thus of a thought. But perhaps Bouillier is also, at heart, more animist—animist in Aristotle's and Stahl's sense—than his expressions would lead us to believe.

---

[14] Francisque Bouillier (1813–99), *Du principe vital et de l'âme pensante, ou Examen des diverses doctrines médicales et psychologiques sur les rapports de l'âme et de la vie* (Paris: Didier et cie, 1862).

He doubtless did not mean to say that the instinct of the soul, in its vital functions, is absolutely and rigorously blind, entirely devoid of intellect and consciousness; how then could it be that this instinct sometimes, as Bouillier shows, enters the circle of consciousness? On closer inspection, he seems very close to believing what Stahl and Aristotle believed. In order for him to fully agree with the doctrine of these profound thinkers, he has only to recognize, and he seems to be not far from doing so, that in the end instinct is still thought, not as it possesses itself in the full freedom of reflection, but captive, as Plotinus represents it, in the bosom of nature, as if under the spell of its own object, and having become, so to speak, by the effect of a kind of fascination, eccentric to itself, alienated from itself.

Let us add that after having taken this step Francisque Bouillier will doubtless recognize—as will those of his opponents whose thought is very close to his own, notably Lemoine and Lévêque—not only, as he says at the beginning of his learned work, that the soul knows and sees itself directly, because its action, which consciousness has as an object, and its substance are one and the same, but also that distinguishing the action of the soul from thought and will, as something deeper and more general, is perhaps to remain attached to one of the incomplete notions whose insufficiency was demonstrated by Descartes, Berkeley, Leibniz. It is necessary to recognize that the action that is the being of the soul, the whole of the soul, the action that is the constant object of its awareness, is not separate from the conception of a goal, of a good to be attained, and is but thought and will.

To these ideas we can relate, as being little different, those developed by Adolphe Franck in a review of Bouillier's work, inserted in the *Journal des débats* of 11 and 13 November 1862; by Chauffard in an article in the *Correspondent* of 25 October 1862, entitled 'Soul and Life'; and by Frédault, in three articles within *L'art médical* of August, September, and October 1862.

XXIV
Old and New Materialisms
On Paul Janet

Paul Janet, in a review of Bouillier's work presented to the Société médico-psychologique, held that the reasons developed by the latter in support of his animism were convincing within the limits of the hypothesis that he had first wished to establish: that vitalism in general had won the day either against organicism, or, a fortiori, against absolute materialism. But Janet did not believe that Bouillier had sufficiently demonstrated the hypothesis, and this is what he has since endeavoured to do himself in an extensive work, first inserted in the *Revue des deux mondes* of August and September 1865, under the title 'Contemporary Materialism', and reprinted in the following year in the *Library of Contemporary Philosophy* with new developments.[1]

In this pamphlet, in presenting the forms that materialism has recently taken in the hands of some German physiologists, and particularly in those of Büchner, a pupil of Moleschott and author of *Matter and Force*, a work published in 1850, which has had seven editions in five years and which has been translated into our language,[2] Paul Janet relates and evaluates the arguments by which it has always attempted, and still attempts, to prove that what is called matter is sufficient to account for everything.

The arguments that Janet opposes to organicism, to the view that matter, once organized, is sufficient for life, can be reduced to the following: first—and this is the argument that, deepened, leads to the animism of Stahl and Aristotle—the concert, the whole is not sufficiently explained by the supposed life of particular and more or less independent organs; second, supposing that the organs are sufficient to explain life, what explains the formation of the organs themselves, if not precisely life?

Independently and, as it were, beneath the organism, how can matter be conceived?

---

[1] Paul Janet's *Le cerveau et la pensée*, a development of his *Revue des deux mondes* articles on materialism, appeared in the Germer Baillière collection *Bibliothèque de philosophie contemporaine* (a collection taken over in 1884 by Félix Alcan) in 1867, not 1866 as Ravaisson claims.
[2] Ludwig Büchner's best-selling work of popular science and philosophy, *Kraft und Stoff: Empirisch-naturphilosophische Studien* (Frankfurt am Main: Meidinger), went through twenty-one editions in fifty years and was first published in 1855, not 1850 as Ravaisson states.

The materialism of our time no longer, in general, explains everything by the passive elements of bodies, but takes as its sole and universal principle an active matter having force within it.

The founders of materialism, Leucippus and Democritus, had claimed to explain the world simply by the figures and situations of corporeal elements; they added, however, in order to account for their encounters and the resulting assemblages, the movements by which they would have been carried in all directions in space. Epicurus, in order to reduce to a minimum the absurdity of these movements without cause, attributed just one natural and primordial movement to his atoms, by which, if nothing came to alter them, they would fall eternally parallel to each other. And in order to explain that there were encounters between them, he dared to give them a mysterious faculty of turning away, of 'deviating' from the natural line of their fall; of declining, in truth, to the smallest degree possible. This was enough for them to meet in the long run, and with declination reduced to so little, the theorists who judged nothing if not by the senses found it acceptable.

Such was materialism in those distant times. In the first period, it had to add to matter movements that nothing material could explain; in the second, it had to add to a supposedly natural movement a second movement, even more visibly bearing the character of spontaneity, of free will.

Understanding that movement cannot be conceived without an activity or driving force, the Stoics saw in matter and force two inseparable elements. This is the doctrine to which materialism is reduced today. Neither matter without force, nor force without matter, says Büchner. But this doctrine is no longer, strictly speaking, materialism, explaining everything by matter alone.

Paul Janet has shown that to attribute force to matter, as an integral element, and to add to it what Leibniz demanded, is to admit that the idea of matter is not that of a thing sufficient in itself, but rather that of a thing to which something else has to supply what it lacks—that it is consequently an idea of an incomplete thing, of a part of being, of an abstraction which adopts the appearance of a true and complete reality only in the term by which we express it.

This is because the idea of matter is really only the idea of that from which a thing is made by giving it a form, and which thus passes from a relatively indeterminate and imperfect state to a state of determination and perfection. Consequently, to look beyond all form for a primary or absolute matter is to arrive truly at nothing.

What, indeed, is the idea of something that has no determinate way of existing? It is the completely abstract idea of pure and simple existence, which is equivalent, as we said in connection with ontologism, to that of nothingness. If, therefore, it seems that in such a theory everything can be explained by matter alone, it is because to the idea of matter there is always attached the idea of something quite different, which constitutes what is attributed to it as perfection. Absolute materialism has never existed and can never exist.

What then is materialism in a particular system? It is the theory that, without following the final consequences of its principle, explains things by their materials, by what is imperfect within them, and in this imperfection claims to find the reason for what completes it. According to Auguste Comte's excellent definition, which we noted above, and with which from the height of his second philosophy he himself judged his first, materialism is the doctrine which explains the superior by the inferior. What makes it false? It is contradictory, as Aristotle said, that the best should produce the worst, that the lesser produce the greater. And when materialism apparently succeeds in accounting, in particular cases, for the superior through the inferior, it is because, by a subreption of which it is unaware, it has already put into the inferior the superior that it believes to spring from it. If we explain intellect by sensation, mind by body, it is, without our realizing it, by means of what is necessarily intellectual in sensation, of what is necessarily spiritual in the crudest body.

It is the finished work that explains the rough draft, the complete, the perfect that explains the incomplete and the imperfect, the superior that explains the inferior. Consequently, it is mind alone that explains everything.

XXV
Organicism and Animism

Vulpian devoted a chapter of his learned *Lectures on the Physiology of the Brain* (1867) to the question of vitalism.[1] He opposes two arguments to the view that grants to vital functions a special principle, different from the properties of organs. First, what is called the vital principle is, he says, always conceived as unitary, and cannot be otherwise. But we see the parts of certain lower animals, separated from each other, continuing nevertheless to live. 'The vital principle, a unitary force, in these animals was therefore divisible. But to say that the vital principle is divisible is to say that it does not exist.'[2] It might be added, in order to strengthen Vulpian's first argument, that considering all organisms, even those of the highest order, as composed of very independent parts is a result of the most advanced physiology. Claude Bernard has put forward the idea that all living beings, plants and animals, are compounds of organisms. Virchow, in his new and profound research on cellular pathology, shows that all living beings amount to a sort of society of cells, which are complete organisms. Second, in a great number of pathological and physiological facts the vital operations do not conform to what would be required for the good of the individual; 'therefore', says Vulpian, 'the various tendencies which had been regarded as attributes of the vital principle, far from acting in a more or less intentional way, as was supposed in this hypothesis, manifest themselves on the contrary fatally, necessarily, blindly. Hence determinism exists in the organic world as in the inorganic world.'[3]

These or similar objections have been proposed from time immemorial; the new facts on which they can be based today have not added anything essential to those which, from antiquity, seemed to justify them: vitalists and animists are therefore not unaware of them. It is true, however, that most often they do not discuss them. Vulpian, for his part, is not unaware of what has been said and what can be said about vital unity, about the obvious concert of functions, and about what he himself calls, when it comes to the regeneration of an organ, 'a sort of conspiration of all the elements'; but he limits himself to saying that 'this is a profoundly obscure fact, and yet it must be admitted'. He does not examine whether this fact does not destroy his theory.

---

[1] *Leçons sur la physiologie générale et comparée du système nerveux*, ed. E. Brémond (Paris: Germer Baillière), by Edmé Félix Alfred Vulpian (1826–87), the physician and neurologist, was first published in 1866.
[2] Ibid., p. 295.   [3] Ibid., p. 307.

Thus, the facts and reasons which establish vital plurality and determination [*fatalité*] are adduced for organicism, while those which establish unity and finality, or intentionality are adduced for vitalism and animism; and on each side there is scarcely any mention of what is opposed to the opinion believed to be true. This may be because the opposing ideas seem absolutely incompatible and that one despairs of reconciling them; it may be that one believes more or less distinctly that by pitting them directly against each other, one would succeed only in neutralizing the observations and reflections, however obviously true they may be, on which each side is based.

However, if the opposing ideas seem irreconcilable here, is this not because they are considered, on both sides, in terms rather than in things, more logically than physically? On both sides, it seems, the notions we consider are taken in the exclusive sense offered by the name that expresses them and which admits nothing of its opposite. But is it really the same in nature? What is logically incompatible is often in nature united, harmonized; nature, to which a higher reason must conform, shows us linked, continuous, and fused together what the imaginative reason constitutive of language slices and separates, by framing, so to speak, notions in words, just as we place different material objects in different places.

Depending on whether we place ourselves at one end or the other of the immense series of beings, or even only at one end or the other of the still extensive series of animate beings, we are inclined either to see in nature only division, multiplicity, mechanism, fatality; or, on the contrary, only harmony, union, and intentional spontaneity. If we consider phenomena such as those offered by the successive formation of a habit, where we see voluntary operations, implying the most complete unity of action, gradually changing into instinctive movements executed as if they surpassed any central activity, by an obscure mechanism, in the multiplicity of the organs, we shall perhaps be more easily led to the thought that, either in the various parts of our being, from its highest to its most minute elements, or in the various orders of existence, where the same differences are found on a grand scale, the same principle exists everywhere, in varied and even contrary forms, and that in the end lower life is only the last degree to which higher life descends, from metamorphosis to metamorphosis. Here, as in other sciences, continuity in progress, in growth and in decay, teaches unity.

XXVI
Neurology after Phrenology

The question of the relationship between the physical and mind, soul, spirit, is raised in its most precise form in the study of the nervous system and, above all, of the brain.

We have said that phrenology, which explained thought by the functions of different and independent parts of the brain, has definitively disappeared from science. A crucial fact, established particularly in recent times by Vulpian, has attacked the very foundations of the theory of the exclusive localization of faculties: it is the fact that the various parts of the brain can act as a substitute for each other, and that only a very small amount of one part of the cerebral matter is needed to carry out, when necessary, the totality of the functions. Vulpian, after having summarily presented the phrenological doctrine and its history, could thus conclude as follows: 'On the one hand, there are as yet no facts that can seriously plead in favour of the doctrine, and, on the other hand, the experimental results and a good number of pathological observations speak against this dislocation of the faculties, with distribution in isolated parts of the grey matter. Gall and his followers, and the philosophers who, in their wake, have sought to institute this sort of cerebral geography, have worked with some ingenuity but without any serious basis; the work must, therefore, be banished from positive biology, from biology based solely on the facts of experimentation and observation. Experience and observation teach us here that the various parts of the cerebral hemispheres, and especially of their grey matter, can act as a substitute for each other; that a relatively small part, especially in animals, can suffice to carry out the functions of the whole; and consequently the doctrine of the location of the various instinctive, intellectual, and affective faculties has no consistency.'

Having set aside phrenology, it remains to define both what is known and what is currently being learnt concerning the relations of the mind, either with the brain, or with the other parts of the nervous system.

As for the brain itself, it has been established that this apparatus or set of apparatuses serves sensibility, imagination, and even thought in a certain sense and to a certain extent. This is the result of the work of Vicq-d'Azyr, Cuvier, Gall, Millier, etc.

Let us note only that although it may have been proved that all of what can be called the antecedents and conditions of thought, sensations, imaginations, etc. cannot exist without the brain, it has not been proved that thought itself, in its central, necessarily simple action, depends in any way on it. In this inner space, there is nothing left of matter, of body, of the organism; nothing of what is extended and multiple. Aristotle said, 'we think without organs': this lofty proposition has remained unshakeable, and probably, for those who know how to hear it, it will never be shaken.

Secondly, it should be noted that, although the various internal operations cease when the brain is destroyed or even profoundly damaged, they are restored after a certain period provided that life remains. This is one of the most important results of Flourens's experiments, according to which the cerebral hemispheres, the greatest expansion of the principal nervous system, come to be replaced, after a certain time, by the striated bodies that form the immediately lower expansion of the spinal cord, whose normal function is to serve instinctive operations.

It has been discovered, therefore, not only that a small part of the brain suffices for all its functions, but that the whole brain can be replaced, for the higher functions which belong to it, by those parts of the nervous system which, in the normal and usual state, serve only immediately lower functions. This means that it is not the organ which causes the function, as materialism maintains, but that it is the function, the action, which under certain physical conditions subjugates and appropriates the organ.

That upper part of the spinal cord which enters the brain, named the medulla oblongata, is the physical seat of instinctive sensations and movements. While the brain carries out the operations by which perceptions are added to sensations and motor volitions are formed, it is in the cerebral isthmus, in the medulla oblongata, that the reception of sensation as well as the home of spontaneous movements are located.

In a word, according to the present state of our knowledge as it is set forth in Vulpian's work, sensations are transmitted by the nerves and the spinal cord, and take on their distinctive and special characteristics in the medulla oblongata; and it is in the brain alone, or at least by means of the brain, that a higher elaboration adds perceptions, ideas to sensations. In the same way, but in the opposite direction, volition begins from the brain, which excites in the medulla oblongata the motor power, which, finally, through the spinal cord and the motor nerves which proceed from it, determine the movement of the muscles.

Although this is the normal order, it is no less true, according to Müller, that when the brain is destroyed or annulled the medulla oblongata becomes the focus of functions, either sensory or motor, that are entirely analogous to the cerebral functions.

Experience has led us to relate to the medulla oblongata the movements of mimicry and language, those of circulation and respiration. Is it not evident that in these movements there is, between the instinctive and the voluntary, a mixture, an intimate fusion, an indivisible continuity?

If we now pass from the medulla oblongata to the spinal cord, from the domain of operations to which reflexive will or at least consciousness extends, we descend, it seems, without return, to that of purely mechanical and blind operations.

Since the work of Robert Whyte, Prochaska, Legallois, and Marshall Hall above all, movements have been recognized in the animal which are a simple reaction to an external impression, a reaction to which the brain and the medulla oblongata are foreign, and which proceed from the spinal cord. These movements, in which we see a sort of immediate, unconscious, and, as it seems, entirely mechanical repercussion or reflexion, are those which have consequently been called reflex actions.

But in the very facts which have been so well recently described by Vulpian, we see animals with only the spinal cord, or even a part of the spinal cord, remaining of the cerebrospinal nervous system, not only respond by movements to external excitations, but also bring together, in order to defend themselves against attack, various movements of independent parts. Are we not allowed to see, with Robert Whyte, Prochaska, Paton, Pflüger, in actions thus co-ordinated, exercises of some power to feel, to perceive, and then to aim at a goal, to tend towards an end, and in these depths of the most obscure vitality, do we not still see something like a glimmer emanating from something that knows and wants? From this, philosophy seems to be able to conclude, as in the not dissimilar question of organicism, vitalism, and animism, that at bottom everything comes back to the same principle, but one that is engaged in conditions of existence which, from the point at which it possesses and governs itself, make it more and more external and foreign to itself.

Just as we have seen Claude Bernard, in a part of his physiological theory, announce the project of extending to all the phenomena presented by living beings the mechanism which seems to reign in the inorganic order, Vulpian, starting from the observation of reflex actions, which he considers to be absolutely mechanical, even though the mechanism is unknown to us, outlines the idea that gradually the same explanation will have to be extended to the phenomena of the instinctive order, and then, finally, to the phenomena of the intellectual and voluntary order. He remarks that if reflex actions are determined by impressions, voluntary actions are similarly determined by ideas. Without examining whether the will, in determining itself according to ideas, does not determine itself—as Leibniz among others has explained, as has, perhaps better, Kant—in a way that does not exclude spontaneity but rather implies it, Vulpian, in starting from the hypothesis that reflexive actions are only a crude mechanism, believes that he can extend this mechanism to the will. 'From this point of view, which is the only true one,' he says, 'volitions, as several modern physiologists admit, can and must be considered as phenomena of cerebral reflex action.' In addition: 'when one advances step by step, from manifestation to manifestation, one is astonished to finally arrive at the question: what is, in reality, a voluntary phenomenon? It may be said that there are very few physiologists who can, in the present state of science, admit the way in which most philosophers consider the will.'[1] By these words, Vulpian means that the state of science no longer permits belief in free will.

Indeed, if we proceed according to a continuous analogy, starting from the supposition of a pure mechanism in the phenomena of the lower order, and gradually extend the same explanation to higher and higher phenomena, it is obvious that we necessarily arrive at the disappearance of all spontaneity.

But it seems on the contrary, although Vulpian holds metaphysics in even less esteem than Claude Bernard, that his researches and discoveries lead, in the end, like those of Claude Bernard, to the demonstration of the proposition, in which metaphysics can be concentrated, that thought and will lie at the bottom of everything, that nature offers only degradations of them, that vital phenomena in all their degrees can be explained, in short, only as so many refractions, in variously perturbed environments, of a unique and universal light.

From the superior nervous system, or spinal centre, if we pass to the inferior system, to that which is composed of the partial and scattered nervous centres that are called ganglia and that preside over the inferior functions of life, some very recent discoveries of physiology seem to confirm and even extend the conclusions that the current state of science concerning the cerebral-spinal system seems to authorize. And there is one philosopher who interprets them more or less in this sense.

Bichat, developing a thought first expressed by Grimaud,[2] under the inexact titles of animal life and organic life, distinguished higher life, generally voluntary and intellectual, from lower life, generally blind and involuntary. Buisson (a relative of Bichat) observed that between the functions of the first of the two lives and those of the second there are intermediate and mixed functions, those of circulation and respiration, those of the lungs and the heart, where instinct and will are mixed. Buisson thus re-established, between the two extremes of life, an intermediary, a middle term.

This was already indicated by the most superficial observation, and was soon to be confirmed by the most exact science.

From time immemorial, the human body had been divided into these three great parts: the head, the chest, the abdomen; the head containing the brain; the chest, the heart and the lungs; the abdomen, the stomach and the intestines. 'The brain, the heart, the stomach, are', said Bordeu, 'the tripod on which life rests.'[3] This is a division that pathology justifies, and whose great importance the recent

---

[1] A. Vulpian, *Leçons sur la physiologie générale et comparée du système nerveux* (Paris: Baillière, 1866), p. 420.

[2] On Grimaud's doctrine of the 'two lives' before Bichat, see Elizabeth A. Williams, 'Of Two Lives One? Jean-Charles-Marguerite-Guillaume Grimaud and the Question of Holism in Vitalist Medicine', *Science in Context* 21/4 (2008), pp. 593–613.

[3] Ravaisson is referring to Théophile de Bordeu, who studied at Montpellier before moving to Paris and publishing several significant works in histology and anatomy.

discoveries of embryogeny have clearly come to prove. As Coste and Bischoff have shown,[4] as soon as the first outline of the embryo in the egg is distinguishable, we recognize three layers, the development of which will form the three great parts of the body: an inner layer, which will become the intestinal organs; an outer layer, which will become the most peripheral organs, the vertebral column with its dependencies; finally, a middle layer, the origin of the heart, the vessels, the lungs.

In moving from the parts of the organism to the nervous system, on which the organism depends, we find that if the functions of the highest life depend on the brain and spinal cord, thus forming the cerebro-spinal system, and if the functions of nutrition and reproduction depend principally on the ganglia, thus forming the 'sympathetic' nervous system, as Bichat said, the intermediate functions of respiration and circulation, in which will and instinct are mixed, depend principally on an intermediate nervous system, formerly called the minor sympathetic system, today the pneumo-gastric system forming the tenth pair of the cranial nerves, which is attached to the upper part of the spinal cord, at the point Flourens has called the vital node, and that cannot be injured without life immediately, by the interruption of respiration, coming to an end. This is an intermediate system since, on the one hand, it originates in the head and within the cerebral-spinal system, and, on the other hand, it becomes ganglionic in form in its endings leading to the heart and the lungs.

Thus, between the two extremes opposed to each other by Bichat, there is a middle ground: a middle ground in the very situation of the parts, between the head and the abdomen; a middle ground in the functions, mixed with will and instinct; middle ground, finally, either in the anatomical constitution, or in the functions of the part of the nervous system on which these organs depend. A middle ground, an intermediary situation and constitution, and at the same time mediation, mediating action. By their special functions, an intermediary of the others, the pectoral organs establish constant and intimate communications between the cerebral and abdominal organs.

Everywhere, therefore, and in every direction, in the organism and in life, there is liaison, continuity.

Some of these facts and remarks, especially concerning the pneumo-gastric nerve, Père Gratry has, in his *Knowledge of the Soul*,[5] collected, related, and combined in such a way as to throw a vivid light on the triple unity of the organism. The aim he set himself was above all to show in the body an image of the soul, and in the soul an image of divine nature, as represented by the dogma of the Trinity; and it is doubtful whether, with such a dominant theological preoccupation, but

---

[4] Ravaisson is referring to the German biologist and embryologist Theodor Ludwig Wilhelm von Bischoff (1807–82) and to Victor Coste (1807–93), who introduced scientific embryology into France and held the first chair in the specialism at the Collège de France.

[5] Gratry, *De la connaissance de l'âme* (Paris: Douniol, 1857).

in following a path once marked out by Platonic philosophy, he succeeded in the eyes of a rigorous science. But his ideas concerning the relations of the functions of the organism, and the consequences he drew from them to establish that it is at bottom the same principle that does everything in the living, will remain as a precious resource for a theory which, as we have seen, is in germination concerning the unity of life and its dependence, in all its parts, on the power of the soul.

'At bottom', says Père Gratry, 'it is always the soul that feels or moves through the nerves and operates in the body. This is the solid doctrine of St Thomas and Aristotle, opposed only by the error of those who suppose that the soul does nothing, either in itself or in its body, unless it wants to and knows it.'[6]

Let us add, once again, only that if it is the soul that acts in the vital functions, this can only be by thought and volition, given that the soul is wholly thought, but perhaps by thought and volition in a way that escapes, so to speak, even itself, and almost entirely surpasses self-awareness by developing beyond it.

---

[6] Ibid., p. 76, n. 2.

XXVII
Instinct

Instinct has been the subject of several important works. Frédéric Cuvier; Flourens, in several articles in the *Journal des savants* and in his treatise *Of Instinct and Intelligence in Animals*;[1] de Quatrefages, in one of his articles on 'The Unity of the Human Species';* Maury, in his *Treatise on Sleep and Dreams*;[2] Vulpian, in the last of his *Lectures on Physiology*; Michelet in *The Bird* and *The Insect*;[3] Durand (de Gros) in his *Vital Electrodynamism*, published under the pseudonym of Philips, and in his *Essays in Philosophical Physiology* (1861),[4] have all endeavoured to determine, with greater precision than had previously been gained, the differences and similarities between instinct and intellect.

The most general and important result of these inquiries was to establish that if man has instincts, and not only intellect, animals do not have only instincts, as was said before the observations of Réaumur, G. Leroy, of the Hubers, and others; that we find in them, especially in the species the least distant from the human being, but also in many others, unmistakable marks of intellect—an intellect, however, which remains below what is commonly called reflection. 'Animals', says Flourens, 'do not have reflection, that supreme faculty which the human mind has of withdrawing into itself. There is here a deep dividing line. The thought that considers itself, this self-seeing and self-studying intelligence, this self-knowing knowledge, obviously forms an order of determinate phenomena, of a distinct nature, which no animal can attain. The human is the only one of all created beings to whom the power has been given to feel that he feels, to know that he knows, to think that he thinks.'[5]

---

[1] Marie Jean-Pierre Flourens (1794–1867), *De l'instinct et de l'intelligence des animaux* (Paris: Hachette, 1851).

* *Revue des deux mondes*, 1861. [Ravaisson's footnote]

[2] L.-F. Alfred Maury (1817–92), *Le sommeil et les rêves: études psychologiques sur ces phénomènes et les divers états qui s'y rattachent* (Paris: Didier et cie, 1861).

[3] Ravaisson is referring to some of the historian Jules Michelet's writings about nature: *L'oiseau* (Paris: Hachette, 1856) and *L'insecte* (Paris: Hachette, 1858).

[4] Joseph-Pierre Durand de Gros (1826–1900), *Electro-dynamisme vital, ou Les relations physiologiques de l'esprit et de la matière, démontrées par des expériences entièrement nouvelles et par l'histoire raisonnée du système nerveux* (Paris: J.-B. Baillière, 1855) and *Essais de physiologie philosophique suivis d'une étude sur la théorie de la méthode en général* (Paris: Germer Baillière, 1866).

[5] Flourens, *De l'instinct et de l'intelligence des animaux*, 4th edition (Paris: Garnier Frères, 1861), p. 59.

Willis had already said, 'Insuper mens humana actione reflexa se ipsam intuetur, se cogitare cogitat.'[6] The Scottish metaphysician James Ferrier has recently also put it just as well: 'The existence of animals is not accompanied by knowledge of themselves, and they have no account of the reason which operates in them; it is reserved for man to live this double life: to exist and to be conscious of existence, to be reasonable and to know that he is reasonable.'[7] Leibniz had said earlier, indicating even more clearly both the fact and its cause, that if, unlike beasts, we can reflect on ourselves, it is because we conceive what it is to be, what is unity, identity, what is necessary truth; and before that Descartes had said: 'We can know that we are only on condition that we know what it is to be.' This is to say that the condition of reflection is that faculty of abstracting and comparing, more generally of intellectually separating and bringing together by virtue of necessary ideas, which is called reason.

After so much learned and ingenious research that has brought to light a thousand as yet little-known traits in which the human being and the beast resemble each other, with which most physiologists, including Vulpian, bring them together to the point of making them species of the same genus, reason remains a mark of an essential and irreducible difference between the human and the animal.

It is no less necessary to add to the scientific achievements of our time remarks recorded in the works of several observers, according to which not only more or less voluntary actions are changed, as we have had occasion to say, by frequent repetition, into habits resembling instincts, but also according to which these habits, being transmitted by heredity, become, in subsequent generations, veritable instincts. Lucas, in his *Philosophical and Physiological Treatise on Natural Heredity*,[8] Roulin in his *Enquiries Concerning some Changes Observed in Domestic Animals Transported from the Old to the New Continent*,[9] and de Quatrefages in his work 'The Unity of the Human Race' have collected many examples of this. These are all important documents that explain to a certain extent, by a gradual transformation of intellectual and voluntary acts, the generation of instincts; a theory proposed formerly by Lamarck, without the support of adequate evidence

---

[6] Thomas Willis, *De anima brutorum, Pars prima, Opera omnia* (Amsterdam: Henricum Wetstenium, 1682), VII, p. 37.

[7] This seems to be based on a passage from James Ferrier's 1838–9 *Introduction to the Philosophy of Consciousness*; see *Philosophical Works of the Late James Ferrier*, vol. 3 (Edinburgh: Blackwood, 1883), p. 49.

[8] Prosper Lucas (1808–85), *Traité philosophique et physiologique de l'hérédité naturelle* (Paris: J.-B. Baillière, 1847 and 1850).

[9] François Désiré Roulin (1796–1874), *Recherches sur quelques changements observés dans les animaux domestiques transportés de l'ancien au nouveau continent* (lu à l'Académie des sciences le 29 sept. 1828) in *Mémoires présentés par divers Savans à l'Académie royale des sciences de l'Institut de France*, vol. 6 (Paris, 1835), pp. 319–52.

drawn from experience, and renewed very recently by Herbert Spencer and, with all the resources of his vast knowledge, by Charles Darwin.

Durand (de Gros), in his *Essays of Philosophical Physiology* (1866), has defended and strengthened with numerous arguments the theory explaining instincts by the hereditary transmission of habits. He has shown that instinctive acts, performed without the living being to which they belong being aware of them, acts that Maury consequently calls 'unconscious' [*inconscients*], and Durand himself 'incognizant' [*inconscientiels*], nevertheless contain intellect. He has shown that to these acts may be assimilated those depending on the spinal cord and even those which, relating to the nutritive functions and other functions of the same order, depend on simple ganglia; he has thus contributed to modifying the vulgar distinction, too arbitrarily made, between intellect and instinct, and, this time, to the advantage of the superior principle rather than the inferior. 'Now', adds Durand (de Gros), 'if certain sensations, certain determinations, exist outside the consciousness that the living being has of all that properly depends on him, if they cannot exist outside all consciousness, if no sensation can be absolutely unconscious, where will consciousness be found? In the particular centres on which instinctive or reflex phenomena depend; and in each of these centres a particular soul must necessarily be placed, in the spinal cord alone a number of *spinal souls*.' We have to understand strictly, without exception, according to Durand, what Lacaze-Duthiers said of invertebrate animals, and before him, Dugès, and before Dugès, Linnaeus and Reimarus: that each living thing is an assembly of living things. 'A living thing', as also Goethe said, 'is never one, but always several.' And, as Buchez remarked in an examination of Durand's first work, it would be necessary, according to the latter, to define man not as an intellect served by organs, but as an intellect served by inferior intelligences.

It is possible, it seems to us, to oppose to Durand (de Gros) the impossibility of understanding, on this hypothesis, how the living forms a whole, which cannot be contested. If it is a characteristic of the most advanced physiology to understand an organism as a society and a kind of federation of smaller organisms, it is still necessary to consider how such diversity is at the same time unity. It will not be denied that, to a certain extent, there is some justification and sometimes much use in considering a being as a society of beings, and, if you will, as a plurality of souls; but it will be necessary in the end to come to a more elevated point of view from which it is possible to see such a plurality, such a diversity, come back to different states of one and the same principle. 'All is one, though each is separate.'

XXVIII
Sleep

The questions of sleep, dreams, and somnambulism differ only slightly from that of instinct.

'We can have a clear idea of instinct', said Cuvier, 'only by admitting that animals have in their sensorium innate and constant images and sensations which determine them to act, as ordinary and accidental sensations commonly determine them. There is a sort of dream or vision which always pursues them; and in all that relates to their instinct, they may be regarded as a species of somnambulists.'[1]

Maine de Biran defined the state of the animal by sensory life, the superior state of the human by the will; in the same way, in his eyes, sleep consisted in the predominance of the sensitive and passive life, freed from the direction that we give it during wakefulness by effort.

Jouffroy believed, on the contrary, that in sleep the intellect and the will remained. 'In this way it can be explained', he said, 'how one wakes up at the time one has prescribed in advance, how one wakes up when some unusual noise occurs, how in sleep one makes very correct reasonings and even discoveries.'[2]

It has been argued that this is true only of a light sleep, which is only a half-sleep.

Lélut, in a *Dissertation on Sleep, Dreams and Somnambulism* read to the Academy of Moral and Political Sciences on 27 March and 17 April 1852,[3] after having explained how little is known about the physical conditions of sleep, made it clear by judicious remarks that in sleep, whether light or deep, intellect and will do not remain, as Jouffroy held, in all their fullness, but that nevertheless they are not, as Maine de Biran had believed, entirely abolished, and that, on the contrary, there is no sleep so deep where, to some degree, they are not present or cannot legitimately be presumed to be present. Lélut also endeavoured to distinguish, in sleep, between the dreams of our different senses as well as between those of our different mental faculties.

When the Academy of Moral and Political Sciences put the question of sleep up for an essay competition, Albert Lemoine won the prize it had proposed. In

---

[1] Georges Cuvier (1769–1832), *Le règne animal distribué d'après son organisation* (Paris: Deterville, 1817), p. 54.
[2] Théodore Jouffroy, 'Le sommeil' in *Mélanges philosophiques* (Paris: Hachette, 1866 [Paris: Paulin, 1833]), pp. 225–42. Ravaisson seems to cite more the spirit than the letter of Jouffroy's text.
[3] Francisque Lélut (1804–77), 'Mémoire sur le sommeil, les songes et le somnambulisme', *Compte rendu de l'Académie des Sciences morales et politiques* (May and June 1856), pp. 1–31.

his dissertation, he supported with many ingenious remarks opinions not so different from those that Lélut had summarily expressed.

Maury, shortly afterwards, published a book entitled *Sleep and Dreams*, composed largely of observations made on himself with great patience and sagacity.[4] The main object of Maury's researches was to prove that sleep is explained by a diminution of the activity of the brain, and principally of those parts of the brain that serve the intellect, a diminution which would allow lower life to dominate, either animal life properly so called, or still more vegetative and organic life; that in this state we are under the influence of hallucinations all similar to those which, in the waking state, mark a progression towards the loss of reason, and that thus sleep and dreams are an intermediary state between self-possession and insanity.

These results seem to be able to serve as a basis for a more complete theory of sleep, one explaining the facts better than those which have been hazarded up to now.

As regards the physiological part of sleep, an English physiologist, Durham, has just established, it is said, a very important fact, which was doubtful until now and even opposed to what was generally held to be true, namely that, during sleep, the influx of blood to the brain is less than during wakefulness. Did we not already know that during sleep there is a tendency to cooling, especially of the extremities? If we compare these facts with those highlighted by Grimaud in particular, which show during sleep a certain increase in the digestive and nutritive forces, that is to say, of the most interior organic life; if we recall that certain animals are more prone than others to metamorphoses which occur for them during deep sleep; if we think of the chrysalis plunged into a sleep where, as Swammerdam first saw, its organs interpenetrate and melt together, returning into something like an embryonic state in order to be reborn transformed; if we remember that great law, signalled by Goethe, according to which nature, in the case of plants, proceeds, in its development, by a succession of alternate concentrations and expansions; if, on the other hand, we relate to this the phenomena presented by physical nature itself, which seems, in sleep, to relax from all external action, and to gather itself into itself in order to renew and remake itself, we may be disposed to think that the observations recently brought together concerning sleep would accord with each other, would be explained if we considered it as the first of the two phases that any organic metamorphosis has to go through, as the regular and necessary period of concentration in which are worked out the conditions of an immediately successive period of development, and, through development, of generation, of creation.

Could we not add that death, which has always been thought to be comparable to a certain extent to sleep, seems to be a supreme concentration preparing for

---

[4] Maury, *Le sommeil et les rêves* (Paris: Didier, 1865).

some supreme renovation? 'What we call generation', said Leibniz, 'is only development and growth; what we call death, envelopment, diminution.'[5] Envelopment and development, concentration and expansion, opposite effects of opposed states of activity, of alternate remission and tension, as Stoicism said. And one could say: successively negative and positive stages of one and the same will. To stop willing is to will again. The man of great spirit who saw most deeply how the metamorphoses that constitute the very existence of the living proceed by alternate contractions and dilations, Goethe, dared to say: 'Birth takes place by an act of will, and so does death.'[6]

---

[5] Leibniz, *Monadology*, §73.

[6] It is not obvious that Goethe ever wrote exactly this, but Ravaisson is relying on the ideas he expressed to Johannes Falk on the death on Christoph Martin Wieland in 1813, ideas according to which on death the chief monad that is the soul releases subordinate monads. See, for example, Caro, *La philosophie de Goethe* (Paris: Hachette, 1866), p. 200.

XXIX
Madness

Insanity [*l'aliénation mentale*] has been the subject of almost as many publications and no less animated discussions as the general question of the relation of the physical to the mind; insanity, above all, in its relation to moral and legal responsibility.

Most of the works on this subject have been written by physiologists endeavouring to demonstrate that thought is a function of the brain; that insanity is an alteration of this function, resulting from some material lesion; that, consequently, there is no responsibility for the insane. One might add that, in this system, in which all spontaneity is replaced by a pure mechanism, the people who are called reasonable are no freer or more responsible, nor in reality more reasonable, than the mad.

Albert Lemoine, in *The Madman before Science and Society*, has developed a completely opposed thesis.[1] Recognizing a principle of thought that is entirely independent of the body, he does not want madness to be able to reach it; he does not want the soul to be sick; he would willingly say with the ancient Stoics that the wise man can have drunk too much, but never be drunk. He admits that in madness sensibility is perverted, the imagination disturbed by vain phantoms; but, behind the disturbance of the imagination and the senses, in madness as in dreams, reason, according to him, remains, and it can be seen working in the insane to draw the best possible advantage from the false data which come from the sickened senses and imagination. Albert Lemoine thus agrees with the materialists, whose declared opponent he is in every other respect, in attributing the origin of madness to lesions of the nervous system. Will it be said that madness often seems to come from purely psychological causes? In these cases, according to him, such causes produce in the brain a disorder which is felt consecutively by the senses or the imagination. But reason cannot, in his opinion, be either consequently or originally damaged.

Could it not be said, then, that if in the system of materialism the so-called reasonable are no more reasonable than the insane, in the system here opposed to them the insane are, in fact, scarcely less reasonable than those who have the advantage of possessing intact senses and a healthy imagination?

Locke, too, had argued that, in order to be insane, one was not deprived of the faculty of reasoning; that one reasoned only according to false suppositions.

---

[1] Albert Lemoine, *L'aliéné devant la science et devant la société* (Paris: Didier et cie, 1862).

Whereupon Leibniz remarked that a particular madman (what we now call a monomaniac) could reason rightly on a false assumption, but 'that a universal madman lacked judgment on almost every occasion'.[2]

It seems indeed, and this is the common opinion, that madness [*la folie*] is quite different from mere hallucinations, the work of sick senses and imagination, and against which reason has some defence. It seems that madness consists in no longer recognizing, as one could do by using one's reason, the disagreement, the contradiction presented by hallucinations, either between themselves, or with veridical perceptions; it seems, in a word, that madness is properly unreason. If reason, absolutely speaking, can never be sick, we might ask whether it is any different for that which is in some way engaged in our condition, and which thus participates in our necessary imperfection?

Esquirol said, as Moreau (of Tours) said after him, that what constitutes madness is a lesion in attention. 'Madness', Baillarger has said, 'is intellectual automatism; it is the state in which the mind, instead of possessing and governing itself, is at the mercy of imaginations or ideas which obsess it'; and Durand (de Gros) subscribes to this definition, under which would fall, in his opinion, phenomena very similar, for him as for Maury, either to dreams or to instinct. We have already recalled that Cuvier assimilated the state of the animal dominated, driven by its instincts to the state of somnambulism. As for the condition of the dreamer, compared with that of the insane, it presents, it seems, this essential difference: that the sleeper, given over to his imaginations, lacks the means of control which perceptions provide for the waking person, while the insane person has these means, but lacks the faculty of making use of them. What then is this faculty? To make it consist of attention, with Esquirol and Moreau (de Tours), of self-possession, with Baillarger and Durand (de Gros), is to make it consist, like Maine de Biran, of the will. But if it is true to say that the faculty of reflecting on ourselves comes from the fact that we are reasonable, can we not say the same of the will? If the madman is alien to himself (*alienus a se*), beside himself, outside of his own centre, is it not because he is outside that which is in some way the common centre of all of us?

If Albert Lemoine's opinion, in what is absolute within it, is not generally accepted, he will at least have contributed, by his ingenious analyses, to making it clear that the madman, even in the most extreme madness, still retains some remainder of reason. Some spark of the light that illuminates every human entering into this world always remains. This was already the sense of Leibniz's 'almost'. Madness consists, it would seem, in making a vicious use of a remainder of reason, just as not being able to use reason at all is imbecility or dementia.

---

[2] Leibniz, *New Essays* II, xi, §13, p. 143.

XXX
Genius

An ancillary question, that of the relations between the higher faculties of intellect and reason or madness, has also given rise to remarkable works.

Lélut, a man of wit and learning, first made himself known by a book, *Socrates' Demon*,[1] in which he undertook to prove, by the examples of Socrates and Pascal and others, that genius was usually linked to some disorder of the mind.

Moreau (of Tours) went further: he wanted to prove, in his *Morbid Psychology*, that great ideas came from the same source as insanity, as madness and instinct; that genius was a 'neurosis'.[2]

Albert Lemoine, in *Mind and Body*, and Paul Janet, in *The Brain and Thought*, have explained what is true in the facts alleged by Lélut and Moreau (of Tours), what is mixed up in them with error, and what Moreau's paradox comes down to.[3]

What remains, after these analyses and criticisms, is that intellectual faculties of a very high order are not incompatible with affections of the nervous system or even with real disorders of the mind. But that genius is more often associated with such disorders than mediocrity of mind, that it has its source in the very focus of mental disorder, that it is simply a form of alienation, are quite different propositions, which Albert Lemoine and Paul Janet have refuted in a way that seems to be unanswerable.

Paul Janet, summing up, said: 'What constitutes genius is not enthusiasm, for enthusiasm can occur in the most mediocre and empty minds; it is the superiority of reason. The man of genius is the one who sees more clearly than others, who perceives a greater share of the truth, who can link a greater number of particular facts under a general idea, who links all the parts of a whole under a common law, who, even when he creates, as in poetry, is merely realizing, by means of the imagination, the idea which his understanding has conceived.'[4]

Perhaps there is some justification in pointing out that, in order to accept wholly Janet's definition, the word reason has to be taken in its broadest sense, and not perhaps in the most ordinary sense. According to Cicero, who here merely echoes Greek philosophy, we have two great faculties: the faculty of

---

[1] Francisque Lélut, *Le démon de Socrates, specimen d'une application de la science psychologique à celle de l'histoire* (Paris: Trinquart, 1856).

[2] Jacques Moreau, *Psychologie morbide dans ses rapports avec la philosophie de l'histoire, ou De l'influence des névropathies sur le dynamisme intellectuel* (Paris: Masson, 1859).

[3] Lemoine, *L'âme et le corps* (Paris: Didier et cie, 1862); Janet, *Le cerveau et la pensée* (Paris: Baillière, 1867).

[4] Janet, *Le cerveau et la pensée*, p. 89.

judging and that of inventing. Now it is usually the faculty of judging that is called reason, not the faculty of inventing. And it is in invention that the strength and greatness of mind that we nowadays call genius is most evident. Genius, by all accounts, consists above all in inventing, in creating.

Creating is particularly characteristic of poetry: *poet* means *creator*. And poetry, according to a great critic (Lowth), is the language of emotion. It is not possible to create, to invent without imagination, and the imagination is not fruitful if it is not moved.

If, therefore, there is no true genius without reason, that is, without judgement, there is something else in genius, since there is something else in invention, in creation, than the faculty of judgement, and therefore something other than reason. If reason is the defining characteristic of the human being, there is in genius something that surpasses man, something that has always been called divine. It was not in vain that Plato said that the poet is a sacred thing, and that in order to create, he must be somehow outside himself, in a sort of delirium. Inspiration, enthusiasm, are indeed of the essence of creation, of poetry, of true genius, and enthusiasm has features in common with madness.

Does that mean that the theory of Moreau (de Tours) is true, and that genius and mania are the same thing? It only means that, just as we can be outside ourselves by falling during illness or a brutal passion below ourselves, which is the alienation of which Moreau speaks, we can also, through a suggestion of what is better than us, better than some of us at least, *quos aequus amavit Jupiter*,[5] be elevated, carried above ourselves. What is in us and is better than us is, according to Plato, the love which always tends upwards as vulgar love tends downwards. The love that is like a god in man, animating the soul itself, the love that carries thought aloft, this is perhaps what we call, what we must call genius.

---

[5] Virgil, *Aeneid* VI, 129; 'to few, great Jupiter imparts this grace' (translation Dryden).

XXXI
Language and Physiognomy

It is still to the general question of the relations between mind and body that the question of signs, which includes the theory of physiognomy and that of language, is perhaps most closely related.

Both have been the subject of important works.

A physiologist who has made himself known principally by new and successful applications of electricity to medicine, Duchenne (de Boulogne), had the ingenious idea of using it also for the study of physiognomy. He applies the rheophore to various parts of the face successively: the muscles contract, and the face expresses particular feelings, particular passions. Duchenne then notes the relations he has thus discovered between certain expressions and certain muscles; in this way, he makes a great step forward in a part of physiology that has remained in a backward state until now, and he provides art with precious discoveries.

The illustrious English physiologist who contributed so much to the great discovery of which Magendie was nevertheless the principal author, to the discovery that there are nerves for movement and others for sensation, Charles Bell, had aimed before Duchenne at knowledge of the laws of physiognomy, but with a completely different perspective. Duchenne wanted above all to gather facts and draw useful consequences for art. Charles Bell's main concern was to discover an explanation of the facts.

The explanation, according to Charles Bell, is that the parts that serve expression also and primarily serve functions of either lower, organic life or higher, relational life. The movements of the body and limbs, attitudes, gestures, express sensations and actions. The same is true, if we look closely, of the modifications of the face, modifications resulting from the play of muscles which do not move, like the others, under the skin, but which hold it and drag it along with them. If the face, by contracting in different ways, expresses different passions, different appetites, it is because this contraction is precisely the mechanical condition necessary for the passion, for the appetite to be satisfied. If, for example, the rictus that retracts the lips backwards, as we see it in all its force in carnivores, is the expression of rage, this is because it is the movement by which the animal prepares to seize and tear with its teeth.

Gratiolet, who was recently and prematurely taken from science, added ingenious and important developments to this theory.

Albert Lemoine adopted it and drew from it a new and quite considerable consequence, by which he separated himself from the school to which he belonged and took a first step in a completely new direction.

Reid had counted among the primitive faculties, which are impossible to resolve into prior elements, the faculty of expressing oneself by signs and of understanding them. Jouffroy had done the same, and, even more so, Adolphe Garnier, who was never afraid to multiply native, irreducible inclinations and faculties. But if expressive signs are only the natural movements for particular actions, there is obviously no need for a special faculty to produce them; and probably no need for a special faculty to understand them either.

Now, if this is so, a key seems to have been found for the much debated question of the origin of language.

Thinking without language, at least thinking distinctly, does not seem possible. Many concluded that man had to receive a ready-made language from a special and direct revelation in order to think. This is the hypothesis to which the name of de Bonald in particular is attached.

More recently, the progress of philology, especially of comparative philology, has led to the understanding that language in its various forms must have developed, like science, like life, according to certain, constant, natural laws. Ernest Renan, in his treatise *The Origin of Language*, summarized this opinion by saying, in agreement with Max Müller, that language is the product of the spontaneity of the human mind.[1] According to these two learned linguists, languages form, in their grammatical constitution, sets, regular systems, which appear as if from a single source, and from this result of philological experience as well as from the apparently self-evident principle that one cannot speak without thinking, they conclude with reason that the human speaks just as naturally as it thinks.

But the fact that a set, a whole is natural does not prevent it from being formed to a certain extent successively and from having causes susceptible of analysis. We can undertake to explain how the edifice of our knowledge was built up; we can also undertake to explain how the edifice, today so vast, so rich in detail, that forms one of our languages, was built up. This is what Albert Lemoine has done with great sagacity, albeit in a summary manner, in developing Charles Bell's principle.

It had already been said and shown clearly that the more or less artificial and conventional signs of which language is formed derive from certain natural signs. We know now, moreover, by Charles Bell's remark, at least for certain cases, what these signs are and how they are explained: we see all the more clearly how we can, voluntarily, extend their use, develop them, transform them, and derive from

---

[1] Ernest Renan, *De l'origine du langage* (Paris: Lévy, 1859).

them a true language. The needs of breathing, of various pressures, make the newborn cry out to attract those who care for it; later the infant will understand the use it can make of this; the infant will repeat it, and thus imitate itself. This is the first language. From this first language, as modified and extended, will arise, with the mutual aid of nature and the will, what we call the words of a language. These words, chained to each other, or modified, inflected, according to laws which are those of thought itself and whose whole is logic, subject to the rules that compose what we call grammar, constitute a complete language.

In these views seem to be found the rudiments of a truly philosophical explanation of the origins of languages.

One consequence to be drawn from this, which has not escaped Lemoine, is that not only does speech not precede thought and not stand as its cause—as de Bonald thought, and also, according to quite different principles, Condillac—but that it is, on the contrary, intellect which, as it is produced, makes organs, a body for itself. And here, as everywhere, we find, at the heart of all creation, the native force of spirit. Whence Lemoine will perhaps also draw some day another consequence—with which he would agree with Plato, Aristotle, Leibniz, Stahl, whose bold conceptions sometimes seem to frighten his wisdom—that, even in the ultimate depths of instinctive spontaneity and purely natural existence, it is thought, it is the will that explains everything, and that the reason for everything is, in short, reason.

This is not to say that thought can easily do without speech. Language is a mirror in which our thought learns to know itself, and without which it seems that it would be for itself as if it were not. 'Light', says Emerson, 'passes through space without being seen; for us to see it, we must meet an opaque body that reflects it. The same is true of our thoughts.' But the mirror is not, for all that, the light or the cause of the light.

'We do not think without images,' said Aristotle, 'and words are images.' 'But,' said Jamblicus, 'things more excellent than images are expressed by images.'[2]

It seems that of language we can say what Emerson said of the universe: 'It is an externalization of the soul'; what Schopenhauer said of the body: 'It is the will made visible; it is the will objectified.'

---

[2] Aristotle, of course, claims that the 'soul does not think without an image' in *De anima* (III, 7), but he does not follow this with a reflection on the relation of word and image, and nowhere, it seems, does Aristotle simply identify words and images (*phantasma*). See Iamblichus, *De mysteriis Aegyptiorum* I, xxi; see *On the Mysteries of the Egyptians, Chaldeans, and Assyrians*, trans. T. Taylor (London: Bertrand Dobell, 1821), p. 80.

XXXII
Science and Probability
Cournot

In the period covered by this report, given that its principles have been much disputed, philosophical research has been concerned above all with these principles, and consequently with the most fundamental questions of metaphysics and psychology. The parts of philosophy dealing with the conduct of our two great faculties, the understanding and the will, namely logic and morality, have given rise to relatively few works.

As far as logic is concerned, apart from the essays on various points of detail by Waddington-Kastus and Antonin Rondelet, special mention must be made of two extensive works by Cournot, *Essay on the Foundations of our Knowledge and on the Characteristics of Philosophical Critique* (1851) and *Treatise on the Linkage of Fundamental Ideas in the Sciences and in History* (1861), and of Duhamel's treatise *Of Methods in the Sciences of Reasoning* (1865).[1]

In both works, Cournot set out to determine the characteristics and goals of the various branches of human knowledge and philosophy. The conclusions he arrives at are not very far removed from those of the positivist doctrine, as first established by Auguste Comte; but he arrives at them by considerations of his own and from which the conclusions themselves become clear.

According to Cournot, philosophy is not a science with a particular object, a world apart of intellectual and moral phenomena as posited by the Scottish school or the eclectic school; nor is it a science of the absolute, as others have understood it. Auguste Comte had it consist of the combined generalities of all the sciences; for Cournot, it consists of a set of views relating to the order and reason of things. These views, however, can only be probabilities, and this opinion, although it is a natural consequence of the principles called positivist, is proper to Cournot.

'The relation of reason and order is extreme,' said Bossuet. 'Order is reason's friend and its object.' This dictum, which Cournot never tires of quoting, is the soul of all his speculations; but it does not have for him the same meaning as it did for Bossuet.

---

[1] Antoine Augustin Cournot (1801–77), *Essai sur les fondements de nos connaissances et sur les caractères de la critique philosophique* (Paris: Hachette, 1851); *Traité de l'enchaînement des idées fondamentales dans les sciences et dans l'histoire* (Paris: Hachetee, 1861); J. M. C. Duhamel, *Des méthodes dans les sciences de raisonnement* (Paris: Gauthier-Villars, 1865).

According to Bossuet, as well as to Plato, Aristotle, Descartes, Malebranche, Leibniz, Berkeley, order has its principle in the universal and eternal reason from which our reason derives. For Cournot, in contrast, what belongs to reason in us can be explained by what belongs to order in things, just as, for Auguste Comte, in the period when he was writing the *Course of Positive Philosophy*, the human being has to be explained by the world, the subjective by the objective.[2] Human intellect must be understood, in his view, in accordance with a saying of Bacon's, which is no less familiar to him than Bossuet's dictum, and according to which he interprets the latter; *ex analogia universi*.[3]

'Chance is not', he writes, 'as many have thought, an expression which signifies only our ignorance; it signifies that which results from the concurrence of independent causes. But however frequent this concurrence may be, it is a fact that in nature regularity is dominant. Hang two pendulums at the two ends of a joist, and they will beat very differently: after some time they are in agreement. Agitate the water at the entrance to a pipe: with some distance all the waves are equal. Now, where there is regularity, constancy, order, there is undoubtedly a reason which is a law; for if it were chance, it would be a prodigious and incredible chance. If there is a law, beyond what we have been able to observe in particular cases, the facts will always be in conformity with it, and this is what experience verifies. In no case, however, will it be a perfect certainty; it will never be anything but more or less probable. Probability may be, so to speak, infinite; and infinite probability, physically speaking, is equivalent to reality, just as the opposite probability, if infinite, is physical impossibility; but it is always, logically speaking, probability.'[4]

Being true of things, this also becomes, by undergoing their action, true of our intellect. The order in things, wherein they have their ground, produces in us the order constituting our reason; reason as what judges things and the other faculties by which we perceive things. The Scottish philosophers and their followers among us, in claiming certainty against scepticism, attributed equal authority to the senses, to memory, to reason, and thus placed all our faculties in the same rank. According to Cournot, this time in accordance with Plato and Leibniz, there is an order, a hierarchy between our faculties; it is through reason that we know anything, that we judge everything. But the highest function of reason is that by which it coordinates and classifies all our knowledge; it consists in determining, by means of induction, with the different degrees of

---

[2] Ravaisson writes 'le monde doit être expliqué par l'homme, le subjectif par l'objectif', but, given the contradiction, he must have meant to write that it is the world that explains man according to the early Comte.

[3] Francis Bacon rejected the idea that the forms of the intellect are the forms of the world; 'all perceptions of sense and mind are built to the scale of man and not the universe' (*omnes perceptiones tam sensus quam mentis sunt ex analogia hominis, non ex analogia universi*); Bacon, *The Instauratio Magna Part II: Novum Organum and Associated Texts*, *The Oxford Francis Bacon*, vol. 9, ed. G. Rees and M. Wakely (Oxford: Clarendon, 2004).

[4] This seems to be a fusion of different passages from Cournot's *Essai*.

probability that they entail, the laws that make up the order of things. This function is philosophy.

Why, in what way is philosophy not science? It is because science presupposes both the precise determination of characteristics, and consequently the logical deduction by which from a given characteristic we conclude with another; in two words, it presupposes definition and demonstration. But this occurs, rigorously speaking, only where things are presented under conditions of exact measurement, that is, under the conditions of extension alone, separated from all others. From this derives the identity of science proper and mathematics, and even, to put it still more accurately, of geometry, to which the other parts of mathematics refer. In philosophy, there is nothing like this. In physical things—even for the simple determination of forms and evaluation of magnitudes, and thus for the experimental verification of geometrical theorems—, continuity, which nowhere allows a precise division to be established, is opposed to any completely exact determination and allows only for approximations; hence the lack of absolute certainty. The ideas of order, harmony, etc. which philosophy apprehends between too many and too diverse elements, do not lend themselves to precise evaluation, to completely characteristic description, to rigorous definition; hence the obscurities, the equivocations, the endless controversies; hence the impossibility that any result exceeds the probable, and this even without a determinate degree of probability. For mathematical elements, probability is measured and calculated like these elements themselves. Philosophical probability is incapable of rigorous determination.

Plato, claiming absolute knowledge for philosophy, was wrong, according to Cournot, to despise what can be attained only by induction and only approximately known. His successors, the academicians, who were closest to the Pyrrhonians, were undoubtedly more aware of the necessary limits of human science.

However much Aristotle may have been concerned with the things of nature, he also had only meagre notions of the idea of chance, and did not think highly enough of it. He was wrong to have the scientific method consist of the syllogism, and was wrong to consider knowledge of absolute existences as the goal of all true science, and especially of philosophy. Bacon, in celebrating induction, did not know well its nature or use; he did not understand well the principle on which philosophical probability is founded.

Descartes saw what later saw Bacon's Scottish successors, who wanted to achieve in the mental order what Bacon had achieved in the physical order, and thereby institute an experimental science of mind: that truth does not come to us indiscriminately and equally through all our means of knowledge, that reason in us is the judge of everything by its ideas. But he did not see, no more than the most consistent of his disciples, Spinoza, the way in which these ideas are necessarily imperfect and limited.

Leibniz understood the nature of continuity better than anyone: he saw in it the secret of the whole of nature; yet he did not adequately understand that continuity and science are incompatible. Far from it, he pushed further than anyone else the ambition to measure everything; hence his intention to express all things by adequate characteristics, which would serve as an algorithm for a universal calculation. What he himself sometimes called 'the indistinguishable', he hoped in vain to define and count. If only he had applied the general theory of combinations, which occupied him from his youth, to the comparison of chances, to the calculation of probabilities! He would have found the only possible philosophy.

Kant, better than anyone else, knew the limits of reason, the impossibility of absolute science; at the same time, he, like Plato and Aristotle, neglected the probable, disdained induction. While seeing well what is not knowable, he did not see enough of what is knowable; he remained in the negative.

To all the theories of the same class as Cournot's theory, can be posed, as we have seen, the question that was so well understood by Sophie Germain's rigorous mind, among so many other excellent minds: however difficult it may be for us to become aware of anything absolute, how can we understand that we know something relative without some notion, however obscure, of an absolute in relation to which the relative is measured? And to Cournot in particular we can address this second question: how can we judge between probabilities? How can we estimate, even approximately, degrees of probability, if not in relation to something fixed and certain? How can we estimate what is probable [*vraisemblable*], as was objected to the half-sceptics of the Academy, if not in relation to the true [*vrai*]? 'Probability', said Leibniz, who made so much of the calculation of chances, and who wanted to make of it a major part of logic, 'is always founded in verisimilitude [*vraisemblance*], or in conformity with truth.'

It is therefore difficult to establish that reason in us—and this is, as we saw, more or less how Herbert Spencer understands it—is the accumulated result of what is constant in the perceptions of external things. Far from each of these perceptions explaining intellect, intellect alone explains them.

We perceive nothing distinctly without the conditions of extension that Stahl called *figurability*, nothing except the very action by which we perceive. And it is the attributes of its own action that the mirror of nature represents, as if displayed in a coarser image, to mind. How can we understand extension, repetition, plurality, if not by unity, of which we become aware only in action?

'Our soul,' says Pascal, 'thrown into the body, where it finds number, time, dimension, reasons about them, and can believe nothing else.'[5] Nothing of all this, however, is intelligible without what comes from the soul itself.

Plato may have been wrong to take too little account of the things of opinion, but he was perhaps not wrong to subordinate opinion to true knowledge. Aristotle

---

[5] This is fragment 535 of Brunschvicg's edition of the *Pensées*.

himself may not have given enough credit to induction, but he was perhaps not wrong to seek, for what is in itself without rule, a rule in reason.

Descartes may have too often focused on the deduction of pure ideas at the expense of experience, whose value, for all that, he knew and which he recommended as much as anyone else; but he may not have been mistaken in proclaiming that it is in relation to the perfect, to the absolute, that everything is ultimately measured.

Concerning Leibniz, a passage from his *New Essays on Human Understanding* is sufficient to defend him against the reproach that he did not sufficiently understand the incompatibility of science and continuity: 'Everything goes by degrees in nature and nothing by leaps, and this rule with regard to changes is part of my law of continuity. But the beauty of nature, which wants distinct perceptions, demands the appearance of leaps and, as it were, musical drops in phenomena, and takes pleasure in disentangling species.'[6] Perhaps he was wrong to extend prematurely the rigour of definitions and the exactitude of calculation to objects of an undulating and elusive nature; but was he wrong to believe that there is reason at the bottom of everything, and that there is in everything, therefore, number, weight, and measure?

'There are things', says Pascal, 'that are difficult to demonstrate in order and which cannot be explained by definitions and principles. But it is not the case, for all that,' he adds, 'that the mind does not do it; but it does it tacitly, naturally and without art.'[7]

At the bottom of everything, then, order and certainty, reason and wisdom; the difficult thing is only to gain knowledge of this inner wisdom that is us, but that is also more than us and better than us.

'The expression of it surpasses all men,' says Pascal, 'and the feeling of it belongs only to a few men.'[8]

Cournot's reflections, supported by numerous examples, will recommend more than ever to the attention of philosophers an important truth that has already been brought to light by the progress of probability calculus and statistics, namely that even where all sorts of series of facts and causes intersect and intermingle as if in inextricable knots, order will be found and the rule will appear; that probability, even where exact calculation appears inapplicable or hardly applicable, can rise so high that it reaches the level of full certainty in practice. It is an eminent service to philosophy to show, by seeking to prove that everything can be reduced to chance, that chance is also a matter of science and philosophy, and to describe oscillations and disturbances in such a way that they reveal in their truth and power the invisible but necessary centre whose action governs them.

---

[6] Leibniz, *New Essays* IV, xvi, §12, p. 473.
[7] This is the first fragment of Pascal's *Pensées* in Brunschvicg's edition.   [8] Ibid.

Nevertheless, under the name of philosophical probability, it is, it seems, physical probability that Cournot has described.

It is physical science, the science of nature which, by induction, by means of analogies, establishes conjecturally the laws of phenomena. And as for what is called probability or mental assurance, it is nothing more than what results from the combination of physical circumstances with mental causes, and ultimately with the will. Physics and chance are not separate. For chances there is a rule; for probabilities, a reason: it is this rule, this reason, that is the object of philosophy.

But, says Cournot, in matters of philosophy there is hardly any agreement: this is proof that we do not go beyond the region of the probable.—On the relations of the different ideas considered by philosophy either between themselves or to physics, it is difficult, indeed, to reach agreement; we do not possess the means of sensory verification that experience provides for physics. This is not to say, however, that one cannot find, as Leibniz said, some *succedaneum*; it is not impossible to conceive for ideas, of whatever order and nature they may be, means of determination and expression; otherwise, how would any discourse and any understanding be possible? And this is why the hope of the grand philosophical calculus dreamed of by two thinkers, two inventors of the first order, is perhaps not as vain as we imagine. In any case, as far as the very source of ideas is concerned, the radical truth which is none other than the very foundation and essence of our spirit, does it not follow from the summary that we have presented of the different systems of our time that there is more agreement than it seems and more than we think? Have we not seen those systems, initially produced by the most pronounced aversion to metaphysics, ultimately gravitate towards the very idea from which they were supposed to have departed without return? The planets, in the vast orbits they describe through space, seemed for a long time to be independent of any common law; a day came when it was discovered that they all obeyed the attraction of a single focus. There is a focus too, there is a sun of the intellectual and moral world. Some new Kepler, some new Newton, will one day make manifest both its reality and its power. We can already feel this reality and power, though we may not yet be able to give a clear demonstration of them.

To recall here a remark by the author of the *New Essays on Human Understanding*, which we have already had occasion to quote, 'general principles enter into our thoughts, of which they are the soul and the tie. They are as necessary there as muscles and sinews are for walking, though we do not think of them. The mind relies on these principles at all times, but it is not so easy to unravel them and to represent them distinctly and separately, because this requires great attention to what the mind is doing, and most people, unaccustomed to meditating, have little of this... This is how many things are posited without knowing it.'[9]

---

[9] Leibniz, *New Essays* I, i, §20, p. 84.

XXXIII
Epistemology
Analysis and Synthesis

Duhamel, a learned geometer, aimed in his treatise *Of Methods in the Sciences of Reasoning* to determine what is to be understood by *science of reasoning*, what are the various kinds of questions that can be asked of it, and what methods should be followed to solve its questions; 'and this', he adds, 'is the whole of logic, if we define it as the art of reasoning'.

Duhamel remarks that, since philosophers have neglected the mathematical sciences, the belief has gradually become established among them that geometers have methods peculiar to them. The truth, he says, is merely that the mathematical sciences are based on simpler and clearer data than any other branch of human knowledge. It is in these sciences that one can best study and understand the methods either of demonstration or of research, or, as is most often said, either of teaching or of invention; but in any science of reasoning, the methods are the same, whatever the subject. This was the view of Descartes and Leibniz, not to mention the ancients; it was also that of Condillac, and perhaps it is only in our own time that the methods of the geometers have been considered as peculiar to them.

'Reasoning', says Duhamel, 'is deduction.' We saw above how Claude Bernard recognized that induction, at bottom, was only deduction; merely hypothetical or conjectural deduction. The deduction or syllogism consisting in concluding from the general to the particular, from a class of individuals to an individual of the class, in repeating of an individual taken separately what has been said of this individual by considering him in a group, is, for Duhamel, an operation so simple that it hardly deserves a name. We may wonder here if the learned author, like Descartes, does not despise too much the art that Leibniz considered very useful, if not in discovering truths, then at least in avoiding errors, and which consists in arranging judgements in the order in which their dependence on each other, with all the diversities developed by the syllogistic, is best shown. In any case, what is important, according to Duhamel, and what must be taught, is the way to direct the deductions or syllogisms in order to reach the goal we propose. These are the methods either of demonstration or of research, the methods by which one sometimes proves theorems, sometimes solves problems, methods that are: synthesis and analysis.

Synthesis consists in deducing necessary consequences from propositions that are recognized as true; according to Duhamel, it is only useful for communicating to others what one knows. The method of discovery, in his opinion, the method which it is important, consequently, to deepen, is analysis.

Analysis consists, for a theorem whose proof is sought, in seeking which proposition can be deduced from it, then which other one can be deduced from it, and so on until one arrives at a proposition recognized as true, and which, moreover, is such that one can, by retracing one's steps, demonstrate by synthesis the theorem that is to be established. For a problem, analysis consists in seeking the consequences resulting from the data, which are known relations of known things to the unknown thing that is being asked about, until a consequence is found by which this unknown thing is determined.

In the case of theorems, analysis thus goes back from the proposed conclusion to a series of others until it arrives at a known theorem; in the case of problems, it goes back from the proposed question to a series of others until one is found that one knows how to solve and that leads to what one is looking for.

Here Duhamel points out that, in order to verify a problematic proposition, it is not enough, as Euclid and Pappus said, to draw consequences until we find one that we know to be true. From a false proposition one can draw consequences that are true. And in the same way for the problems proper, in order to know if what is asked is executable, it is not enough to start from what is asked, and, from consequence to consequence, arrive at something that is definitely executable. It is also necessary that what is asked can be done through this thing. In short, it is necessary, starting from what is provisionally taken as a principle, to arrive at a consequence from which it can in turn be concluded, thus at a proposition that can be inverted, a reciprocal proposition.

This is because what is deduced from a thing and is thus, logically speaking, its consequence, is something without which it cannot be; it is, in other words, a necessary condition of that thing. Now a necessary condition of a true thing is necessarily true.

'According to Pappus, analysis as practised by the ancients', said Leibniz, 'was the procedure of taking the proposition which is to be proved and deriving consequences from it until something given or known is reached. I have noted that for this to be effective the propositions must be reciprocal ones, so that a synthetic demonstration can move backwards along which the analysis has followed.' And again: 'Analysis makes use of definitions and other reciprocal propositions that provide a way of reversing the process and finding synthetic demonstrations.'[1]

Duhamel has rediscovered, through his own meditations, these too often forgotten ideas and given them new and useful developments.

Ampère too, as we can see from what has just been published of his philosophical works, had observed very well that consequences only rigorously prove the truth of a principle in so far as they lead to some relation of reciprocal dependence.

---

[1] Leibniz, *New Essays* IV, xvii, §6, p. 484 and IV, xii, §6, p. 450.

Leibniz and Ampère had also seen clearly that in physics one does not arrive, as in the sciences based on definitions, at reciprocal propositions; but, as they remarked, the great number of true consequences which are drawn from the hypothesis, without giving rise to a perfect reciprocity, nor consequently to a perfect demonstration, provide at least a high probability, which can approach it infinitely.

In his examination of the principal theories that have been proposed up to now concerning reasoning and methods, Duhamel passes a very severe judgement on Condillac's theory, which nevertheless seems to be only a consequence of Leibniz's: in his eyes, it has no value. Condillac had believed that reasoning consisted of simple transformations of the same proposition; he relied above all on the example of algebra, which proceeds by series of equations. Ampère had already rejected this thought and pushed far away what he called 'this ridiculous identity'. Duhamel remarks that, in successive systems of equations, what is identical is only the values successively given to the unknowns, and that consequently one can call these successive systems only equivalent and not identical. Ampère said the same in a memoir of the year XII *On Abstract Ideas*, that two ideas which offer the same object, but considered differently, must not be called identical but equivalent.[2] Destutt de Tracy, in his *Logic*, had made a very similar observation. Perhaps, however, the gulf between Condillac on the one hand, and de Tracy, Ampère, and Duhamel on the other, is not enormous. Condillac, however absolute his language may have been, did not claim that, in the successive propositions that deduction links together, and even in a series of equations, there is no difference of any kind: he only wanted to point out a radical identity beneath the differences.

In reasoning, in general, as Aristotle, Leibniz, and Euler have explained, the mind relies on ideas containing each other. But a perfect demonstration is one that goes back to a proposition wherein the subject is as much contained in the predicate as the predicate in the subject, to, that is, a reciprocal proposition, which is a definition. All the consequences are then only different forms of the principle; this is what always happens in mathematics, and this is why we can, from a given property of a quantity, deduce all the others. And, finally, demonstration is absolute or categorical, without anything hypothetical, only if it descends, as from its first principle, from a proposition which is justified by itself; and such propositions are identical propositions, which belong especially to philosophy, and which are like immediate expressions of reason itself.

Perhaps, therefore, Condillac did not advance an entirely untenable paradox when he said, in terms that can be found in Leibniz, that the basis of logic was identity. He himself, moreover, often spoke, instead of identity, of analogy in order to

---

[2] Ampère's *Mémoire de l'an XII* was not published in its entirety, but fragments of it were included in Barthélémy-Saint-Hilaire's 1866 *La philosophie des deux Ampère* (Paris: Didier), which included some of the correspondence of Ampère with Maine de Biran and the commentary of his son, Jean-Jacques. Like the young Biran, Ampère senior was a follower of Condillac and the Ideological school.

characterize the relations of successive propositions. This is enough to show in what sense his ordinary expressions must be taken, and that, by the succession of identicals, he meant only what Leibniz calls the succession of equivalents (*substitutio aequipollentium*). Did not the latter also say: 'Things which can be substituted for each other without the truth suffering for this are identical'?

In any case, just as Cournot, even as he cuts off from philosophy its most special and highest nature, has contributed to restoring it to what it requires in breadth and generality, so too Duhamel, although he does not claim to be working for the advancement of philosophy, has not served it any less, by contributing with his remarks to bringing it back into possession of method in all its generality, and consequently to restoring to it the use of procedures of demonstration or research which in our time it abandoned almost entirely to the geometers.

It remains, in order to clarify the matter, to remove the opposition that is still so often established between deduction, on the one hand, which is identified with synthesis, and, on the other, analysis or, as Duhamel calls it, reduction; as if deduction and drawing consequences were not the same thing, and as if, by employing either analysis or synthesis, one was doing something other than drawing consequences. 'In synthesis', said Descartes with his ordinary and superior clarity, 'one deduces from the known the unknown; in analysis one deduces from the unknown the known in treating the unknown as known, the known as unknown.'[3]

It will also remain, and this is a task that may tempt Duhamel someday, to examine, as well as the rules of analysis, those of synthesis, which is confused, according to Leibniz, with the theory of combinations, and wherein consequently lies the key to invention no less perhaps than in analysis, which is only an inverted form of it.

Perhaps we could even say that genius, whose own nature is invention, has its method; that this method consists in the combination of relationships (*dissita conjungit*), and that this is synthesis.

The philosophy of our time has been reproached for often appearing to be more concerned with literary perfection than with scientific accuracy, for preferring indications and summary descriptions, in more or less figurative terms, to definitions, which are the only sources of proofs, and inductions to true demonstrations. Hence the abandonment of logic. The time has come, perhaps, finally to leave the indeterminate and the uncertain behind, and to seek to determine ideas with precision, and, instead of wrapping them in forms that hide their relationships, to produce them detached, distinct, and arranged according to their logical order. Leibniz never tired of demanding this. The vain and interminable disputes of the scholastics did not come, he said, from the fact that they employed regular forms of reasoning, which, on the contrary, can only greatly contribute to understanding and agreement, but from the fact that they started from poorly

---

[3] It is not clear that Descartes ever wrote anything exactly like this; he does not in the Second Reponses to his *Meditations*, where he discusses analysis and synthesis as methods.

determined principles, from definitions that were only apparent, and that could always be eluded by making distinctions. It is necessary to define precisely, he kept repeating. One must also know how to renounce, if need be, 'the beautiful appearances of regular discourse'. And again: 'In order to reason with evidence, one must know how to maintain some constant formality (to express one's reasoning in such a form that the principles and the consequences are perfectly distinct). There will be less eloquence and more certainty.'[4] The time also seems to have come, in order to use methods appropriately, to examine their nature in greater depth.

As far as method in philosophy in particular is concerned, recent years have seen a growing abandonment of the hopes that had been founded on what was called the psychological method, and have seen come to prominence the idea that the proper function of the mind is to know itself.

In 1865, the Academy of Moral and Political Sciences put the question of *The Role of Psychology in Philosophy* up for competition. The prize was shared between Nourrisson and Maurial.[5] There is no indication in Adolphe Franck's official report on this competition that Nourrisson had departed from the ordinary maxims of the Scottish and eclectic schools; but Maurial, in his dissertation, seems to have illuminated anew the mind's direct knowledge of itself. Already in an earlier book, *On Kant's Scepticism*, he had endeavoured to prove that the radical vice of the system of the author of the *Critique of Pure Reason* was 'to have excessively diminished and reduced to almost nothing the crucial fact of the immediate perception of the soul'.[6] In the dissertation that gained the favour of the Academy of Moral and Political Sciences, he applied himself especially to distinguishing the experience that the soul has of itself from the experiments of physicists, and to show that instead of being limited to simple phenomena, 'it extends to the depths of our person or of the soul itself'. And it must be added that Adolphe Franck seemed to give his assent to the ideas expounded by Maurial. He himself, moreover, had already expressed similar ideas in several articles in the *Dictionary of Philosophical Sciences*.

We must also mention a remarkable account of Caro's *Idea of God*,[*] by Lachelier, in which this young writer briefly but clearly characterized how the reflection that 'within the concatenation of inner phenomena, recognizes the free activity of the mind' differs from the mere observation of phenomena considered apart from their cause.

---

[4] Leibniz, 'Letter to Princess Elizabeth' (1678) in Leibniz, *Philosophical Essays*, ed. R. Ariew and D. Garber (Indianapolis: Hackett, 1989), p. 239.

[5] Félix Nourisson, *La nature humaine: essais de psychologie appliquée* (Paris: Didier, 1865). Emile Maurial's dissertation seems not to have been published.

[6] Emile Maurial (1814–70), *Le scepticisme combattu dans ses principes: analyse et discussion des principes du scepticisme de Kant* (Paris: Durand, 1857).

[*] *Revue de l'instruction publique*, June 1864. [Ravaisson's footnote].

XXXIV
Moral Philosophy

Since Jouffroy's *Course on Natural Right*, the most remarkable philosophical writings relating to morality, along with the learned and ingenious essays of Paul Janet and Ernest Bersot, have been those published by Jules Simon: *Liberty, Duty*, and *Natural Religion*.[1] However, in these writings, the author was concerned less to explore the principles of his moral doctrine and that of the school to which he belongs, than to develop the general rules of conduct which derive from them, and to mark their independence from the dogmas of positive or revealed religion.

We have already said that theologians censured this philosophy, which stands quite apart from religion, and which they have described as 'separate philosophy'. While maintaining the necessary independence of philosophy from any other authority than that of evidence and proof, it is to be hoped that it will not deprive itself, so as to ensure all the more this independence, of the high metaphysical or other truths contained in religious faith. Perhaps, indeed, a morality which, remaining within the circle of 'nature' and 'reason', would not seek its roots where nature and reason have theirs, in the supernatural and supra-rational principle expressed, in the religious and moral order, by the law of love and sacrifice, which was already known to the religions of the East, and which Christianity has brought into such great light, would be an incomplete morality, one that is narrower, in many respects, than that of the Gospel, than that of the Old Testament, than that of Buddhism itself.

Many periodicals have recently made known a school of morality that calls itself 'independent'; independent not only of any religion whatsoever, but of any metaphysics, of any belief, for example, in the existence of God and in a future life. Such is the thesis maintained by Bayle and by all those who called themselves 'free thinkers' in the seventeenth century, that atheism and morality are not irreconcilable. Today, as then, it seems that there is reason to doubt that a moral theory can be constituted, if not on the mobile and fragile basis of material interest, outside of any conception of the moral ideal represented by the name of God. 'To consider morality as independent of all metaphysics', said a great thinker, 'is to consider practice as independent of all theory.'

---

[1] Théodore Jouffroy, *Cours de droit naturel* (Paris: Hachette, 1843); Jules Simon, *Le devoir* (Paris: Hachette, 1853); *La religion naturelle* (Paris: Hachette,1856); *La liberté* (Paris: Hachette, 1859).

The crucial question of freedom has not given rise to any special and remarkable writings, except perhaps those of Lequier, published after his death by Charles Renouvier, which we have already mentioned. Bonifas, in a thesis defended a few years ago before the Paris Faculty of Humanities, has forcefully defended human liberty against what he, with others, believed was opposed to it in the determinism of the author of the *Theodicy*. In a chapter of Charles Dollfus's *Philosophical Meditations* (1866) entitled 'On Free Will', we find summarized in a phrase that deserves to be noted what has perhaps been said most accurately concerning the relationship between volitions and their motives. 'From the fact that the will always depends on the motives which determine it, must we conclude that the will is not free? No, because the motives that determine *me* are *my* motives. By obeying them, it is I myself that I obey, and freedom consists precisely in depending only on oneself.'[2]

Under the title of *System of the Moral World*, Charles Lambert has developed a theory of immortality, according to which it would be the privilege of those who, by the use they make of their freedom, would acquire for their souls the strength to live without end.[3] That such a theory has arisen and has not been received without favour proves how strong is the preoccupation with spiritual and moral activity among the thinkers of our time. However, once such activity has been studied more closely, it is perhaps more difficult to persuade oneself that it can ever cease once it exists, and one will more readily believe, with Descartes and Leibniz, that what has thought, even if only for a moment, will always think. And not only, according to the latter of these great authors, will that which has once thought eternally think, but each of our thoughts contains something of all that we have ever thought, something of all that we will ever think. As, indeed, there is no movement which does not depend on all the movements that have ever been accomplished, and which must contribute to all those which will ever be accomplished, there is no thought in which all that has been does not resound more or less obscurely, and which must subsist and propagate itself, without ever dying out, as in eternal vibrations. Each soul is a central point where the universal light is reflected from all sides, from a thousand different angles, and not only each soul, but each of the thoughts, each of the feelings through which its immortal personality is constantly produced from the depths of the infinite.

Wiart, in a book published in 1862, has examined *The Principles of Morality as a Science*.

The Scottish school and the eclectic school generally limit themselves to appealing, in order to regulate human conduct, to a certain number of maxims which are considered to be self-evident, or even, more simply still, to relying on what is called the judgement of conscience for the moral appreciation of either

---

[2] Charles Dollfus (1827–1913), *Méditations philosophiques* (Paris: Lacroix, 1866).
[3] Charles Lambert, *Système du monde moral* (Paris: Lévy, 1862).

ideas or actions. This is the doctrine that de Strada calls, as we saw above, *evidentism*, and whose origin he relates to Descartes.

To proceed in this way, dispensing with proofs and referring to common sense, to the general idea of duty, to conscience, amounts, according to Wiart, to suppressing science. And he shows by numerous examples how it follows that prejudices peculiar to a particular time and country are set up as rules of morality, or even that each individual takes his own fantasy as the only law. On the contrary, there is, in his opinion, a principle which accounts for all prescriptions and measures their value as well as that of actions, and this principle is utility. However, as Bentham presented it, the principle of utility is confused with egoism, which destroys all morality. According to Wiart, it must be combined with Jouffroy's principle that we tend and must tend towards what is the universal end of humanity. In the reconciliation of these two ideas, that is, in the maxim of universal utility, lies the true principle of moral science. In other words, the best action is that which serves the greatest number the most.

It can hardly be disputed that the best actions are those which are most generally useful, that most serve the common good, and that, consequently, general utility can be a test in the appreciation of morality. But, whether for each or for all of us, what exactly is the good, and consequently what is useful, or what serves the good? This is the main question, on which all the others depend.

Will we still be content to answer with Kant, and after him with the eclectic school: it is duty, or what reason commands? It is a question of knowing what one must do, what reason commands. If one asks for an explanation of what reasoning is, saying that it is explained by a faculty of reasoning is not to answer, but only to replace a word by another equivalent word, at the most only to classify, to categorize. In the same way, answering the question: 'What should be done?' by saying we should do 'what it is our purpose to do' is still not to say anything, or it is not to say enough, if we do not also explain in what our purpose consists. This is to fail to leave behind the insufficient generalities that Wiart reproaches, not without reason perhaps, the eclectic school for clinging to.

We could leave behind this circle of abstract and general terms, which consists in defining duty by the good or by a purpose, and the good or the purpose by duty, by defining the good, for example, as the Greeks, and particularly the Stoics, did, by the beautiful, and then the beautiful by harmony and unity, or again by what determines love, or by love itself.

'Religion', says Pascal, 'is God present to the heart.' Through the heart, therefore, according to Pascal, we feel God, and that is religion. This is, in the end, the thought that inspired Charles Charaux to write his thesis defended before the Nancy Faculty of Humanities and entitled *Of Moral Method, or Of Love and Virtue as Necessary Elements of all True Philosophy*.[4]

---

[4] Charles Charaux (1828–1908), *De la méthode morale, ou De l'amour et de la vertu comme éléments nécessaires de toute vraie philosophie* (Paris: Ladrange, 1866).

After having remarked that, even in the physical and mathematical sciences, great progress has been made only under the impulse given to the will by the increasingly visible beauty of the order which is discovered in an equally marvellous unity and variety, Charaux seeks to establish that, a fortiori, for the truths of a still higher kind that are the object of philosophy, together with the action of the intellectual faculties, the constant contribution of the moral faculties is necessary. He remarks that the psychology which reigns everywhere today takes little account of moral sensibility, and attributes to it no part in science. 'Yet', he says, 'the God whom my reason conceives as the capital truth, as the supreme principle of all philosophy, my heart, too, affirms in its own way, and woe to him who does not hear this double testimony!'

Pascal said: 'The heart has its reasons, which reason hardly knows.'[5] He also said that 'the heart has its order'. He added: 'This order is not in principles and demonstrations: it consists principally in digressions on each point which relates to the end, to show it always'; and finally: 'This order which Jesus Christ, St Paul, St Augustine followed, is that of charity.'[6] In this passage by Pascal, compared with his profound remarks on the art of persuasion, there lies doubtless the germ of a 'moral method'. If Charaux has not yet tried to develop it or even to define it with precision, at least he has the merit of having called attention to this important truth, that thought, which is an action and a faculty of the soul, is not enough for philosophy, that it needs the whole soul, and, if one can distinguish parts in the soul, that it needs above all the one which seems to be its principal and best part. Did not Socrates—he with whom, after Anaxagoras, begins high philosophy, Plato's master, and, through him, that of Aristotle; he who, comparing himself to the Sophists puffed up with false knowledge, said 'I know nothing'—add, in order to clarify at least the source of his awareness of his ignorance, the beginning of a true science: 'I know nothing but the things of love'?

According to Plato, and even more, perhaps, according to Aristotle, if we get to the bottom of the latter's thought, it is in the idea of the good, in the idea of love, which corresponds to it and explains it, that the last word on all things lies. And today, after so much research and experience, given that we see more clearly than ever that the inside of things, so to speak, is the soul, and that the innermost part of the soul is the will, how can we fail to recognize that it is in the innermost part of the will itself that the deepest source from which all science springs is hidden? Is not true love, or love of that true good which itself is only love, indeed wisdom? And what is science, if, to recall an idea of Aristotle, the world is not a bad drama made up of unrelated pieces; what can it be if not the whole of the divergent forms and, so to speak, of the projections and reflections in lower spheres of a primary science, which is that of the first and universal principle, and which we call, with an excellent name, wisdom?

---

[5] This is fragment 277 in Brunschvicg's edition.
[6] The three sentences belong to fragment to 283 in Brunschvicg's edition.

XXXV
Aesthetics

A part of philosophy which is closely related to morality, namely aesthetics, or the theory of beauty, was the subject of a competition organized by the Academy of Moral and Political Sciences in 1857, the result of which was announced in 1859. This competition produced two distinguished works: one, by Chaignet, which received an honourable mention; the other, which was awarded the prize, by Charles Lévêque.[1]

In his skilful analyses of existing aesthetic theories, Chaignet endeavoured above all to distinguish from the idea of beauty those which seem close to it and with which it has often been more or less associated or confused, principally the ideas of the good [*le bien*], and consequently, of goodness [*le bon*] and moral perfection.

One of the most brilliant and perhaps also one of the strongest parts of Victor Cousin's philosophy is the one addressed by his lectures on beauty, where, developing a theory advanced by Reid, which goes back through Shaftesbury to Plato, he seeks to establish that beauty is a more or less complete expression of spiritual and moral perfection. Chaignet professes to belong to the eclectic school. Nevertheless, and although he admires the great views of Kant, Schelling, and Hegel, those 'founders of aesthetics, which since then', he adds, 'has not advanced a single step', he hesitates to commit himself, like Victor Cousin, to their efforts to establish that beauty, far from being only the set of pleasant impressions that objects make on our senses, is the expression of the absolute in what is relative, of the infinite in the finite, and consequently, of the intelligible by the sensory, or of the moral by the physical. He is not prepared to admit either that the beautiful is closely related to the good, or, consequently, that, speaking precisely, beauty can be attributed either to virtue or to God himself.

Summing up the doctrines of St Augustine, which derived from Greek philosophy, St Thomas said: 'The good is the object of desire, therefore it is what pleases. When the object is such that it pleases by the knowledge of it, not by sense alone, it is what is called beautiful. The beautiful is therefore the good, but the good responding to thought, to reason. The good in itself, the absolute good, corresponds to something deeper, which is love.' It seems that, in the light of these

---

[1] Antelme-Edouard Chaignet (1819–1901), 'Les principes de la science du beau', *Comptes-rendus des séances et travaux de l'Académie des sciences morales et politiques* 55 (1861), pp. 369–445; Charles Lévêque (1818–1900), *La science du beau étudiée dans ses principes, dans ses applications et dans son histoire*, 2 vols (Paris: Durand, 1862).

simple notions, the obscurities that Chaignet finds in the doctrines of the greatest thinkers, from Plato to Schelling and Hegel, can be cleared up.

Charles Lévêque has endeavoured to define what beauty consists of exactly. Dissatisfied with the most widespread theories which have it consist either in proportion, or, and this amounts to the same thing, in variety combined with uniformity, or in simple unity, or in the relationship of the finite to the infinite, beauty seems to him to be the expression of the constitutive characteristics of the essence of all being, and these characteristics are, according to him, greatness or power and order; here are to be found, let us note in passing, Malebranche's two principles. Let us also add that, like several of his predecessors, Lévêque seems to find genuine beauty where grandeur is subject to order, and, in contrast, the sublime where order yields to grandeur.

Victor Cousin, mainly in his last works, seemed inclined to define beauty by force; and in his polemic against the philosophy that reduced beauty to what pleases the senses, he had always excluded from true beauty any idea of pleasure. Charles Lévêque is faithful to the eclectic doctrine on this point too: he excludes from the idea of true beauty what he calls 'charm' [*le charmant*]. However, given his taste in the appreciation of beautiful things, one might suspect that from this theory, whose rigidity is perhaps not without aridity, he will be led to a broader theory, wherein beauty would perhaps find a more complete explanation.

The word *force*, as we have had more than one occasion to remark, in being nearer to expressing something positive and real than those of *substance* and *cause*, is nevertheless still the expression of an incomplete idea, which has a definite value only as a sign or logical equivalent of particular material phenomena. It should also be noted that Lévêque himself admits into the idea of force, together with the idea of power, from which it hardly differs, that of order as necessary to complete it, because it includes the end towards which the force tends and the way in which it tends towards it; and again, tending towards an end is at bottom to will it. If, therefore, we admit with the ingenious and learned author of *The Science of Beauty* that the explanation of beauty must be sought in what explains the very constitution of being, and that, in turn, the explanation of the constitution of being is given by force, then soon, it seems, we shall have to recognize, with Leibniz, that, in order to find under this abstract term 'force' something positive and real, something really distinct from the material of phenomena, or of movement, we must grasp tendency, and in tendency itself, at bottom, the will; and that, consequently, the claim that beauty expresses force acquires its full meaning only in the claim that beauty expresses will. By means of a further step in the reflection through which we become aware of ourselves, we shall find that volitions, in turn, cannot be completely explained by themselves, that they need a principle, a cause, of which they are, as Malebranche said, only partial manifestations. What is this cause? Precisely that which, by universal agreement, beauty best expresses, and which it also brings into being. Indeed, despite the theories that, for fear of reducing beauty to a purely material and sensory pleasure, dismiss any idea of pleasure, is it not a manifest character of all beautiful things that they please us, and that they please us by a secret magic that, according to expressions that are as acute as they are worn out, fascinates us, charms us? This charm is to be found above all in what is called grace; and this grace that somehow goes, beyond the still outer region of the intellect, to the soul itself, that comes to move the heart, does it not seem to derive, rather than from insensible matter, or from magnitude, or from the form which orders it, from the heart itself and from the depths of the soul?

If the general idea of the good [*du bien, du bon*] can be explained by beauty, it would seem that in the final analysis beauty, at least supreme beauty, comes down to the good *par excellence* which is like the ground of perfection, the very essence of the divine, and which we call goodness [*bonté*]. But to be good in this superior sense is to love. It is therefore, it seems, ultimately love that is the principle and reason of beauty.

'After art', says Schelling, 'has given things the character which imparts to them the aspect of individuality' (could one not say the same of will?), 'it takes a further step: it gives them grace, which makes them loveable, by making them seem to love. Beyond this second degree, there is only one more, which the second announces and prepares: it is to give things a soul, by which they no longer only seem to love, but love.'

'The good', Plotinus said, 'is that which gives to things graces, and to what desires them love [*les amours*].'

The good is therefore love itself.

But the sublime? one may ask. Does this mean that it has to lose the high rank that it has always possessed, and that, especially since Kant, seems to be irrevocably assured for it? Not at all; but the sublime, which reigns supreme in the beautiful, is not simply, as is too often said, and by Kant himself, what borders on the terrible. The sublime is that which exceeds all limits. But what is frightening is foreign, and therefore limited and separate. The infinite is that which, as the book of Wisdom says, penetrates everything by its purity, occupies everything, fills everything. Particular wills, threatening to others, are limited: therefore, nothing truly, absolutely exceeds any limit except that which knows no obstacle or resistance, the immensity of love. This is why there is still something above the sublime of the Old Testament, which is essentially terrible, namely the sublime that begins in Buddhism and is completed in the Gospel, that of sweetness and peace, the sublime of sacrifice.

'We perhaps should not say', as we read in Aristotle, 'that order and grandeur constitute beauty, but only that there is no beauty without order and grandeur.' If order and grandeur, which constitute perhaps the admirable, are indeed only conditions of beauty, is not what grounds its essence what makes it lovable? In relating what we might call the principal categories of aesthetics to the most generally accepted primordial elements of divine and human nature, and which we would also find in the succession of the great epochs of history, that is to say, to the triplicity of power, intellect, and love, might we not say that the sublime of the terrible responds to power, the cause of grandeur; that the beautiful properly so called belongs to intellect, the cause of order; and that to love responds the superior and properly supernatural sublime, which forms the most excellent and truly divine beauty, that of grace and tenderness?

Aesthetics is not only an important part of philosophy: considered in its principles, where it is identified with morality, it becomes philosophy itself. We have seen emerge from the movement of contemporary ideas and from the reflections it suggests the general result, one which any high metaphysics has always at least glimpsed, that what must explain the world, nature, is the soul, the spirit. If, therefore, beauty is the soul's motive, what makes it love and will—and thus act, which is to say, live, which is also to say, be, since for the soul, and indeed for all substances, being, living, and acting are the same thing—, namely beauty, and especially the most divine and perfect beauty, contains the secret of the world.

XXXVI
Summary and Manifesto for a New Spiritualist Philosophy

Let us summarize in a few words what results from the preceding survey.

According to the philosophical doctrines that prevailed in the previous century—doctrines which arose from contempt for the imperfectly defined supra-sensory principles that had satisfied the Middle Ages, and from the almost exclusive preoccupation with material phenomena whose regularity and constancy, which had been poorly known in the past, now seemed to suffice to explain everything—everything is limited to bodies and their relationships. What was called the 'philosophy of nature', with its physical and moral consequences, was supposed to constitute the whole of philosophy. By the beginning of the century, it was generally recognized that these doctrines give an insufficient account of our ideas and beliefs that go beyond nature, and of nature itself. A philosophy came to be formed that re-established faith in the principles that the senses do not teach, but which our intellect demands and demonstrates to itself. Soon it had gained the upper hand among us, and, introduced into public education by teachers of great authority, it has reigned almost alone to this day.

Still dominated by the guiding idea of the previous century that the primary source of all knowledge was to be found in an experience reaching no further than phenomena, and that, consequently, the method of observation, which is that of the natural sciences, was the only method, the new philosophy, at least in so far as it did not borrow from other methods, could provide only incomplete notions and insufficient demonstrations of the principles it wished to re-establish. It was not possible to prove, if we were to proceed as it limited itself to proceeding, that these supposed principles were not, as Kant had said, mere conceptions, by means of which we would represent things under certain conditions of order and unity, without anything really existent corresponding to them.

In recent times, moreover, the philosophy in question has ended up, with those who pushed its maxims to their final consequences, with a theory that admits, beyond sensible phenomena, only idealities, through which nature would be regulated, it is true, but which would nevertheless be deprived of all reality. This is a theory constituting what can be called, consequently, a system of idealism; not, in truth, of that absolute idealism which reduces all reality to ideas, but of a mitigated idealism, which, granting reality to the phenomena which experience makes known to us, attributes to that which differs from these phenomena, and which serves, moreover, to explain them, only the kind of existence belonging to mere ideas.

In the face of a metaphysics which gave to the intelligible principles of sensible phenomena so little reality, the philosophy that reduces everything to these phenomena could not fail to return, and our time has indeed seen the reappearance of a new materialism under the name of positivism.

However, since the time when materialism found such a welcome, things have changed in many respects.

We have had more than one occasion to point out in the course of this survey that materialism generally originated in the sciences that consider the elementary conditions and the simplest properties forming the material basis of nature, that is, among the mathematical and physical sciences. Living things, in contrast, especially as one rises in the organic hierarchy, where one somehow feels the soul approach, teach spiritualism, as do, even more so, things of the moral or aesthetic orders, because there the consideration of the whole, of order, of harmony dominates that of the detail of the parts; in other words, because there the consideration of form dominates that of matter.

Now, in our time, we remain less willingly within the limits of the sciences whose object is the matter of nature, without any regard for those which deal with things of a more complex and higher order, without any commerce either with the sciences of life, or with the fine arts and with the poetry which forms their basis, and, in general, with studies of the intellectual and moral order. Materialism, therefore, under these powerful influences, hardly remains true to itself, but, in being gradually modified and altered, is changed into a different theory that is more or less imbued with spiritualism.

Indeed, we have seen the doctrine that calls itself positivism, or the doctrines which closely resemble it, after having begun by reducing everything to more or less complex combinations of geometrical and mechanical elements, and to the crude mechanism of the communication of their movements, finally resort—in order to explain the combinations themselves, at least when it comes to things of a higher order that are so complicated and so harmonious, as well as the origin of movements—to some organic and creative idea, to some regulating ideal, to some cause, in a word, both efficient and final, very similar to the principles invoked by the philosophy they intended to combat. We have also seen the more or less materialist theories of our time also lead, at a greater or lesser distance from spiritualism, to a kind of idealism.

The causes to which one must relate these two opposite kinds of philosophy—with one, it may be said, considering only the matter of things, while the other considers also their form—are evidently to be found in the dominant preoccupation, on the one hand, with existence at its lowest point, in its most elementary state, and on the other, with existence at its highest point, with complete and absolute existence. If, therefore, we seek, not these causes, but their immediate effects, in other words, if we examine the two different ways in which they direct minds, and which lead them to entirely opposite results, we find, it seems, that these two ways are those followed in the two major parts of any method that we call analysis and synthesis.

Any object which we propose to know can be considered either in its elements, or in the unity of its form. The elements are the materials; the form, their mode of assembly. To decompose an object or an idea, to resolve either into its elements, is to decompose it into its material. When a whole is broken down into its elements, these into others, and so on until we arrive at indecomposable elements, it may seem that we have explained this whole, that we have given a complete account of it. This is perhaps true of those things whose properties are scarcely other than those of their elements, things of the geometrical and even mechanical order, where the parts fully explain the whole, and can serve to explain it a priori. Consequently, if we extend to a higher order what we have found to be true of the lower order formed by the set of general material conditions, we believe that we can explain objects, whatever they may be, by decomposing them.

In contrast, it is possible to consider in things the mode of union of the materials, or form; to consider how they are assembled and combined with others. This is the point of view of combination, or complication, or synthesis. This perspective is essentially that of art, since art consists above all in composing, in constructing; it belongs, in particular, to poetry, which ceaselessly brings together, associates, marries together the most distant objects; it is the perspective, finally, of science itself whereby it participates in the nature of art, whereby it is above all inventive. The art of combining what is given serves, at least as much as analysis, to solve problems. Induction is most often described as essentially consisting in enumerating the elements of facts, which is the work of analysis. However, as the discoverer of infinitesimal calculus, he who made so many other important discoveries, said a long time ago: 'If induction, considered as the operation of gathering observations, is not accompanied by a certain art of guessing, little progress will be made.'[1] And this art of guessing, as he rightly said, and, as we have seen an eminent inventor of our time clearly explain, consists, after having broken things down into their ultimate parts, in forming hypotheses, on the basis of analogy, that explain their relationships. These hypotheses are modes of assembly or combination; combination, composition, synthesis, the opposite of analysis.

Leibniz said, it is true, that the source of invention was analysis, which made known the properties of the primary elements; but wherever he wished to penetrate more deeply into the question of methods, he said that analysis, by breaking things down into their elements, was useful above all for judgement, but that what was most useful for invention was synthesis.

---

[1] Ravaisson is paraphrasing here Leibniz, *New Essays* IV, xii, §13, p. 454.

If synthesis is of great utility in the sciences, particularly in those whose objects are the highest and most complex, it is of even greater utility in the science that goes beyond all physical and sensory experience, in philosophy.

Our synthetic judgements are not limited to bringing together the elements of things in the whole which they have offered or can offer, as phenomena, to our experience. There are others by which we go beyond all that sensory experience presents to us. These are the ones that Kant highlighted under the name of synthetic a priori judgements. However, by seeing in them only an application to the objects of experience of the conditions of the sensory order without which we cannot imagine them, perhaps he did not seek the principle high enough. It is not only to the laws of extension and duration that we subject, by our synthetic a priori judgements, the objects offered to us by our senses, but to higher laws from which those of extension and duration perhaps derive.

We have the need for perfection, we carry within us its type [*le type*]: it is according to this type that we judge everything.

Nothing comes from nothing, said ancient wisdom from the earliest days.— Nothing happens, nothing exists, said Leibniz, for which there is no reason. According to a dictum of Spinoza that we have already cited, nothing is conceivable if not in the form of eternity; we could say more generally, if not in the form of infinity or perfection; maxims that are, at bottom, equivalent. If nothing comes from nothing, it is necessary that, since all relative existence is nothing compared to absolute existence, everything must ultimately come from infinite and absolute existence. Since everything has a reason, it is necessary that, from reason to reason, everything is justified by a reason that justifies itself, by, that is, the infinite and the absolute. Hence the synthetic judgement by which we attribute, a priori, to every fact a cause.

Descartes said: to judge that a thing begins, that a thing is new, is an intellection or thought which the senses do not explain; it is a 'pure intellection'. He could have added, and this is perhaps what he was thinking: it is an intellection implying the idea of what is, opposed to what is not, of what is eternally, opposed to what begins, the idea of that against which all beginnings and all ends are compared and measured.

We cannot understand, said Hamilton, and we have already referred to this, how something should begin, absolutely speaking; and this is the basis of what philosophers call the axiom of causality. If something seems to us to begin, we immediately assume it somehow to have a prior existence in what we call a cause.

There is more: everything that happens not only comes from somewhere, but also goes somewhere. We conceive it as necessary that the cause contains, together with the reason for the beginning, also the reason for the end towards which the direction tends. Every cause is thus conceived as exceeding the effect on all sides and as embracing the finite with its infinity.

It is not only, as Kant thought, that all phenomena appear to us to be determined by a time and a space which limit them in every sense and to which no limits can be given. Beneath these sensory and external conditions of existence, the phenomenon is a change or movement; and movement requires, in order to explain what is unitary in its multiplicity, something simple from which it proceeds. Moreover, as an imperfect thing that is as it were on the way to being, movement implies a principle that provides it, at each moment of its progress, with what it acquires, and which, consequently, is in actuality what it is becoming. This principle from which movement emanates as from its source, this necessary ground and substance of movement, is tendency or effort; effort that is not, like the movement by which it manifests itself, an object of the senses and of the imagination, but rather what our most inner awareness, in the unique type of the will, makes known to us.

If we are dealing only with the details of physical and mechanical phenomena, it does not seem absolutely impossible, at least initially, that in order to explain one phenomenon, another phenomenon would suffice; we may not see that in order to explain that which is imperfect in itself, we must always turn to that which is perfect, complete, and absolute. In the presence of organized beings, it is quite different. A very complicated machine stands before us: if we examine it with the penetrating eye of a Pascal or a Leibniz, the complication appears to go to infinity; yet everything conspires and concurs in it. Here we no longer conceive only in a vague and indeterminate way that there must be a cause: we state that the cause must be something analogous to what is for a machine that we have made, for a work of our art, the idea according to which it is composed and ordered, the thought that makes all the pieces work together towards the same end. In other words, in the presence of the ever so complex unity of organized beings, the synthetic judgement by which we relate it to a cause is determined and completed. Instead of remaining, for the explanation of phenomena, with a simple idea of efficient cause or force, conceived as a principle of movement, an idea which is incomplete and as it were empty, we now arrive at the idea, fuller and closer to our inner experience, of a cause which, from the beginning of its operation, implies the end as its goal, of a cause that is final at the same time as it is efficient, efficient by the very fact that it is final, and whose perfection, at least relative, is the reason for the existence of all those elements which find their completion in it alone, of all those means which find their utility only within it. Such is the synthetic judgement by which, in the presence of organized beings, and better still in the presence of intelligent and moral beings, we complete, by the idea of perfection, to which they aspire in their very existence, what is imperfect in them.

This is the point at which arrive, through the use of synthesis, and though perhaps to a degree unknowingly, all the theories that we have seen converge, from very different starting points, towards the same idealism.

On this path, we cannot stop at any particular and imperfect idea. With Plato, with Kant, with the authors of most of the idealist theories we have examined, it is necessary, degree by degree, to arrive at a supreme ideal of which all the particular ideas offer only partial aspects, incomplete applications, limitations.

Analysis, descending from decomposition to decomposition to more and more elementary materials, tends to break everything down into absolute imperfection where there is neither form nor order. Reducing, as Auguste Comte said so profoundly of materialism, the superior to the inferior, reducing thought to life, life to movement, movement itself to a change of relations of crude, entirely passive bodies, it reduces everything, in Leibniz's phrase, to inertia and torpor. And if it is true, as antiquity had already seen, and as Aristotle and Leibniz demonstrated, that to do nothing, not to act, is truly to be nothing, it can be said that analysis, applied on its own, tends by degrees towards nothingness.

Synthesis, rising from composition to composition to higher and higher principles of composition, increasingly free of material limitations, tends to explain everything by absolute perfection, which nothing limits; it therefore tends from degree to degree towards infinity.

However, if we limit ourselves, as idealism does in the various systems we have seen leading to it, to conceiving the principle of composition from which matter takes its form under the general notion of a unity through which material diversity is co-ordinated—which is defined, moreover, only by removing particular and differential circumstances, just as we distinguish plant in general from particular plants, just as we dislocate from the species their genus, and this is how Plato and Malebranche seem, at least at first sight, to have understood what they call 'ideas'—then, instead of the ideal being the final perfection in relation to which the phenomena that one wants it to explain represent but imperfection and a beginning, it really represents only their vaguest outline and briefest sketch. The ideal thus understood, and this is also how the aesthetics called 'idealist' conceived it, is not properly, as idealism would like it to be, a form or unity in which the material phenomenon is contained, but on the contrary a condition that this phenomenon implies, just as a figure implies a simpler figure, as a notion contains a more elementary notion. We arrive at the ideal thus conceived not by way of synthesis, as it seems at first, but by way of analysis. Presented as an end towards which the movement of nature tends, on closer examination we find only the conception of a simpler state, to which we reduce an existence by stripping it of its attributes, and, from idea to idea, while we think we are rising from perfection to perfection towards absolute perfection, we are, on the contrary, advancing by simplification, and consequently, by progressive generalization towards the idea of 'being' in general, which is only the expression, in our understanding, of the last degree to which abstraction can descend, and which, deprived of any other determination, is very close to being confused, as Hegel saw, with the idea of pure nothingness. In this way, and Aristotle reproached the Platonists for this, we only descend by degrees from a given point of perfection to ultimate imperfection.

These two quite different doctrines, the one admitting in things only what our senses show us, the other believing that the essence of things is contained in the ideas formed by the understanding, by abstraction, thus both use a similar method, the first breaking things down into their material elements, the second, after having first related them, through a sort of synthesis, to an idea, and, believing itself to rise from this first synthesis to more and more comprehensive syntheses, but in reality only decomposing the idea into the logical elements that are its matter, both go along different paths in the same direction which leads them away equally, though diversely, from the perfection and fullness of reality, both tending towards the same abyss of emptiness and nullity.

Materialism, in imagining itself arrive by way of analytical simplification from the accidental to the essential, only reduces everything to the most general and elementary conditions of physical existence, which constitute the minimum of reality.

Idealism, in wishing to arrive, by generalization, which eliminates as accidental the specific and differential characteristics, at what is highest in the intelligible order and at the ideal of perception, only reduces everything, on a path opposed to that which it intended to follow, to the most elementary logical conditions, which are the minimum of perfection and intelligibility.

The problem is that idealism has not placed itself, any more than materialism, at the only point of view from which it is possible to recognize the accidental that must be excised or neglected, which is the work of analysis, in order to arrive, by veritably synthetic means, at what is essential. This is the point of view from which we directly and fully perceive what is essential, namely the point of view of the consciousness of the absolute that is inner activity where reality and perfection coincide and become one.

When we return, so to speak, into ourselves, we find ourselves amidst a world of sensations, feelings, imaginations, ideas, desires, volitions, and memories, a boundless and bottomless mobile ocean, which is still all ours, which is nothing other than ourselves. In what way 'ours', in what way 'ourselves'? Because at every moment and everywhere within this multiple inner vortex, we form from its elusive diversity assemblages, ensembles, whose link is a unity which is none other than the very operation by which we form them.

If, indeed, we look for the way in which this cause, which is ourselves, does what it does, we find that its action consists in the determination, by thought, of an order or an end to which the unknown, latent powers enveloped by our complex individuality adjust themselves. We propose to ourselves a particular object, an idea, or an expression of an idea: from the depths of memory there immediately emerges all that is useful in the treasures it contains. We will a particular movement, and, under the mediating influence of the imagination, which somehow translates into the language of sensibility the proposals of the intellect, elementary movements emerge from the depths of our being, of which the desired movement is the end and completion. Thus, according to the ancient fable, docile materials arrived, at the call of a song, and arranged themselves, as if all by themselves, into walls and towers.

What is the idea that our thought proposes to itself, and which calls up, as from the height of its perfection, our inferior powers? It is our thought itself at the highest point of active reality that, within its particular limits, it can attain. What are these powers which it attracts and which find in it their fulfilment, their realization? Ideas too, ideas which are also ours, that still belong to our thought, though in a state where it is beside itself and foreign to itself.

Experience shows that the mainspring of the whole of inner life is thought or intellectual action which, from a state of diffusion and confusion where it has, as it were, only a virtual existence, recalls itself, brings itself back, by a continual movement of recomposition into the unity of consciousness, into active existence, and from a state of sleep and dream returns ceaselessly to the waking state. If the stones of the fable obey a melody that calls them, this is because in these stones there is something that is also melody, however muted and secret it may be, and that, when pronounced, expressed, is drawn from potentiality to actuality.

It must be added that, if the relative perfection of our thought is the cause of all that happens in us, this relative perfection has itself its cause, which is absolute perfection.

Our personality, consisting in our intelligent will, is in the whole of what we are, according to the ancient expression, a genius, that is to say a special generating principle, or a god, a particular god, whose empire has its limits; this genius, this god produces nothing, can do nothing without the superior virtue in which it participates, the universal God, who is absolute good and infinite love. And this great God, according to a famous saying, 'is not far from us'. The superior measure against which we compare and measure our conceptions, or rather which measures them in us, the idea of our ideas, the reason for our reason, is 'more interior to us than our interior';—'it is in it, through it, that we have all that we have of life, movement and existence'. It is us, one might say, even more than we are us, we who are constantly and in a thousand ways alien to ourselves.

While Malebranche said that we see everything in God except ourselves, of which he thought we had only an obscure feeling, perhaps we should say that we see everything in God because it is in him alone that we see ourselves.

In short, it is by means of a synthetic operation that, given a particular fact, we do not simply relate it to a fact preceding it or merely reduce it to a more general and simpler fact—and these are the two degrees of the determination of what is called the physical cause—but rather relate it to a true cause, that is to say, to the action of a higher perfection.

But this synthetic operation, which is especially, as opposed to analysis, the philosophical method, has a necessary principle. This principle is the method properly so called (if a simple and indivisible operation can still be called a method) of high philosophy, of metaphysics: it is the immediate awareness, in the reflection on ourselves and by ourselves on the absolute in which we participate, of the ultimate cause or reason.

All perspective is relative to a point, a single point. Seen from everywhere else, it offers only disproportions and discordances; seen from this point, it becomes fitting in all its parts, and presents a harmonic whole. It can be said that the universal perspective, which is the world or the universal harmony, has as its point of view, its only point of view, the infinite or the absolute.

The absolute of perfect personality, which is infinite wisdom and love, is the perspectival centre from which can be understood the system formed by our imperfect personality, and, consequently, the system formed by any other existence. God serves to comprehend the soul, and the soul, nature.

This intimate constitution of our being, which a direct consciousness makes known to us, analogy makes us find it elsewhere, and then everywhere. It is according to this unique type of interior organization that we grasp all the beings described as organized, things which have in themselves, whatever their complexity, and more evidently in the contrast to this very complexity, the principle and the end of their movements, or, better, a cause which is their principle in that it is their end; things which, like God, like the soul, though to a lesser degree, are the causes of themselves, things which are more or less the analogue of persons.

If, after the soul, we consider that with which it is immediately connected, that is to say, the organism, we see that the highest of its functions, and the one in which we must perhaps seek the ultimate explanation of all the others, is that it moves itself. How can we better define the organism than by saying that it is a machine that gives itself movement?

Aristotle already remarked that the most perfect of organisms, that of man, is eminently distinguished from all others by the superiority of voluntary movements and their instruments. Is this function of spontaneous movement, which thus attains, in the most perfect of creatures, the highest perfection, not the universal function by which, in different and more confused forms, as we descend the organic scale, all others are carried out?

According to ideas very recently expounded by Claude Bernard, and which summarize with superior clarity those that he had previously developed in his *Introduction to Experimental Medicine*, all the phenomena which take place in organized bodies are reducible to physical and chemical phenomena, and are all quite similar to those that inorganic things offer us, and which our art can reproduce. What is special is the way in which these phenomena are realized by means of apparatus whose formation we cannot understand and which our art is absolutely powerless to imitate. Could we not add that this special way in which physico-chemical phenomena are realized in living beings consists in the fact that the latter, by spontaneous determinations, within milieux to which these determinations are relative, provide for the parts situations through which particular physico-chemical phenomena are immediately produced, and that, consequently, just as organisms as a whole can be defined as machines that move themselves, each of the organs of which they are composed *ad infinitum* can be defined as a special automatic instrument of movement? Can we not say, moreover, that these machines themselves, these special devices, products of an art which surpasses us, are the result, guided by this art, of a harmonic conspiration of spontaneous elementary movements? Finally, if we cannot understand how living machines are formed and repair themselves, nor consequently imitate them, is this not because they are the result of spontaneous elementary movements that escape, as Stahl saw, all the conditions of imagination, and that cannot, consequently, be objects of calculation and reasoning?

And the same goes, one might conjecture, for the imperceptible internal movements by which what one might dare to call the organization of inorganic bodies, i.e. crystallization, is produced. As for physical and chemical phenomena, whether in organized bodies or in others, the tendency of present-day science is to reduce them to particular forms of mechanical phenomena, to special combinations of movements, and, instead of explaining these movements by affinities or attractions that can be accounted for only by veritably intentional determinations, similar to those of organized beings, to analyse them as mere effects of the impulsion from surrounding bodies, in conformity with the general principles of the physics of Descartes and Leibniz. And when we arrive at the impulse, the shock, and the resulting communication of movements, it seems, said Cuvier, that everything is explained, in taking this simple phenomenon, accustomed as we are to encountering it everywhere, to offer an adequate explanation of itself. And it also seems, consequently, that science itself is this theory of universal mechanism that reduces all the functions of more or less organized beings and all physico-chemical phenomena to the propagation of movements by impact.

However, this apparently simple phenomenon will be found, if we look at it closely, still to contain what everywhere it was supposed to replace: spontaneity.

In the communication of motion by shock, there is nothing, it seems, but passivity. Leibniz, however, has highlighted a fact of springiness or elasticity, and this fact can only be understood, as he has shown, by imagining, not that the movement of the moving body perishes in order to be reborn in the body which is struck, but that, by a mutual action and reaction, the inner movement by which the parts were previously animated is merely transformed into a movement of transport of the whole and vice versa. Now, if the movement in the shock, instead of being annihilated and reborn, is only transformed; if, consequently, through so many encounters, there always remains the same quantity of force, this is because the body, once animated by a movement, maintains itself in it. This is the inertia that Kepler first introduced into mechanics, of which it became the first principle, and in which Leibniz brought out a persistent tendency, which is certainly opposed to the will, with its changing resolutions, but which is, at bottom, of an analogous nature. What to the soul is the innate tendency to preserve the action that is its very being and, when disturbed by foreign influences, to restore it, inertia, with its spring effect, is to the body.

Thus, even in admitting that living beings do not manifest anything analogous to the soul which, in us, knows itself, and that they can be brought back to the condition of crude bodies; and even in admitting that from these bodies we must, a fortiori, excise any principle of order and unity in order to reduce them to mere heaps of material particles held together by random external movements, which is the materialist theory, it is still necessary, in order to understand the laws that the crudest matter follows in its movement, to join to the idea of this matter the idea of something which, under the typical but vague name of 'force' or 'power', is no less an analogue and derivative of will and thought.

There is more: independently of the different laws of motion, the idea of motion in general itself implies something other than what is material and external in it. Descartes, who knew very well how to find in the mind the source from which the idea of action is drawn, but who was afraid at the same time of granting any of this activity to nature, defined motion solely by the successive relations of bodies in space. Leibniz showed that it is not possible to determine in what way a body in motion differs, in each of the places it occupies, from what it is at rest, unless we add that in each place it occupies it tends towards passing to another. All motion, at bottom, is therefore tendency. Tendency or effort, says Leibniz, is what is real in motion; all the rest is mere relations. Bodies therefore receive from other bodies, as he also says, only limitations or determinations of their tendency. The tendency itself is innate to them with its primitive direction, and, to find its origin, we have to go back to the power that created them. This is, at bottom, the same demonstration by which Aristotle once proved that, in order to explain motion, it is necessary to go back, beyond the succession of phenomena—be it eternal, as he thought—to a first mover that is not itself in motion, but in an immaterial action, from which emanates what is somehow the internal source of motion. Everything is carried out mechanically, said the thinker of pre-established harmony, and by this he meant that each phenomenon has a determining reason in another phenomenon; but, he added, the mechanism itself has a principle which must be sought outside matter and which metaphysics alone makes known to us.

By this he meant that, if each movement has its physical condition in an external movement, it has its effective principle, its cause in an action that is explained, in the final analysis, only by the power of the good and the beautiful. 'The principles of mechanism, of which the laws of motion are the consequences, cannot', he says, 'be derived from what is purely passive, geometrical or material, nor can they be proved by the axioms of mathematics alone. To justify the dynamic rules, it is necessary to have recourse to real metaphysics and to the principles of attraction [*convenance*] that affect souls and which are no less exact than those of geometers.'[2]

'The source of mechanism', he says, 'is the primitive force; in other words, the laws of motion, according to which the derived forces or impetuosities are born from this force, derive from the perception of good and evil, from what is most attractive. Efficient causes thus depend on final causes; spiritual things are by nature prior to material ones, as they are also prior to them in the order of knowledge, since we see the soul, which is intimate to us, more directly than the body, as Plato and Descartes remarked.'[3] To these two names he could have added that of Aristotle. Perhaps it is also permissible to go beyond the terms of this memorable passage. Since physical causes are not efficient causes, but only conditions whose order of succession represents in reverse the degrees of perfection from the end to the means, perhaps it is permissible to say: efficient causes can be reduced to final causes.

In this way, as the profound thinker that we have so often quoted said, 'the connection of causes with effects, far from establishing an unbearable fatality, rather provides a means of lifting it'.[4]

Everything has a reason, as Leibniz said. This entails that everything has its necessity. And, indeed, without necessity, no certitude; and without certitude, no science. But there are two sorts of necessities: an absolute necessity, which is logical necessity, and a relative necessity, which is moral necessity and which can be reconciled with freedom; two sorts of reasons, one of logic and one of attraction [*convenance*].

There is an absolute necessity. This, in the final analysis, comes back to the principle that a thing cannot not be what it is, to the principle of identity, from which derives the further principle that itself constitutes the ground of all reasoning: what contains a thing contains all that the thing contains. Reasoning, it seems, does not advance in a progressive manner from the simple to the complex but, on the contrary, from the complex to the simple. To reason is to go from an idea to the ideas that it contains, and thus to more elementary ideas without which it cannot be; a consequence is really a condition. The necessity resulting from the relations of containing and contained, which is present in the ideas thus compared to each other, is the one to be found in mathematics, which is merely logic applied to quantity.

---

[2] Leibniz, 'Conversation of Philarète and Ariste, Following a Conversation of Ariste and Theodore' in *Philosophical Papers and Letters*, ed. L. Loemker (Dordrecht: Kluwer, 1989), pp. 618–28, p. 625.

[3] Leibniz, 'Epistola ad Bierlingium' (1711) in *Die philosophischen Schriften von Gottfried Wilhelm Leibniz*, ed. C. J. Gerhardt, vol. 7, p. 501.

[4] Leibniz, *Theodicy* §55.

Another sort of necessity is that which determines the agent to do the best; this necessity hardly excludes, like the first, freedom: on the contrary, it involves it. The sage cannot not do good. Is he any the less free for that? Less free is rather the one enslaved by the passions, he who floats without certainty between good and evil. The sage, in choosing the good, chooses it infallibly, but at the same time with the freest will. This is perhaps because the good, the beautiful, is in reality nothing other than love, which is the will in all its purity, and because wanting what is truly good is to will oneself.

'There is', says Leibniz, 'geometry everywhere and morality [*la morale*] everywhere.'[5] In other words, there is geometry in morality and morality even in geometry. Indeed, morality, which belongs to the soul and to the will, insofar as it contains relations of identity and difference, of equality and inequality, is subject to geometrical necessity; and, on the other hand, if geometry excludes, in its development, any purely moral necessity, it still seems to have, judging by the most recent work to have explored the question, to have as its primary foundation principles of harmony that perhaps have to be conceived—as Descartes, who made everything depend on God's free decrees, doubtless conceived them—as the sensory expression of an absolute and infinite will. 'There are those who assert', said Aristotle, 'that mathematics has absolutely nothing in common with the idea of the good. Are not order, proportion, symmetry forms of beauty?'[6]

The geometrical order as a whole, at least when understood in a narrow sense, can be opposed to the moral order, and thus geometry can be distanced from philosophy, but Plato had reason to stipulate that the philosopher should first of all be a geometer.

Nature, now, is not, as materialism taught, all geometry, and thus all absolute necessity and fatality. Morality enters into it; it is as if mixed with absolute necessity, which excludes contingency and will, and with relative necessity, which implies them. That is not all: morality is the principal form. Nature—if we put to one side the accidents that, although disturbing to a degree its regular course, on closer inspection can be seen to fall under the same laws—everywhere offers constant progression from the simple to the complex, from imperfection to perfection, from weak and obscure life to an increasingly energetic life. Each degree within it is, moreover, a goal for what precedes it. This produces an absolute necessity and a relative necessity in two opposing senses. Within logic there is an absolute necessity of a proposition in relation to its conditions; in nature, there is an analogous necessity of an end to its means. The end, indeed, entails the means. But the end imposes itself only according to the relative necessity that determines

---

[5] Leibniz wrote in a letter to Bossuet: 'On peut dire qu'il y a de l'harmonie, de la géometrie, de la métaphysique, et pour parler ainsi, de la morale partout [there is harmony, geometry, metaphysics, and, so to speak, morality everywhere]'; *Sämtliche Schriften und Briefe*, ed. Deutsche Akademie der Wissenschaften zu Berlin, Darmstadt, series II, vol. 2, p. 516.

[6] This is a loose rendition of Aristotle, *Metaphysics* XIII, 1078a 32–7.

the will. This is why, as a general rule, no event ever entails, with an absolute and geometrical necessity, a subsequent event. It is only in a derivative and improper sense that it can be considered as its cause. It is only ever one of its elements, the negative element, as we saw above, of a relative necessity, of the same nature as the necessity belonging to the reasons by which our free will decides, a moral necessity that does not prevent, and that rather implies that the cause that it is said to be determining determines itself. It is only in being duped by a sort of mirage inverting appearances that materialism, when it finds necessity in nature only in reversing the direction of its development, claims to apprehend its immediate sense according to the progressive order of time.

Fatality in this world, at least according to the regular course of things, and putting accidents to one side, is therefore just an appearance; spontaneity, freedom is the truth. Far from everything occurring according to brute mechanism or chance, everything occurs by the development of a tendency towards perfection, towards the good, towards beauty, which is in things like an internal spring by which the infinite pushes them, like a weight the infinite bears on them and thereby makes them move. Instead of submitting to blind destiny, everything obeys, and obeys willingly, a wholly divine Providence.

This is not to say, returning to the beliefs of the first epochs of humanity, that we have to persuade ourselves that everything occurs in nature according to arbitrary volitions that would always undermine our forecasts and thus make any science impossible. If the will, like life, whose principle it is, is at the heart of everything, the will, like life, comes in degrees.

In the infinite, in God, will is identical to love, which itself is not distinct from absolute good and absolute beauty. In us, the will, full of this love that is its internal law, but also in commerce with sensibility, which presents images to it of the absolute good altered in some way by the milieu into which they are drawn, often errs—uncertain about this infinite good towards which, entirely free, it would always tend—towards those imperfect goods to which it gives away a part of its independence. In nature, to which we belong by the inferior elements of our being, the will, illuminated only by a glimmer of reason, stands as if under the powerful influence of the particular form representing nature, which it seems to obey in a wholly passive obedience. It is no less true that, all the way down into the darkest regions of corporeal life, it is a kind of obscure idea of the good and the beautiful that explains the primary origin of movements; that in the end what one calls physical necessity is only, as Leibniz said, a moral necessity that in no way excludes, that on the contrary implies, if not freedom, then at least spontaneity. Everything is ruled, constant, and yet radically voluntary.

From the inner and central point of view of self-reflection, the soul does not only grasp itself as, at bottom, the infinite from which it emanates: it sees itself, it recognizes itself, more or less different from itself, by degrees, all the way to the extreme limits where, in the dispersion of matter, all unity seems to vanish, and all activity seems to disappear in chains of phenomena. From this point of view, since everything that develops in nature can be found in the soul, we can understand Aristotle's statement that the soul is the site of all forms; since all objects appear to us as representing, by forms in space, the phases that the soul traverses in the succession of its states, we can understand Leibniz's statement that body is momentary mind; and since, finally, the soul itself, in the progress of its life, unfolds in a successive manner what pure spirit contains, in a somehow undivided present, we can understand this other dictum of the same thinkers, summing up in a brief formula the whole spirit of high Platonic doctrine, that what is developed in the variety of the finite is what the infinite concentrates in unity. Nature, one might say, is like a refraction or dispersion of spirit.

If this point of view is that of true knowledge, does this mean that it must become the exclusive point of view of all science? Far from it. Natural phenomena occur in time and space, under the laws of quantity, in definite relationships to certain other phenomena. Determining these conditions is the business of experience, with the guidance of reasoning; the different sciences, in the detail of the facts with which they are concerned, in the successive determination of what are called physical causes with their quantitative or mathematical particularities, do not have to follow other methods; and the superior science of intellect, the final arbiter of all the steps taken by the inferior sciences, does not have to intervene directly here.

'It is necessary', says Pascal, 'to keep a thought in the back of one's mind, and to judge everything by it; but meanwhile to speak like the people.'[7] The thought 'in the back of one's mind', which must not prevent us from speaking in each particular science the language proper to it, that of physical appearances, is metaphysical thought.

This is not to say either that the science of the spiritual can never do anything for that of the natural. It is true that the natural and physical sciences are to a certain extent independent of metaphysics; it is also true that they can be of great use to it; for such is our constitution that we do not easily understand what is purely intelligible, if not in the sensory terms that offer us, as it were, a coarser image of it. But it is also true, and of a higher truth, that the sensory can be understood only by the intelligible, that nature can be explained only by the soul. In the science of organized beings, from Hippocrates and Aristotle to Harvey, Grimaud, Bichat, and Claude Bernard, nothing of any importance has been found without the more or less express assumption of a determining purpose of the functions, of a harmonic concert of means. In physics, the most important laws have arisen from the use of these more or less avowed hypotheses: that everything is realized, as far as possible, by the shortest paths, by the simplest means; that the least possible

---

[7] This is fragment 336 of Pascal's *Pensées* in Brunschwicg's ordering.

force is expended and the maximum effect is always produced—all variants of a general rule of wisdom. In general or elementary cosmology, especially since Copernicus and Kepler, there has been no great discovery not suggested by some application of an express or tacit belief in universal harmony.

When, therefore, an exclusive physical science believes that it can absolutely banish or replace all metaphysics, it can be said, literally, that it knows not what it is doing. Newton said: 'Physics, beware of metaphysics!' This was to say, as Hegel remarked somewhere, 'Physics, beware of thought!' But who can, and what science in particular, do without thought? There is no scientist, no inventor above all, who does not make use at every moment, even if unwittingly, of the principle that everything is, in essence, intelligible, and therefore conforms to intellect; and the greatest inventors are those who have made the most use of it. In this material world of phenomena, where experience finds, under the name of physical causes, only simple conditions, it cannot orient itself and advance without being enlightened by the idea of a true cause, of a cause that is both efficient and final, which is none other than immaterial spirit. Just as spirit seems to be the universal substance, so it is the universal light.

These are the most general results to which it seems that the philosophical movement of our time, as far as we have presented it, must lead. Idealist theories—on which, as we have seen, most systems come to an agreement despite so many other differences—tend towards these results as if towards their natural completion. In some of the other doctrines that we have expounded, the very same results can be seen in more or less distinctive features. In the end, it is easy to foresee a future in which they will form a body of doctrine.

In the days following our last revolution, when, tired of recent unrest, people feared anything that might seem likely to move minds, philosophy had become the object more of fear than favour. It was felt that its longstanding role in public education had to be greatly diminished and that it had to be reduced, at least in name, to logic. At the same time, the annual competitive examinations for the appointment of teachers in this part of education were abolished. Philosophical studies were affected by this, and for some time they seemed to be less cultivated than in the past. From this state of things, however, it followed that the tradition of the doctrines which had reigned alone for nearly a quarter of a century in our schools, without being entirely interrupted, lost its strength and its ascendancy. In minds freed from its authority and left to themselves, perhaps pre-existing germs of new thought began to emerge. A few years ago, on the proposal of the present Minister of Public Instruction, whose first act it was, philosophy was resumed in the state schools, with its old title, with the place it had formerly occupied within them, and a special examination for the reception of those teaching it was re-established. In the public lectures forming part of these examinations, examinations in which several young masters have shone brightly, we have seen the production, instead of the theories which had reigned since the advent of eclecticism, of pronounced tendencies towards the ideas to which these theories, as well as those analogous to them, seem about to give way. We could cite, as signs of these tendencies, several works recently presented either to the highest levels of the Faculty of Humanities, or to the annual competitions on questions of philosophy or the history of philosophy by one of our academies specializing in such studies. Given these signs, it is possible to foresee a philosophical epoch whose general character will consist in the predominance of what may be called a spiritualist realism or positivism, having as its generating principle the consciousness that mind has in itself of an existence, on which all existence depends, which is nothing but its activity.

Let us say a few more words to clarify the meaning of these expressions and to define their scope.

By spiritual action, by thought and will, are we to understand, as we do with sensory qualities, a mode of a subject from which it differs? Leibniz, at least if we take his expressions literally, would have understood it thus; he would not have dared to follow Descartes in the bold idea that thought is not a mode of the soul, but its substance, its very being. How to understand—as the founder of metaphysics had said, and with reason, it seems—that the action to which reasoning leads us as if to a first cause is a mode of something else? This other thing would be the first cause, or it would be a third thing again which would hold them together, and from the one would bring out the other. So let us not imagine the first cause as something that would first exist and which, in addition, would think, as something like Spinoza's substance having thought as an attribute, and other attributes perhaps, without its ground being thought, and which would be, as Aristotle put it, like a thinking stone. On the contrary, we must admit that the primary and absolute existence, of which any other offers us only a limitation, the only perfect substance, is thought; that being and thinking, as the ancient Parmenides said already, are, rigorously speaking, the same thing.

Consequently, the consciousness that the first cause has of itself, which is the essence of our own consciousness and the primordial source of all intellect and all life, is not such that the infinite being, in contemplating itself, considers in its thought something different from this very thought, but that perfect, absolute thought, according to the formula that crowns Peripatetic metaphysics, is thinking of thinking.

Such a conception surpasses us, it is true; we understand intellect only under conditions of distinction, of the opposition of subject and object, of thought and existence. Still, in the infinite and the absolute, such conditions vanish. 'It is not possible to understand', said with great reason the very man who sometimes hesitated to admit entirely Aristotle's and Descartes's idea because it seemed to him too incomprehensible, 'how the variety of ideas is compatible with the simplicity of God. But neither do we understand the incommensurable and a thousand other things whose truth is not unknown to us, and which we are entitled to use in order to explain others that depend on it.'

The same is true of Descartes's statement, which we have already mentioned, that God is the cause of himself. This means, as the author explained, that if we follow the path prescribed by reason, going back for each fact to a cause that explains it, when we arrive at God and seek in the same way the reason for his existence, we find that he cannot have one outside himself, and that consequently he can be defined as 'that which is the cause of itself'.

The same is also true of a third proposition from which the a priori proof of God's existence is derived, a proof which many find difficult to admit, and in which Kant has nevertheless rightly shown, as we have already said, the necessary foundation of all other proofs: namely, that in God essence and existence, in other words, virtuality and reality, power and actuality, are one and the same. If from finite things, where we conceive a possibility that an actual cause comes to realize, we rise, by the suppression of their limits, to the conception of an infinite being, we find that its possibility is that of something which nothing can limit or prevent, and that by this very fact it implies real existence.

These two propositions, which state that in infinity fact and cause, essence and existence, are one and the same, enclose each other as equivalent abstract expressions of one and the same positive idea, in which reason and experience are merged. And this idea is that of the wholly active and consequently wholly spiritual nature of complete or absolute existence. From this nature it follows that the object and the subject of thought, of will, and of love, are but one and the same thing, which is thought, will, and love; a flame without material support, as it were, which feeds on itself. Such is the unique conception in which opposites, separated everywhere else, merge as if in a living and luminous unity.

Now, in explaining sensory phenomena, the world, nature, if there remains, apart from this pure action, only something that plays the role of matter with respect to a form from which it receives order, beauty, unity, what is to be understood by this thing, deprived of that which constitutes reality and consequently also intelligibility? It is, Leibniz said, after Plato, something negative, which, in the creature, limits by its imperfect receptivity the perfection and the natural infinity of the cause.

Leibniz noticed that all numbers could be formed on the basis of just unity joined to zero, which gives a system of binary and no longer decimal arithmetic, and that in the same way all colours could be formed with just light and shadow, as Goethe also said; and he saw in these facts symbols of the general constitution of nature, for which a principle of absolute or infinite reality and a principle of limitation suffice. He imagined a medal that would express these ideas, presenting, on the front, the sun tinting clouds with its light, and, on the reverse, a series of numbers formed by the combination of unity and zero, with this exergue: *omnibus ex nihilo ducendis sufficit unum*.

Aristotle had shown that, since the positive principle of reality exists in action, the opposite principle could only be defined, like all matter compared to the form that orders it, by the idea of possibility, which action alone realizes. Is that to say that beyond everything that really exists, there is something that is only possible, that is only potential, such as we sometimes imagine what we call a prime matter? To be in some way without actually being is a contradiction, it seems. To be merely possible, in fact, is not to be anything. So pure possibility is, as Leibniz again remarked, only an abstraction of our understanding. There is no real power without some tendency towards action. But tending towards action is already to act; tendency is action.

But in what, comparatively speaking, is only virtual, from where would action come from, if not from that which is its unique source? How then to understand tendency, if not as action stopped, prevented, suspended? Now, if we go back to the first cause, to the infinity of the free will, how to understand that something outside it, a nothing, a void, could in any way prevent it and suspend its action for a single moment? It seems, therefore, that the origin of an existence inferior to absolute existence cannot be understood except as the result of a voluntary determination, by which this high existence has of itself moderated, deadened, extinguished, so to speak, something of its omnipotent activity.

The Stoics, in their very physical language, defined the first cause, or the Divinity, as a burning ether, at the maximum of tension; matter as the same ether relaxed. Could it not be said, in a similar way, that what the first cause concentrates in its immutable eternity, it unfolds, so to speak, relaxed and diffused in those elementary conditions of materiality which are time and space; that it thus lays down, as it were, the basis of natural existence, a basis on which, by the continuous progression that is the order of nature, from degree to degree, from realm to realm, everything returns from material dispersion to the unity of spirit?

God made everything out of nothing, out of nothingness, out of that relative nothingness that is the possible; he was the first author of this nothingness, as he was of being. From what he annulled in a way and annihilated from the infinite fullness of his being (*se ipsum exinanivit*) he has drawn, by a kind of revival and resurrection, all that exists.

In almost the whole of the ancient East, and from time immemorial, an ordinary symbol of the Divinity was this mysterious, winged, fire-coloured being, which consumed itself, annihilated itself in order to be reborn from its ashes.

The old Heraclitus, one of those who, in physical forms of language, began metaphysics, said: fire is the substance and cause of everything; what is called matter is fire which of itself has diminished, is extinguished; the world, with its order and its progress in order, is fire which rekindles itself. The Stoics, as we saw earlier, said the same; and the Stoics said, like Heraclitus, that fire, the primitive fire, the true fire is reason, is soul.

According to Indian theology, and also according to the theology of the mysteries of Greek religion, the Divinity had sacrificed itself in order to form creatures from its members.

According to Jewish theosophy, granting to the world more of a share that compromised what belonged to God, God was everywhere; then he voluntarily, concentrating into himself, left behind a void where from a kind of residue of his being all other beings emerged.

According to the later Platonists, who combined the conceptions of Greek philosophy with those of Asiatic theology, the world originated in a lowering or, to use a term familiar to Christian dogmatics, a condescension of the Divinity.

According to Christian dogma, which is confined to the moral order, but which nevertheless contains as it were the germ of a principle of general metaphysical and physical explanation, and in a way a virtual philosophy, God descended through his Son, and thus descended without descending, into death, so that life might be born from it, a life that is entirely divine. 'God became man so that man might become God.' The spirit, lowering itself, became flesh; the flesh will become spirit. Liberality, the source of justice itself, is the characteristic virtue of great souls; the supreme name of the Christian God is grace, gift, liberality; extreme liberality by which, freely indeed, he gives himself, creates from his own being his creature, nourishes it with his own being, makes it similar to himself and divine as himself. 'You are gods.'

These thoughts are still those, if we are not mistaken, that our modern systems gravitate towards, without excepting those which seem to or wish to depart the most from them. The truth has shown itself to us where it has been experienced, from the earliest times, in almost every country. Only today it shows itself to us, perhaps, more nakedly and more fully. We understand better, it seems, than antiquity itself what it meant when it said: 'Eros was the first and is still the most powerful of the gods'; or: 'God is charity.'

It would be easy, if the scope of this work allowed it, to show in the main philosophical conceptions to which countries different from ours have given rise in recent times, tendencies all similar to those which seem to us to dominate or to be close to dominating in the theories which our country has produced. Let us only mention the latest systems that led, in Germany, to the great movement of renovation which Kant began there: the system by the completion of which Schelling ended his glorious career, of which the absolute freedom of the will, in opposition to Hegel's logical mechanism, forms both the ground and the crowning moment; Schopenhauer's system, where the principle which explains everything is similarly the will; that of Lotze, who, in maintaining with experimental science the mechanical connection of phenomena, ends up reducing them, from a higher point of view, which is that of metaphysics, to manifestations of a radical activity that is fundamentally spontaneous, and to reduce all true existence to infinite spirit and love.

But in this general movement by which thought is tending to dominate materialist doctrines once again, and from a higher position than ever before, the smallest share in it will perhaps not belong to the homeland of Descartes and Pascal.

Our fathers, from the earliest times, believed profoundly in immortality, a belief which has as its principle the knowledge of the infinite, of the divine within us. Whence, said the ancients, their indomitable valour. They were praised for possessing to a supreme degree eloquence or the gift of persuasion, along with courage, the mark of greatness of soul that consists in giving, if necessary, one's own life. And it was, in their opinion, by eloquence that one was most assured of victory. Indeed, they represented their hero *par excellence*, the symbol of their genius, in the guise of a man around whom one could see several others entwined in golden chains coming out of his mouth. This was to express in a mute language the idea that the greatest power is persuasion. And whoever knows how to persuade knows how to make himself loved, and is great enough to give himself up, to sacrifice himself: 'Be great, and love will follow you.' Thus Christianity was nowhere better and more quickly accepted than among our fathers. Is not Christianity summed up in the dogma, which contains with the best of all ancient wisdom the cherished thought of our ancestors, that love alone is the author and master of everything? From this same thought, from this thought of love and devotion, which is the basis of heroism, chivalry was born among us in the Middle Ages.

If the French genius has not changed, there will be nothing more natural for her than the triumph of the high doctrine, which teaches that matter is only the last degree and, so to speak, the shadow of existence, over systems that reduce everything to material elements and to a blind mechanism; which teaches that real existence, of which everything else is only an imperfect sketch, is that of spirit; that, in truth, to be is to live, and to live is to think and to will; that nothing occurs without persuasion; that the good and beauty alone explain the universe and its author; that the infinite and the absolute, of which nature presents only its limitations, consist in spiritual freedom; that freedom is thus the last word on things, and that, beneath the disorder and antagonisms which trouble the surface where phenomena occur, in the essential and eternal truth, everything is grace, love, and harmony.

Index

aesthetics 8, 13, 33–5, 184–7
art (*fine art*) 3, 8, 13, 19–20, 33–4, 40, 77, 184–9, 192
affinities 42, 134, 197
Ampère 27–9, 32, 47, 176–7
analysis 25, 29, 33, 60, 73, 84–8, 112–16, 117, 167, 175–8, 190, 193–6
animism 8–9, 139–49, 152
antinomies 124–6
association of ideas 63, 134–8
attraction 13–15, 42, 48, 87, 134, 197
Augustin, St. 84, 111–15, 120–1, 126, 183–4

Bailey, S. 7, 56, 62–3, 69, 135
Bain, A. 7, 56, 62–3, 92, 135–6
beauty 33–5, 40, 44, 47, 88, 95, 173, 183, 184–7, 200–1, 206, 208, 676
biology 7, 14, 60, 73–5, 88, 150
Barthez, P.-J. 9, 105, 140
Bergson, H. 1, 3, 4, 8, 10, 14–15, 133
Berkeley, G. 5, 24–5, 34, 51, 57, 63, 70–2, 83, 85, 144, 170
Bernard, C. 6, 103–8, 112, 138, 148, 152–3, 175, 196, 202
Bichat, X. 9, 140, 153–4, 202
Bordas-Dumoulin, J.-B. 38–39, 130–2
Bossuet, J.-B. 31, 98, 101, 120, 123, 200
Bouillier, F. 9, 31, 141–5
Boutroux, E. 15
brain 10, 54, 81, 125, 136, 148, 150–4, 160, 162
Broussais, F.-J.-V. 54–5, 106, 140

calculus 23, 112–15, 131, 173–4, 190
Canguilhem, G. 7, 10–11
Caro, E. 4, 88, 99, 117–18, 161
causation
 final causation 7, 13, 15, 46, 75–6, 81, 94, 101, 107, 189, 192, 199
 efficient causation 15, 101, 189, 192, 199, 203
certainty 12, 45, 65, 94, 105, 112, 119, 125, 127–9, 170–3, 179, 200
chivalry 77, 208
Christianity 22–2, 48, 50–2, 95, 109, 116, 120, 180, 208

Comte, A. 1, 6–8, 12, 16, 55–61, 64–79, 80–1, 83–87, 91–2, 96, 100, 104, 106–7, 135, 147, 170, 193
Condillac, E. 5, 27–9, 84, 168, 175, 177
contingency 13–15, 200
continuity 9, 23, 90, 115, 149, 151, 154, 171–3
Cournot, A. 12, 15, 169–174
Cousin, V. 2–4, 8, 11, 30–40, 47, 51, 83–4, 97–8, 109, 141, 184–5
creation 3, 14, 41–3, 46, 90, 107, 160, 165, 168
crystallization 197

deduction 73, 85, 111, 112, 171, 173, 175–7
De Strada (Jules-Gabriel Delarue) 118, 122–129, 182
Descartes, R. 4–5, 10, 21–4, 28, 30–3, 39, 50, 58, 60, 62, 68, 84, 94, 101, 104, 112, 117–19, 125–7, 129–31, 140, 142–4, 157, 170–3, 178, 181–2, 191, 197–200, 204–5, 208
determinism 8, 105–8, 181
divinity 14, 22, 89, 97, 206
dreams 156, 159–62
Duruy, V. 1–3, 6

eclecticism 2–5, 11, 30–41, 50, 80, 83–4, 86, 98–100, 109, 115, 127, 134, 139, 141, 169, 179, 181–2, 184–5, 204
effort 5, 20, 27, 67, 101, 136, 159, 192, 198
Emerson, R. W. 51, 168
empiricism 7, 29, 32, 35, 68, 91, 137
epistemology 175–9
eternity 50, 70, 137, 191, 206
evolution 1, 8, 11, 14, 106

fetishism 77–8
Fichte, J. G. F. 84, 111
Fourier, C. 5, 47–9
Franck, A. 31–2, 38, 105, 134, 144, 179
freedom 12–13, 21–4, 42, 48, 94–5, 116, 121, 126, 144, 181, 199, 200–1, 207–8

Galileo, G. 113, 129
Gall, F. 54, 106, 150
geometry 39–40, 60–1, 64, 93, 127, 131, 171, 200
Germain, S. 6, 66–8, 71, 118, 172
grace 13, 48, 165, 186–7, 207–8

habit 5, 9–13, 15, 25, 37, 75, 134–9, 142, 149, 157–8
hallucinations 139, 160, 163
Hamilton, W. 36, 56, 70, 92, 117, 124, 135, 191
Herbart, J. 135, 138
Hume, D. 5, 25–7, 35, 56, 63, 68, 70–1, 79, 83, 85–6, 134–6
Hegel, G. W. F. 5, 40, 62, 109–111, 116, 118, 120, 123–4, 184–5, 193, 203, 207

idealism 32, 76, 96, 101, 188–9, 192–4
imagination 9, 22, 25, 68, 123, 140, 150, 162–5, 192, 194–5, 197
immortality 50, 52–3, 78, 95, 118, 181, 208
inclination 48, 68, 136, 167
induction 12, 14, 33, 35–6, 38–9, 63, 69–71, 85, 95, 104–5, 111–13, 118, 122, 170–175, 178, 190
insanity (see also *madness*) 139, 160, 162, 164
instinct 9, 11, 63–4, 91, 126, 135, 139, 142–3

Janet, Paul 4, 8, 31, 38, 81, 99, 107, 145–7, 164, 180
Jouffroy, T. 4, 30, 36–8, 83, 159, 167, 180, 182

Kant, I. 5, 11, 14, 23, 26–8, 31–2, 38, 42, 56, 80, 92–3, 111, 117–18, 123–4, 133, 142, 152, 172, 179, 182, 184, 186, 188, 191–3, 205, 207
Kepler, J. 12, 174, 198, 203

Lachelier, J. 14, 82, 102, 179
Lagrange, J.-L. 60, 66
Lamennais, F. 6, 41–7, 91, 109
Leibniz, G. 13–14, 16, 20–6, 31–4, 39, 42, 47–8, 50–1, 62, 64, 66, 68–71, 73, 82, 84, 90, 96, 98, 100, 101, 104, 110, 112–15, 118, 123, 127, 129–131, 136–40, 144, 146, 152, 157, 161, 163, 168, 170–9, 181, 185, 190–3, 197–206
Lemoine, A. 9, 142–4, 159, 162–4, 167–8
Leroux, P. 5, 11, 50–3, 78
Littré, E. 7, 54, 61, 66, 69, 80–82, 91–2
love 5, 13, 15, 23, 41–3, 53, 76–8, 95, 116, 118, 128, 165, 180, 180–4, 186–7, 195–6, 200–201, 205, 207–8
Locke, J. 25–7, 32–3, 62–4, 66, 104, 119, 162

Madness (see also *insanity*) 9, 139, 142, 162–5
Malebranche 24, 31, 71, 118, 120, 130–1, 142, 170, 185, 193, 195
materialism 7, 9, 20, 24, 45, 54, 61, 65, 68, 74, 81, 87–8, 93, 100, 105, 108, 122, 126, 129, 139, 145–7, 151, 162, 189, 193–4, 200–201
mathematics 38, 58–60, 73–4, 77, 85, 88, 90–1, 112, 114, 123, 130, 171, 177, 199–200

memory 10, 50–1, 57, 94, 134–7, 140, 170, 194
metaphysics 2–3, 12–15, 20, 26, 36–8, 40–3, 45, 47, 53, 56–7, 60–1, 66, 75, 77–8 84–6, 89–92, 95–7, 100–102, 113–14, 117, 122–33, 153, 174, 180, 187, 189, 196–207
method 3, 21, 33, 35, 37–39, 62, 73, 77, 80, 83–7, 89, 96, 103–4, 109–16, 122, 125–8, 156, 169, 171, 175–9, 182–3, 188, 190, 194, 196, 202
Mill, J. S. 7, 54, 56, 59, 62–4, 66, 68–70, 73, 75, 80, 85–6, 92, 104, 111–12, 117

necessity
  moral 13–15, 24, 64, 102, 105, 199–201
  mechanical 13, 15, 71, 106
Neoplatonism 30
neurology 150–5
Newton, I. 12, 48, 113, 134, 174, 203

occasionalism 142
ontologism 119–21, 146
organicism 9, 139–41, 143, 145, 148–9, 152
organisation 159

pantheism 79, 95, 109, 112, 117
Pascal, B. 5, 22–3, 34, 47, 76, 95, 109, 112, 117
perfection 20, 22, 34–5, 39, 43–4, 47–8, 52, 69–70, 76, 78, 96–102, 110–15, 117, 130–1, 146–7, 163, 176, 184, 186, 191–5, 199–200, 205
phrenology 54, 150–155
physiology 36, 54, 57–8, 60, 80, 82, 104, 106, 139, 148, 153, 156, 158, 166
physics 3, 6–7, 20, 27, 38, 47, 58, 60–1, 64, 67, 71–4, 88, 106–8, 123–4, 130–1, 133, 170, 174, 177, 197, 202–4
physiognomy 9, 166, 167
Plato 3–4, 14, 19–20, 30–32, 34, 38, 41–2, 46, 50, 52, 62, 64, 66, 73, 76, 93–4, 101, 104, 111, 115, 120, 123, 140, 155, 165, 170–2, 183–5, 193–4, 199–200, 202, 205, 207
Plotinus 31, 42, 50, 84, 101, 144, 186
positivism (*see also* Comte) 1, 4, 6–8, 12, 55, 57, 59, 61–70, 73, 75–88, 91, 92–6, 104, 118, 122, 129, 134, 137, 140
  spiritualist positivism 1, 4, 7, 8, 12, 129, 189, 204
Praxiteles 19–20
probability 12, 49, 69, 113, 169–177

Quatremère de Quincy, A. 33–4

reflex 10–11, 25, 27, 39, 106, 151–2, 157–8
relaxation (as principle of existence) 12–14

religion 3, 7, 40, 44, 51, 57, 66, 77–9, 85, 89, 109, 117, 121, 125, 141, 180, 182, 207
Reynaud, J. 5, 11, 50–3
Royer-Collard, P.-P. 29

Saint-Simon, H. 5, 6, 31, 47–50, 53–8
Saisset, E. 4, 31, 38–9, 115, 117–18, 142
Schelling, F. W. J. 5, 30, 40, 111, 184–6, 207
Scottish philosophy 2, 3, 5, 27, 29, 32–3, 36–8, 80, 83–6, 98–9, 127, 157, 169–71, 179, 181
sleep 9, 142, 156, 159–163, 195
socialism 5, 6, 11, 46, 49
sociology 7, 55, 60, 74–5
Socrates 34, 52, 164, 183
Spencer, H. 7, 56, 62–3, 66–7, 69, 80, 96, 135, 158, 172
Spinoza, B. 24, 28, 31, 56, 70, 95–6, 117–18, 130–1, 171, 191, 204
Spiritualism 4, 7, 8, 13, 32, 45, 54, 61, 88, 93, 102, 118, 143, 189
spontaneity 27, 71, 105–6, 146, 149, 152–3, 162, 167–8, 197, 201
Stahl, G. E. (*see also* animism) 9, 105, 108, 139–45, 168, 172, 197
Stoicism 3, 5, 20, 161
sublime, the 185–7

substance 5, 19–20, 24–6, 33–8, 41, 43, 56, 61, 71, 83, 85, 92, 101–3, 127–8, 130–1, 138–9, 142, 144, 185–7, 192, 203–6
Swedenborg, E. 49, 53
synthesis 26, 73–4, 77, 86, 123, 175–6, 178, 190–4

Taine, H. 7–8, 81, 83–8, 90–2, 94, 96–7
tendency 67, 91, 100, 136, 140, 143, 160, 185, 192, 197–8, 201, 206
theology 14, 32, 41–5, 51–3, 57, 89, 95–6, 100, 109, 111–17, 119, 121, 131, 207
time 14, 23, 28, 33, 42, 53, 57, 70–2, 85, 90–3, 95, 99–100, 114, 125, 127, 130, 136, 172, 192, 202–2, 206
Turgot, A. 58

Vacherot, E. 4, 31, 97–103, 109–111, 120, 123
virtuality 102, 205
vitalism 7, 9, 106, 139–145, 148–9, 152
Vinci, da 21, 129

will 4–5, 9–10, 12–14, 20, 22–24, 43, 46, 71, 77–8, 89, 92, 94, 97, 101, 112, 116–18, 135, 153–4, 159, 161, 163, 168, 169, 174, 181, 183, 185–7, 192, 195, 198, 200–1, 204–8